CIRCLE OF UNITY
Bahá'í Approaches to Current Social Issues

CIRCLE OF UNITY

Bahá'í Approaches to
Current Social Issues

Edited by Anthony A. Lee

Kalimát Press
Los Angeles

Manufactured in the United States of America

Library of Congress Cataloging in Publication Data

Main entry under title:

Circle of unity.

1. Baha'i Faith—Addresses, essays, lectures.
I. Lee, Anthony A., 1947– .
BP370.C57 1984   297'.89178   84-11203
ISBN 0-933770-28-6

TO
GLENFORD E. MITCHELL
who inspired a generation of Bahá'í youth
with a new vision of social action

CONTENTS

Continued

viii   *Contents*

Introduction

A NYONE FAMILIAR WITH THE Bahá'í teachings will recognize that they embody a progressive social program. Indeed, it might be said that, at least in comparison to other religions, the Bahá'í Faith is primarily oriented toward social reform. It is certainly the only world religion that defines consciousness of the unity of mankind as its central theme and dedicates itself almost single-mindedly to the achievement of that goal.

Of course, the Bahá'í teachings also offer guidance to and demand change from the individual believer, who is called to the highest standards of personal morality and spiritual development. But it is clearly stated in the Sacred Writings of the Faith that no amount of individual saintliness will, by itself, achieve the result of overturning the unjust and oppressive social conditions which exist throughout the world today. Shoghi Effendi, the Guardian of the Bahá'í Faith, has declared:

Let there be no mistake. The principle of the Oneness of Mankind—the pivot round which all the teachings of Bahá'u'lláh revolve—is no mere outburst of ignorant emotionalism or an expression of vague and pious hope. Its appeal is not to be merely identified with a reawakening of the spirit of brotherhood and good-will among men, nor does it aim solely at the fostering of harmonious cooperation among individual peoples and nations. . . . Its message is applicable not only to the individual, but concerns itself primarily with the nature of those essential relationships that must bind all the states and nations as members of one human family. It does not constitute merely the enunciation of an ideal, but stands inseparably associated with an institution . . . It implies an organic change in the structure of present-day society, a change such as the world has not yet experienced.

(*World Order of Bahá'u'lláh*, pp. 42–43)

Bahá'u'lláh Himself called for political, economic and social reform throughout His Writings. He specifically condemned the tyranny of absolute rulers and the oppression of the masses, deplored war and the race for arms, denounced high taxation for military expenditure, approved a parliamentary form of government, called for the creation of an international order, and so forth. However, the most popular summary of the Bahá'í social teachings has come to be embodied in the "twelve principles" first enunciated by 'Abdu'l-Bahá during His travels to America in 1912. This synthesis of Bahá'í ideals, the product of the mind of 'Abdu'l-Bahá, was boldly proclaimed from public platforms during His journey across the continent. On occasion, these statements—on the equality of the sexes and on interracial unity, for example—became headline material. They directly addressed the most serious and controversial social issues of the day.

The usual list of twelve principles is:
1. The oneness of mankind,
2. The independent investigation of truth,
3. The elimination of prejudice of all kinds,
4. The equality of men and women,
5. Agreement between science and religion,
6. The common foundation of all religions,

7. Religion must be the cause of harmony and unity,
8. Spiritual solution to the economic problem,
9. Universal education,
10. A universal auxiliary language,
11. An international tribunal,
12. World peace.

The list seems tame, almost commonplace, by today's standards: a Bahá'í teacher in the 1980s might be told often by unimpressed inquirers that they already believe in these principles and see no need of joining a religion to affirm them. But in 1912, the program outlined by 'Abdu'l-Bahá was so progressive, so universal and enlightened, that it startled and attracted the thinking public. The nation was then in the midst of a hot debate over women's sufferage, we might recall. 'Abdu'l-Bahá's unequivocal stance on the issue was remarkable. Likewise, the issues of world peace—Teddy Roosevelt, President of the United States from 1901 to 1909, had popularized the virtues of war; science and religion—as Darwin's theory was still new; worker's rights—in a climate of labor riots; the call for abolition of extremes of wealth and poverty—in a country where there was plenty of both; and racial equality—in a fully segregated America—were very much more current and more fiercely contended than they are today.

The principles are a brilliant testimony to the genius of 'Abdu'l-Bahá, His ability to draw out from the unlimited potential of the Writings of Bahá'u'lláh those implications which were best suited to a particular social context—ideas which might catch the imagination and demand the admiration of the public. It should not be thought, however, that the twelve principles exhaust the possibilities of social concern inherent in the Bahá'í teachings. 'Abdu'l-Bahá Himself repeatedly stated that His listing was not comprehensive. He varied the list considerably on different occasions. And, a number of principles were proclaimed which have since received little attention in the Bahá'í

Community. The Bahá'í principle of equality of men before the law, for instance, is seldom discussed (*Paris Talks*, pp. 132, 154–55). Likewise, the principles of an equal standard of human rights (*Bahá'í World Faith*, pp. 240–41), the establishment of the House of Justice as the blending of church and state (*The Promulgation of Universal Peace*, p. 455), spiritual brotherhood (Ibid., p. 170), etc.

Nonetheless, in 1912, the principles that were taken up by the Bahá'í Community as "the twelve" provided a new and immensely appealing statement of Bahá'í beliefs which could be presented to thinking people as a modern, fully enlightened, and progressive social program. The Bahá'í Faith offered a unique blend of religious commitment and keen social consciousness.

With no need to give further thought to its stance on social issues, the community turned to other tasks. The expansion of the number of believers was given first priority. This was followed by the building of the Administrative Order under the direction of the Guardian. Later, the full energy of the Bahá'ís was focused on the international expansion of the Faith. Recently, more attention has been given to the challenges of strengthening Bahá'í Community and family life. As we have made steady progress in each of these areas, we have had little time—and little need—to philosophize about the application of the principles of the Faith to the changing needs of society. We have kept our minds on more urgent business, and have demonstrated, often heroically, the strength and vitality of the Bahá'í Community.

Today, however, it has become increasingly difficult to ignore the need to take a new look at the social principles that Bahá'ís have repeated for over seventy years. While the message of the Faith is still vital and progressive, our approach to current issues has become rather outmoded. The familiar twelve Bahá'í principles are still universal, but to the sophisticated reader the list today appears more a register of platitudes than a progressive social program.

Shoghi Effendi himself was perhaps the first to point out the need for a rethinking of the universal principles of the Faith. In 1949, in response to a question of an individual believer on the subject, his secretary wrote on his behalf:

> It seems what we need now is a more profound and coordinated Bahá'í scholarship in order to attract such men as you are contacting. The world has—at least the thinking world—caught up by now with all the great and universal principles enunciated by Bahá'u'lláh over 70 years ago, and so of course it does not sound 'new' to them. But we know that the deeper teachings, the capacity of His projected World Order to recreate society, are new and dynamic. It is these we must learn to present intelligently and enticingly to such men!
>
> (*The Individual and Teaching*, p. 28)

The Guardian here clearly explains that it is the task of the believers, and particularly the responsibility of Bahá'í scholars, to take up the business of applying the teachings of Bahá'u'lláh to the changing needs of world society. To now, there has been little response to his call for a "more profound and coordinated Bahá'í scholarship." Perhaps the time has come for the attention of the Bahá'í Community to be turned once again to its social teachings. Building on the foundation laid by 'Abdu'l-Bahá, a new and challenging approach to the problems of contemporary society can be developed.

BAHÁ'ÍS HAVE SOMETIMES been reluctant to enter into discussions of social issues, even among ourselves, because of the Bahá'í teaching concerning the nonpolitical character of the Faith. This principle has often been misunderstood to forbid Bahá'ís from taking part in the affairs of their government or to prevent them from participation in any advocacy or social action. Some Bahá'ís have gone so far as to suggest that Bahá'ís should shy away from involvement in any controversial issue. In extreme cases, the principle of noninvolvement in politics has been used by some as an excuse to remain indifferent to, and even ignorant of, current events, to refrain from voting, and to free themselves from all social concerns.

There is no question among believers that Bahá'ís are obliged to refrain from participation in party politics. The Guardian of the Faith made this clear on a number of occasions. But there is considerable confusion about just what politics is. 'Abdu'l-Bahá Himself addressed this question, saying:

> The Bahá'ís must not engage in political movements which lead to sedition. They must interest themselves in movements which conduce to law and order. . . . Nevertheless, a Bahá'í may hold a political office and be interested in politics of the right type. Ministers, state officials and governor-generals in Persia are Bahá'ís, and there are many other Bahá'ís holding governmental positions; but nowhere throughout the world should the followers of Bahá'u'lláh be engaged in seditious movements.
>
> (*The Promulgation of Universal Peace*, p. 238)

It seems likely that much of the confusion among Bahá'ís on this issue stems from the fact that the word *politics* in English has a wide range of meanings, and it is only in a specific sense that politics is forbidden in the Faith. It will therefore be useful for us to examine some of the many definitions of the word as it is used in various contexts:

The total complex of relations which bind together the members of a society. This broad definition of politics is often found in classical political philosophy. Politics in this sense is also called the *political economy* or the *body politic* (a term used by 'Abdu'l-Bahá). Bahá'ís clearly are not expected to refrain from politics in this sense. It would be impossible to do so in any case, without withdrawing from society completely.

The science of government, or perhaps *the art of government.* Politics in this sense refers to the skills and principles needed for the proper functioning of government, that is, political science. Again, the Faith has nothing against such knowledge. The Bahá'í Scriptures, in fact, devote a good deal of attention to this kind of politics, 'Abdu'l-Bahá's *The Secret of Divine Civilization* and *Treatise on Politics* being prime examples.

The decision-making processes of government. The machinery of elections, deliberation, legislation, etc. is what is intended here. And again, Bahá'ís are free to involve themselves, as long as they do not join a political party in order to do so. Bahá'ís vote in elections; Bahá'ís may also run for office, as many do each year, usually as judges, members of boards of education, city planners, and the like.

The struggle for power within government among parties and factions. This definition of politics brings us to an area where Bahá'ís must exercise caution. Bahá'ís may not join political parties and should not ally themselves with any faction that would compromise the universal character of their commitment to the Faith. Nonetheless, there is nothing against urging action by one's representatives through the legitimate channels of government. Our recent advocacy in Congress on behalf of the Bahá'ís of Iran is an example of how this may be done within the laws of the Faith. But, the political struggle for power or legislation may also tempt compromise with the high ideals and principles of the Faith. Such compromise must always be rejected.

The dishonest or self-serving manipulation of persons and institutions to achieve personal goals. Used in this way, as in *playing politics,* the word is recognized by everyone—

including politicians—as negative. Of course, politics in this
sense is also forbidden to Bahá'ís.

On the other hand, Bahá'ís are not prevented from engag-
ing in social activism, even in public demonstrations:

> That Bahá'ís may take part in demonstrations was made
> clear by Shoghi Effendi when a number of Bahá'í stu-
> dents at the University of Chicago joined a protest
> against racial prejudice and carried a placard with the
> word Bahá'í on it. Mr. Ellsworth Blackwell asked the
> Guardian: 'Is there anything wrong in the protesting of
> Bahá'í student groups against racial prejudice along with
> other student organizations?' The beloved Guardian re-
> plied through his secretary (January 1948): 'He does not
> see any objection to Bahá'í students taking part as
> Bahá'ís in a protest such as that mentioned in the clip-
> ping. On the contrary, he does not see how they could re-
> main indifferent when fellow students were voicing our
> own Bahá'í attitude on such a vital issue and one we feel
> so strongly about.' (*Bahá'í News*, Insert, June 1964)

It is the positive duty of every Bahá'í to demonstrate the
tenets of his Faith in deeds, as well as in words. The need
to make our actions say the same thing as our words in relation to Bahá'í social principles will inevitably lead to the
realm of social action. Such action is a necessary extension
of commitment to the teachings of the Faith, especially—as
the Guardian implies above—when others are voicing our
own Bahá'í ideals so publicly.

Since the Bahá'í Community has, of necessity, paid little
attention to this issue in the past, the imperative to do so
now is overwhelming. The Guardian called for such initiative on the part of the believers, and especially the youth,
as early as 1932:

> The present condition of the world—its economic insta-
> bility, social dissensions, political dissatisfaction and in-
> ternational distrust—should awaken the youth from their

slumber and make them inquire what the future is going to bring. It is surely they who will suffer most if some calamity sweep over the world. They should therefore open their eyes to the existing conditions, study the evil forces that are at work and then with a concerted effort arise and bring about the necessary reforms—reforms that shall contain within their scope the spiritual as well as social and political phases of human life.

(*Bahá'í News*, November 1932)

Bahá'ís have often hesitated to "arise and bring about the necessary reforms"—have refrained from involvement in, say, the peace movement, or any form of social action—in the mistaken belief that simply by becoming Bahá'ís and working to strengthen the Bahá'í Community we have absolved ourselves of all responsibility to also work for the betterment of society (outside of Bahá'í channels). Some have taken this view to extremes.

I remember listening in horror to a conversation between two devoted believers. One wanted to get involved in assisting Southeast Asian refugees—the so-called boat people who were at that time streaming out of Vietnam and Cambodia. She felt that the Bahá'í teachings on the unity of mankind required that she do something to help in such a desperate situation, and she argued that all people of the world have a responsibility to assist when so many are in need. The other believer advised her that anything that she could do to help the refugees would be an insignificant drop in the bucket; that rather she should turn all her energies to Bahá'í teaching and administrative work and let others help those in need. He admitted that all people of the world have a responsibility to help the homeless Southeast Asians *except the Bahá'ís*, since we believe in the unity of mankind and so have more important work to do!

Such a position is clearly untenable and comes close to open hypocrisy. The Guardian of the Faith repeatedly called on Bahá'ís to participate in the activities of other groups working for Bahá'í ideals. This, not only to find opportunities to teach the Faith, but also to "imbue with the spirit of power and strength such movements." (*Bahá'í Administration*, p. 126) In other words, Bahá'ís have a contribution to make to such movements which is positive and unique.

Naturally, when Bahá'ís become involved in social action, we must guard against becoming involved in partisan issues which will identify us with one party or the other; we should refrain from actions that are violent, or illegal, or contrary to Bahá'í law. But this leaves a vast field of social service still open. We cannot retreat from this field out of fear or overcaution, especially as the Bahá'í Faith begins to emerge from obscurity, if we wish to be taken seriously by enlightened and progressive people.

IT IS THE INTENTION of this book to respond to that challenge. The authors hope that this collection of essays will signal a new level of awareness of the need to address current political, social and economic issues from a Bahá'í perspective.

Finally, we must note that the articles presented here represent only the views of their respective authors. They are not intended to be authoritative statements of Bahá'í positions on the questions addressed. Naturally, anyone is free to disagree completely with the opinions expressed here. Indeed, we have intentionally presented differing views on the same topics within the volume itself.

Rather than being a final or comprehensive statement of the Bahá'í position, it is hoped that this collection will open the door to discussion and dialogue within the Bahá'í Community. We are confident that through such a process of consultation within the community powerful insights will emerge to provide us with new tools to face the social crises of our time.

ANTHONY A. LEE
LOS ANGELES

CIRCLE OF UNITY
Bahá'í Approaches to Current Social Issues

A Worldwide Movement for Peace

By Brad Pokorny

T HE HISTORY OF THE PEACE MOVEMENT in this century has been one of great hope and tragic failure. At
each new and cruel turn of the arms race men and women
in the West have taken to the lecture halls, the political
soapbox, and to the streets in their search for peace. Then,
as each new war came, they faltered, unsuccessful. Before
World War I, for example, people organized to oppose the
Dreadnought—early battleships that could level a city with
offshore gunfire. The ships and the war came anyway. Before World War II, aerial bombardment was the new terror,
and thousands organized in Britain and America to stop the
coming horror. Their fears proved well founded: millions
died from strategic bombing during that war.

In 1945, a pillar of fire changed the world: the atomic
bomb became the symbol of ultimate peril. Successive
movements attempted first to control the bomb, then to
ban it, and then to limit its proliferation through diplomatic
negotiation. Currently, hope for many rests in "freezing"
the current balance of terror.

In a follow-up to his widely-acclaimed book on the issue
of nuclear war, *The Fate of the Earth*, Jonathan Schell
wrote last January in *The New Yorker* of a new awakening

3

for peace in America. Although still uncertain in extent and consequences, he wrote: "It promises to be one of those great changes of heart in mankind—such as the awakening to the evil of slavery in the nineteenth century—that alter the psychological and spiritual map of the world . . ."[1]

Yet Schell also noted that, other than the so-called nuclear freeze, the current peace movement offers little in the way of a long term plan to abolish the bomb and the terror it holds. "The peace movement," Schell wrote, "like the world as a whole, is in need of proposals for action which are commensurate with the hopes that it has raised, and are answerable to the moral standards it uses to measure present policies. If no such proposals are forthcoming, the peace movement seems sure to dissipate, just as peace movements in the past have dissipated."[2]

For Bahá'ís, the challenge is equally thorny. Wary of partisan political movements, yet urgently concerned about the world situation, many Bahá'ís are uncertain about how best to act on their desire to see peace. In addition, Bahá'ís have not always had answers for those in the peace movement who ask us what we are doing *now* to stop the arms race. Some of us have faced criticism for talking too much about the future, about the long range solutions to war, rather than the immediate needs of the world.

In the last few years, however, as the Faith has begun to emerge from obscurity on the world scene, it has taken on a new face, revealing new forms. It is like watching an artist paint from a charcoal sketch: as bits and pieces are colored in one finally begins to understand the final picture.

Almost from the start, the Bahá'í Faith has been as much a movement for peace as a religion. About one hundred years ago, Bahá'u'lláh, the Prophet and Founder of the Bahá'í Faith, wrote: "God's purpose in sending His Prophets unto men is twofold. The first is to liberate the children of men from the darkness of ignorance, and guide them to the light of true understanding. The second is to ensure the peace and tranquility of mankind, and provide all the means by which they can be established."[3]

Today, a careful examination of the worldwide activities of the Bahá'í Community will reveal that Bahá'ís have been carefully—if often somewhat unknowingly—building the foundation for an international grassroots movement for peace. It is a movement that embodies many of the best elements of recent proposals for world peace. Its activities include: educational efforts to promote the new kinds of thinking necessary to establish a warless world, forging a template for a new political order, and organizing the world's people into a network for peace. Its methods include a new format for nonadversarial decision making, heart-to-heart grassroots organizing, and carefully planned intercultural exchanges. On top of all that, the Faith offers what this war weary world needs most: a spiritual power to change humanity's collective consciousness so that war becomes forever unthinkable.

Nearly every feature listed above has been suggested or proposed by leaders in the peace movement in recent years. The urgent need for new modes of thinking to deal with the nuclear age was first voiced by Albert Einstein and has since been echoed by others in the peace and disarmament movement.[4] Peace thinkers have long recognized the need for a new political order—a new organization of global politics that will insure that the bomb is forever banished—and not simply pushed out of sight.

Schell writes most eloquently of this particular problem, speaking of the need to "reinvent politics" so that the nuclear peril will not reemerge in some future time of hostility. In addition, many peace writers have concluded that the current crop of world political leaders are too bound by self-interest and too set on the preservation of the status quo to make the radical changes needed for disarmament. They have begun calling for a movement to change things from the bottom up, for a movement that aims at the hearts of ordinary men and women instead of the hardened arteries of the world's political leaders.

To understand how the worldwide activities of the Bahá'í Faith answer these issues, we must first examine the Bahá'í social principles in a new light. Rather than a litany of progressive but somehow unrelated ideas, we should understand that the principles outlined by Bahá'u'lláh's son, 'Abdu'l-Bahá, more than seventy years ago constituted an integrated system of new values aimed at building a peaceful world.

Since its founding, the Bahá'í Community has spent most of its energy promoting itself. Yet even in that apparently self-serving activity, Bahá'í teachers have been educating people to new ways of thinking about peace. Anyone who attends a fireside (a living room lecture on the Bahá'í Faith) is exposed to a set of progressive principles. And whether one ultimately embraces the Faith or not, understanding those principles surely has an effect on one's thinking. For embodied in the Bahá'í principles is an agenda for social progress that both matches the deepest wishes of the world's peoples and provides a cogent call for action.

The need for a social agenda that goes beyond a simple cry of PEACE! or STOP FIGHTING! has long been felt by many peace thinkers. The charter of the United Nations, for example, pays homage to the basic ideals of justice, human rights, and social progress in its preamble. Yet that body has been unable to get the world's nations to put those principles and ideals into action. The Bahá'í principles, however, because they are so universally felt—and because they are being spread at the grassroots level—offer something more. Let us consider each as a prerequisite for peace.

The oneness of humankind. Any new thinking about peace must begin with the understanding that all men and women are brothers and sisters. While that may sound like a simpleminded platitude, the kind of human unity envisioned by Bahá'ís goes beyond traditional religious concepts of universal love. To cite popular slogans, the concept embodies notions of *spaceship earth, planetary citizenship, world solidarity,* and more. Bahá'ís believe that humankind must embrace the idea that what harms anyone or any group, also hurts every other person or group on the planet; equally, whatever benefits one, benefits all. Hungry bellies in India, poor education in Africa, or any of a thousand injustices around the world are the concern of us all.

This principle implies, as the Guardian of the Bahá'í Faith has said, a "wider loyalty" to the world at large. It insists on "the subordination of national considerations and particularistic interests to the imperative and paramount claims of humanity as a whole, inasmuch as in a world of interdependent nations and peoples the advantage of the part is best to be reached by the advantage of the whole."[5] A true understanding of this principle would eliminate the basis for most wars. People in the Soviet Union are not our enemies. Rather, our foes are the outmoded concepts and misunderstandings that keep us apart.

The equality of men and women. While this is a simple matter of social justice to many in the world today, Bahá'ís believe that equality between the sexes is also a prerequisite for lasting peace. In 1912, 'Abdu'l-Bahá traveled to America and spoke repeatedly on behalf of women's rights. "When perfect equality shall be established between men and women," He said, "peace may be realized for the simple reason that womankind in general will never favor warfare. Women will not be willing to allow those whom they have so tenderly cared for to go to the battlefield. When they shall have a vote, they will oppose any cause of warfare."[6]

This tendency foreseen by 'Abdu'l-Bahá more than seventy years ago is clearly seen today. Recent polls show women are far more concerned about nuclear disarmament than men, and pollsters expect the women's vote, or the so-called gender gap, to play an important role in future politics. Women are at the forefront of peace movements around the world—whether it be trying to stop the deployment of missiles in Britain or at the Women's Peace Camp in Romulus, New York.

The elimination of prejudice. Bahá'ís seek to eradicate every last vestige of racial prejudice—along with prejudice based on class, economic, national, or religious distinctions. It is not hard to see the connection between prejudice and war. Racial or nationalistic differences have long been used to whip up hatred toward an enemy, making it easier for soldiers to overcome any moral or religious reluctance to kill. Whether the enemy was the *Hun,* or the *Nip,* or *Gook,* each derogatory term served to dehumanize soldiers on the opposing side. The problem we face in the nuclear age is to overcome ideological prejudice, which by itself accounts for much of the gulf between the United States and the Soviet Union.

The harmony of science and religion. The belief that science and religion are two sides of the same universe, rather than diametrically opposed viewpoints, is an essential element of theology in the Bahá'í Faith. Science, Bahá'ís believe, is humankind's best tool for learning about the physical nature of things; while religion shows us the path to understanding what is beyond. It is a principle that makes a deep faith in God possible for the many who might otherwise be atheists or agnostics.

As a prerequisite for peace, however, this notion also contains an important message: until we temper our scientific research with the moral and spiritual guidance of religion, it will continue to produce such horrors as the exploding bullet, mustard gas, napalm, and the atomic bomb. At the same time, unless we begin to apply the standards of scientific reasoning to our religious beliefs, fanaticism will continue to divide us, justify holy wars, and breed hatred.

This principle also warns us against the illusion that the problem of war can be solved by science. It alerts us to the trap of believing in the "technological fix." War is a moral problem: whether it be bigger bombs or outer space Star Wars weapons, we cannot invent our way out of the arms race. New machines will not save us from ourselves.

The elimination of extremes of wealth and poverty. There can be no justice in a world where some starve while others gorge themselves in materialism. In the Bahá'í vision of the future, both poverty and superwealth will become things of the past. Indeed, the new cry in the disarmament movement is for peace *and justice*—part of a growing recognition that no simple treaty between the superpowers will end war. As long as the Third World suffers in poverty, there can be no peace in the developed countries. This fact will be more acutely felt as new methods for separating uranium and plutonium from radioactive materials become simpler and cheaper, making nuclear weapons available to smaller nations and terrorist groups. In addition, advances in gene biology threaten to make a small inexpensive laboratory an arsenal shop of the highest order. Unscrupulous governments that are unable to satisfy their people will turn to such weapons unless measures are taken to address the economic injustice in the world.

Education for all. In the early 1960s, the United States recognized that development work around the world contributes to peace. It named its showpiece development agency the Peace Corps. Bahá'ís are also working to establish such Third World development projects, understanding that a prerequisite for lasting peace is the academic, moral, and spiritual development of the world's peoples. Currently, most education lacks the dimension of moral and spiritual training. In the Bahá'í view, such elements are essential. Peace must become a part of the curriculum. In some countries now, children drill with mock rifles or learn to throw grenade-shaped mallets as part of school sports. We must counter this with universal education aimed at the development of humanity's peaceful side. Outside the Bahá'í Faith, this understanding that education is essential for peace can be seen developing as teachers rally to the peace movement and to proposals for new institutions like the National Peace Academy.

The right to an unfettered search for truth. This principle defines the freedom and individual rights we must strive for in our new and peaceful world order. It is an acknowledgment of every individual's right to search for meaning and understanding. It carries an implicit guarantee that governments cannot abridge this right, either through secrecy, censorship, or police-state tactics.

A genuine understanding of this principle is indispensable to bringing about the change in consciousness so many have been calling for. For Bahá'ís, this idea is more a command than a pleasant homily. Humankind must work hard to cast off the outworn ideas and limited concepts of the old era to survive in this new one. The awakening of every individual is part of this; and each person's search for truth is a part of that awakening. 'Abdu'l-Bahá wrote: "The fact that we imagine ourselves to be right and everybody else wrong is the greatest of all obstacles in the path towards unity, and unity is necessary if we would reach truth, for truth is *one.*"[7]

A universal auxiliary language. One of the stumbling blocks to peace has been our failure to communicate with each other. The installation of the hotline between the United States and the Soviet Union in the early 1960s was an acknowledgment of this fact. But communication is nothing without understanding. For Bahá'ís, understanding can only come from an interchange of people and ideas on a global scale. Bahá'ís are actively making this interchange.

As a basic activity of their Faith, Bahá'ís are encouraged to move and settle in other countries. Called *pioneering* in the Faith, this is not done simply as missionary work. Rather, it is considered one way of beginning to build a global community and a sense of universal understanding that is necessary if we are to have peace.

One step in that process is a universal auxiliary language. Bahá'ís suggest that either a new or an existing language be chosen and taught in all schools on the planet—in addition to whatever native language is used. "The day is approaching when all the peoples of the world will have adopted one universal language and one common script," Bahá'u'lláh wrote. "When this is achieved, in whatsoever city a man may journey, it shall be as if he were entering his own home. These things are obligatory and absolutely essential."[8]

The common foundation of all religions. For Bahá'ís this understanding is central to any basis for a lasting peace. Many scenarios for World War III begin with a confrontation between the superpowers in the Middle East. Conflicts over religion, sad to say, fuel hostilities in that part of the world. Young men on various sides of the conflicts there take strength and guidance from religion as they prepare to kill other young men who worship the same God according to the teachings of their own religions. The fundamental teachings of Judaism, Christianity and Islam, the three major religions there, preach that there is only one God. For Muslims, this is especially so, as both Judaism and Christianity are considered precursors of Islam. There can be no more powerful way to end war in the Middle East than to promote the idea that God is one and that all religions, in their essence, agree. And that, of course, is the central tenet of the Bahá'í Faith.

If all these principles were fully accepted by humanity, great strides would be made in the eradication of war. The Bahá'í Faith is more than a system of values, however.

Bahá'u'lláh also created a concrete administrative structure for the Faith. In this structure is a model for the kind of new world politics that must eventually guide this planet's affairs if we are to survive in the nuclear age. Using this structure, the international Bahá'í Community has already begun building what one could call a worldwide network for peace.

In *The Fate of the Earth*, Jonathan Schell spends the first two chapters describing the likely effects of World War III. It is a gruesome tapestry he weaves. Not only would most human beings and animals on earth be destroyed, but for anyone who did survive there would be a "second death" of culture, knowledge, and civilization—including the loss of generations of unborn children. Schell writes: "Because the nuclear peril, like the scientific knowledge that gave rise to it, is probably global and everlasting, our solution must at least aim at being global and everlasting. And the only kind of solution that holds out this promise is a global political one."[9] "The task we face," he says later in the book, "is to find a means of political action that will permit human beings to pursue any end for the rest of time. We are asked to replace the mechanism by which political decisions, whatever they may be, are reached. In sum, the task is nothing less than to reinvent politics: to reinvent the world."[10]

Various aspects of the Bahá'í administrative order could serve as a model for this reinvention of politics. The Bahá'í system of administration provides a proven method for reaching decisions for a world constituency. Bahá'ís have their own method for worldwide democratic elections, for example. Over the last twenty years, Bahá'í elections have successfully brought together men and women of all races and nationalities to choose the Universal House of Justice, the nine individuals who lead the Bahá'í world community. Bahá'ís from countries without democracy or from nations with no history of self-determination participate in these elections. As well, Bahá'í elections are nonpartisan and are structured to weed out leaders who might seek to subvert the system for their own personal or political gain. Instead, Bahá'í elections, by their emphasis on spiritual qualities, tend to produce leaders of a different sort: men and women who are not committed to only one small constituency or special interest group, but who rather desire the good of all over the favor of the few.

Decision making in the Bahá'í Faith is based on a process called *consultation*, a nonadversarial method of arriving at clear and rational conclusions. Currently, many in the peace movement recognize the need for a new form of democratic decision making, having concluded that the old political order is defective. Some peace and antinuclear groups are already practicing a method called consensus decision making. Bahá'ís stand ready to offer the principles of consultation to a world that is tired of partisan bickering and political infighting.

Additionally, the Bahá'í administrative structure has distinct local, national and international units (called local and national Spiritual Assemblies). Each Assembly is a decision making body of nine people elected by its Bahá'í Community. And in the separation of local, national and international authority are safeguards that work to avoid the problems of bureaucratic overcentralization.

The extent to which this system has been developed is also worth noting. As of 1983, there were more than 25,000 Local Spiritual Assemblies around the world. Bahá'ís, in fact, reside at more than 112,000 localities in more than 340 countries and major territories. There are 135 National Spiritual Assemblies. The Universal House of Justice is located in Haifa, Israel. All together, it is truly a world-embracing order.

Bahá'ís, then, should be aware—and they should help others understand—that the very structure of our Faith is in reality an answer to what Jonathan Schell and others in the peace movement have been calling for. Our task in the 1980s is to make this known, to build bridges to the peace movement, and to offer our assistance in building a peaceful world.

"Unification of the whole of mankind is the hall-mark of the stage which human society is now approaching," wrote the Guardian of the Bahá'í Faith. "Unity of family, of tribe, of city-state, and nation have been successively attempted and fully established. World unity is the goal towards which a harassed humanity is striving. Nation-building has come to an end. The anarchy inherent in state sovereignty is moving towards a climax. A world, growing to maturity, must abandon this fetish, recognize the oneness and wholeness of human relationships, and establish once for all the machinery that can best incarnate this fundamental principle of its life."[11]

Ultimately, Bahá'ís believe, this machinery will evolve into a world federation, operating on the principle of collective security, in which all the world's nations would unite and stand ready to put down any aggression of one nation against another. Such a system would require a world legislature, representing all the nations and peoples of the planet. A world executive, backed by an international military force, would carry out decisions arrived at by the world legislature. And a world tribunal would adjudicate and deliver the final verdict on any disputes that might arise between nation-members.

That long-term vision may seem too much for those who are already burdened with the immediate peril of nuclear weapons and the current standoff between the superpowers. So let us return to what the Bahá'í Faith offers the peace movement now. A theme that has come up repeatedly among those who think and write about peace is the need to somehow "change the hearts" of humankind. It is a realization that the real issue of the nuclear age lies not in counting missiles or megatons, but in the nature of humanity itself. "It is in the hearts of men that the evil lies," wrote Bertrand Russell in 1961. "The vast instruments of terror that have been built up are external monuments to our own evil passions. Nothing in the nonhuman world affords any ground for existing hostilities. The trouble lies in the minds of men, and it is in enlightening the minds of men that the cure must be sought."[12]

While this notion of changing hearts and minds has long been voiced by peace thinkers, few have suggested how this task might be accomplished—or considered how far the change must go. Serious reflection leads to the inescapable conclusion that the change must be radical. We have seen great technical wonders in this century. We have put men on the moon, we have eradicated once incurable diseases, we have constructed consumer societies that, in some countries, provide the mass of people with more entertainment, comfort, transportation, and luxury than kings of old ever hoped to possess. Yet neither the best intentions of our greatest humanitarians, nor the most well-conceived plans of our wisest thinkers, nor the cream of our political leaders have succeeded in moving us back from the precipice of war. Instead, we have only moved closer.

In recognizing that failure, the time has come to look somewhere else for our healing. Bahá'ís look toward the new Revelation brought by Bahá'u'lláh. Among the roughly three million Bahá'ís around the world are men and women who were once followers of every religion practiced by humanity. There are Bahá'ís who were former Christians, Muslims, Jews, Hindus, Buddhists, and Zoroastrians. Followers of American Indian religions, members of various African tribes, and even staunch former atheists have become Bahá'ís. The Bahá'í Faith is not only universal in its teaching—it is universal in its embrace.

Throughout history, religion has moved humankind to its

highest achievements and proved that it can sustain itself far longer than the ideas or leadership of any political ruler. Wrote 'Abdu'l-Bahá: "The will of every sovereign prevaileth during his reign, the will of every philosopher findeth expression in a handful of disciples during his lifetime, but the Power of the Holy Spirit shineth radiantly in the realities of the Messengers of God, and strengtheneth Their will in such wise as to influence a great nation for thousands of years and to regenerate the human soul and revive mankind."[13]

This kind of spiritual power is again manifest in the Bahá'í Faith. More than twenty thousand early believers suffered martyrdom rather than recant their beliefs. And today in Iran, Bahá'ís have again given their lives and faced persecution to demonstrate the same commitment and fortitude.

In studying the Bahá'í Faith, one discovers certain concepts that by their very nature tend to shake off old thinking. The idea that all the world's religions are a progressive expression of God's will is a revolutionary concept. Understanding that concept, I believe, tends to break down the kind of simplistic, black-and-white thinking that is associated with the militaristic strategies that have set the world wobbling on the edge of a nuclear cataclysm.

The process by which spiritual forces change people is hard to describe or characterize, for it varies from individual to individual. Some people simply come to know about this new reality after a spiritual experience. Others work to transform themselves through long hours of prayer, meditation and practice. Still others feel changed by visions, dreams or other events. For some it is the social experience of working with others toward a common goal. No matter how it happens, it is essential to the creation of a more peaceful world. "If the inner landscape of our souls does not change," writes Schell, "the outer landscape of the world will not change, either."[14]

The Bahá'í Faith, then, in addition to its status as an emerging world religion, must also be classified as a global peace movement. While Bahá'ís may not be marching in the streets or standing in silent vigils, most are consciously trying to spread the new age principles that must be adopted if there is to be peace. They do this by telling people about Bahá'u'lláh. As those who are told realize that God has once again sent a messenger to earth and that He has come teaching world peace, their hearts are touched and their thinking is changed. For a Brahmin in India, that may mean a new recognition that the lower castes are brothers and sisters all the same; for an African it may mean accepting without prejudice the people in a neighboring tribe; for a man in the Middle East, it may mean a new understanding of the status of women. For an American, it may confer a new hope about the possibility of peace—both without and within. The latest call among activists in the peace movement is for just such a worldwide, grassroots movement for peace.

"From Iceland to Tasmania, from Vancouver to the China Sea spreads the radiance and extend the ramifications of this world-enfolding System, this many-hued and firmly-knit Fraternity," wrote the Guardian of the Bahá'í Faith, "infusing into every man and woman it has won to its cause a faith, a hope and a vigor that a wayward generation has long lost, and is powerless to recover. They who preside over the immediate destinies of this troubled world, they who are responsible for its chaotic state, its fears, its doubts, its miseries will do well, in their bewilderment, to fix their gaze and ponder in their hearts upon the evidences of this saving grace of the Almighty that lies within their reach—a grace that can ease their burden, resolve their perplexities, and illuminate their path."[15]

As Bahá'ís, the challenge is clear. We should, as the Guardian urges, be active in the social movements that are in harmony with our ideals, aiming to build bridges between those movements and our own. And we should do this without compromising our commitment to noninvolvement in partisan politics. At the same time, we must not forget where the real answers are. "The true cause of the ills of humanity is its disunity," wrote the Universal House of Justice. "No matter how perfect may be the machinery devised by the leaders of men for the political unity of the world, it will still not provide the antidote to the poison sapping the vigor of present-day society. These ills can be cured only through the instrumentality of God's Faith. . . . The Bahá'í Community is a worldwide organization seeking to establish true and universal peace on earth."[16]

We must let people know about this vast and world-embracing peace movement. By striving to better understand this great Cause ourselves, we must be prepared to offer our help to those who are searching for answers to the greatest peril of our day.

Notes

1. Jonathan Schell, "Reflections—The Abolition," *The New Yorker Magazine*, 2 (January 1984) p. 38.

2. Ibid., p. 66.

3. Bahá'u'lláh, *Gleanings from the Writings of Bahá'u'lláh* (Wilmette, Ill.: Bahá'í Publishing Trust, 1952) pp. 79–80.

4. ". . . the unleashed power of the atom has changed everything save our modes of thinking and we thus drift toward unparalleled catastrophes."—Albert Einstein.

5. Shoghi Effendi, *The Promised Day Is Come* (Wilmette, Ill.: Bahá'í Publishing Trust, 1941) p. 127.

6. 'Abdu'l-Bahá, *The Promulgation of Universal Peace* (Wilmette, Ill.: Bahá'í Publishing Trust, Second Ed., 1982) p. 167.

7. 'Abdu'l-Bahá, *Paris Talks* (London: Bahá'í Publishing Trust, 1912) p. 136.

8. *Gleanings*, pp. 249–50.

9. Jonathan Schell, *The Fate of the Earth* (New York: Avon Books, 1982) p. 108.

10. Ibid., p. 266.

11. Shoghi Effendi, *The World Order of Bahá'u'lláh* (Wilmette, Ill: Bahá'í Publishing Trust, 1938) p. 202.

12. Bertrand Russell, *Has Man a Future?* (New York: Simon and Schuster, 1962) p. 45.

13. Peter Muhlschlegel, *Auguste Forel and the Bahá'í Faith* (Oxford: George Ronald, 1978) p. 27.

14. "Reflections," p. 40.

15. *World Order of Bahá'u'lláh*, p. 201.

16. *Messages from the Universal House of Justice, 1968–1973* (Wilmette, Ill.: Bahá'í Publishing Trust, 1976) p. 46.

The Antinuclear Movement and the Bahá'í Community

By Robert T. Phillips

T HE IMAGES ARE NUMBING, excruciatingly sad, yet almost poetic in their gray finality. The last three survivors in the film *Testament*; Jason Robards as the dying old man revisiting the rubble of his home in what was Kansas City in the T.V. movie *The Day After*; the horror of the photos in Hiroshima exhibits; the facts, tears and fears mirrored in the slides, video tapes, and lectures sponsored by antinuclear groups of students, health professionals, women's organizations, and others. In the 1980s, America and much of the world have finally begun to face the reality of life, or the end of life, in the nuclear age.

Where in this vast and growing awakening known as the peace movement or the antinuclear movement is to be found the organized efforts of the Bahá'í Community? What do the seekers of the Light have to do with humanity's greatest darkness? It is the purpose of this chapter to explore the major threat of our time, of all time—nuclear war. The exploration will focus primarily on the political and social conditions that have made nuclear weapons the foundation of the national defense policies of the world's superpowers. It will also explore the possibilities for change, for averting global destruction, both in terms of the Bahá'í teachings on peace and war and of how those teachings, in interaction with the world at large, shape the role of the Bahá'í Community as the potential spiritual leader of the antinuclear movement.

"... The unleashed power of the atom has changed everything save our modes of thinking and we thus drift toward unparalleled catastrophes," wrote Albert Einstein. It is this way of thinking, our current model of reality, that is both the genesis of the problem and the clue to the solution. Behavioral science has demonstrated repeatedly that human actions spring from individual and communal beliefs and values. These are reinforced by training and education through such mediums as the home, school, religion, and commercial advertising. It is our beliefs about such things as our country, its political and economic system, national security, and our enemies that ultimately create our political reality. That reality is starkly defined in the following statements:

Reduced to numbers, the world's arms race and its effects on human life easily lose touch with reality. The most fertile imagination will boggle at:
☐ a current world military budget of $660,000,000,000 a year (an increase of 10% from the preceding year);
☐ a stockpile of over 50,000 nuclear weapons;
☐ 25 million men and women under arms;
☐ 1 billion people living under military-controlled governments;
☐ more than 9 million civilians killed in "conventional" wars since Hiroshima.[1]

And:

At Hiroshima, humanity reached an historical convergence of its capacity for evil and its genius for science.

Incredible advances in technology have enabled the age-old problem of war to lead the world to the brink of its own annihilation. Humanity seems to be rapidly moving toward a fatal point. The nuclear arms race has taken us from a mere two bombs in 1945 to more than 50,000 in 1981. In the next few years, the U.S. and the Soviet Union plan to add thousands more nuclear weapons to their already bulging stockpiles. Nuclear arms proliferation brings perhaps the most uncontrollable dimension ever to this already unstable situation.[2]

The quotations are endless, as is our ability to chronicle our dilemma rather than solve it. All of us, Bahá'ís and non-Bahá'ís, live under the nuclear shadow. It is a reality we have all helped to create. Before it can be changed, or before it ends human life, we must find its roots within us and change ourselves. The Guardian of the Bahá'í Faith, Shoghi Effendi stated:

How great . . . the responsibility . . . upon the present generation of the American believers . . . to weed out . . . those faults, habits, and tendencies which they have inherited from their own nation. . . . Nor must they overlook the fact that the World Order, whose basis they . . . are now laboring to establish, can never be reared unless and until the generality of the people to which they belong has been already purged from the divers ills, whether social or political, that now so severely afflict it.[3]

What are some of the "faults, habits, and tendencies" that have led to our nuclear dilemma? Or to put it another way, what are the beliefs about nuclear war that Bahá'ís have inherited from American political culture? We will examine a few of these major beliefs and briefly comment on how they influence Bahá'ís and erode the ability of the Bahá'í Community to act on the Bahá'í teachings on peace—teachings that support a radical departure from current public policy on the production, use, deployment, proliferation, and significance of nuclear arms.

National Security. Ever since 1512 when Machiavelli, in his treatise *The Prince,* articulated a political view of society separated into political entities, each locked in a ceaseless struggle with its rivals for ascendancy, war has been seen as the legitimate tool of foreign policy when diplomacy fails. In such a world, military strength has become the measure of the successful nation and the ultimate guardian of national security.

Our current model of national security assumes that the maintenance of peace and the protection of national sovereignty depends on the possession of sufficient nuclear weapons. Yet, it is the great irony of nuclear weapons that they are the first weapon, devised "in the national interest," whose use and impact transcends national boundaries. The existence of nuclear weapons has led to the greatest insecurity man has ever known—the omnipresent threat of global destruction. Nonetheless, these weapons are justified daily by political leaders as necessary for the preservation of American, or Russian, or French, or Chinese, or "Free World" security. Just as Bahá'u'lláh's declaration that the *"earth is one country and mankind its citizens"* introduces a new vision of a unified global society which transcends national boundaries, so do nuclear weapons with their radiation and atmospheric effects remove the possibility of preserving the security of any nation through the resort to nuclear war to resolve international conflict.

The source of this dilemma lies within our own beliefs about political life. Nuclear war is not a natural disaster, but a conscious choice by political leaders as a political and military policy to preserve national security. Such a political consciousness, limited in its vision to the nation state as the final source and arbiter of human rights, is incapable of dealing with the global phenomenon of nuclear war. As

Schell has written in his important book, *The Fate of the Earth*:

> Thus the peril of extinction by nuclear arms is doubly ours: first, because we have it in our power to prevent the catastrophe, and second, because the catastrophe cannot occur unless, by pursuing our political aims through violence, we bring it about . . . nothing could be more crucial to an understanding of the practical dimensions of the nuclear predicament than a precise understanding of what nuclear weapons have done to war, and through war to the system of sovereignty of which war has traditionally been an indispensable part.[4]

Given the bankruptcy of current policies on national security, what is the source of security envisioned by the Bahá'í teachings? More importantly, how can these teachings be actively infused into the popular movement searching for a public policy capable of averting nuclear disaster? 'Abdu'l-Bahá spoke out forcefully in 1875, for collective security as the political doctrine to achieve universal peace:

> True civilization will unfurl its banner . . . whenever a certain number of its distinguished and high-minded sovereigns . . . shall . . . arise . . . to establish the Cause of Universal Peace. They must make the Cause of Peace the object of general consultation, and seek by every means in their power to establish a Union of the nations of the world.[5]

'Abdu'l-Bahá goes on to speak about national security and the necessary military and weapons policies to achieve and protect that security.

> . . . The size of the armaments of every government should be strictly limited, for if the preparations for war

and the military forces of any nation should be allowed
to increase, they will arouse the suspicion of others.
The fundamental principle underlying this solemn Pact
should be so fixed that if any government later violate
any one of its provisions, all the governments on earth
should arise to reduce it to utter submission . . .

Observe that if such a happy situation be forthcoming,
no government would need continually to pile up the
weapons of war, nor feel itself obliged to produce ever
new military weapons with which to conquer the human
race.[6]

It is useful to note with what practical details 'Abdu'l-
Bahá deals with the policy issues raised by the existence of
armaments and war. Bahá'ís should follow this example in
their approach to nuclear arms.

The overwhelming physical and psychological fact about
nuclear weapons is that there are thousands of them, fully
armed, ready to fire, aimed directly at you and me, and
much of the rest of humankind. Defusing this intensely personal threat must be an integral part of any credible Bahá'í
program on nuclear war. Programs that talk only of the
oneness of mankind and the achievement of peace through
universal faith will not be responsive to the fear and anxiety
most people experience, consciously or unconsciously, living in the nuclear age.

Personal and National Survival. Much has been written,
often with gallows humor, concerning the absurdity of our
civil defense measures to counter a nuclear attack. Yet
there is a powerful current of political and military policy,
born out of traditional thinking about war, that maintains
that this country can fight and win a nuclear war. What else
could explain the continuation of the arms race long past
the point where deterrence, in terms of the U.S.'s or the
U.S.S.R.'s ability to destroy each other many times over,
has been achieved? The narrow nationalistic mentality

which promotes nuclear weapons, and also plans for defending against them, is a mentality which sees as an option the possibility of using and surviving nuclear war.

Such major public thinkers as Edward Teller and Herman Kahn have assured us that:

> . . . this much is certain: Properly defended, we can survive a nuclear attack; we can dig out of the ruins; we can recover from the catastrophe . . . as a nation, we shall survive, and our democratic . . . institutions will survive with us, if we make adequate preparations for survival now—and adequate preparations are within our reach and our capabilities.[7]

Or more recently, in an article called "Victory Is Possible," Colin Gray and Keith Payn insist: "If American nuclear power is to support U.S. foreign policy objectives, the United States must possess the ability to wage nuclear war rationally."[8]

This idea of a "manageable catastrophe" is not alien to Bahá'ís. Along with their fellow citizens, many Bahá'ís have assumed that nuclear war is survivable and that social existence as we know it would continue. In fact, it would not be unreasonable to assume that there are some Bahá'ís who look to nuclear war as the necessary precursor to mass enrollment in the Bahá'í Cause. They believe that only such a cataclysmic shock could qualify for the event necessary to create the Lesser Peace or political peace envisioned in the Bahá'í Sacred Writings. Such thinking, to the degree it exists, leads to a dangerous passivity regarding the responsibility of the Bahá'í Community to work aggressively to transform the political consciousness and the accompanying public policies that lead us toward nuclear war.

There is a growing body of scientific and medical literature that persuasively suggests that even a partial nuclear exchange would be such a blow to the planet that human life would cease to exist. In such a case, Bahá'u'lláh's vision of a New World Order would be still-born.

Two scientific reports have recently been published, dealing with the probable effects of nuclear war upon the earth's climate and the life of the planet. The first discovery is already widely known within the scientific community of climatologists, geophysicists, and biologists here and abroad, and has been confirmed in detail by scientists in the Soviet Union. Computer models demonstrate that a nuclear war involving the exchange of less than one third of the total American and Soviet arsenal will change the climate of the entire Northern Hemispere, shifting it abruptly from its present seasonal state to a long, sunless, frozen night. This will be followed after some months by a settling of nuclear soot and dust, then by a new malignant kind of sunlight, with all of its ultraviolet band, capable of blinding most terrestrial animals, no longer shielded from the earth by the ozonosphere. In the same research, new calculations of the extent and intensity of radioactive fallout predict the exposure of large land areas to much more intense levels of radiation than expected. The report is referred to as TTAPS . . .

The second piece of work, by Paul Ehrlich and 19 other distinguished biologists, demonstrates that the predictions of TTAPS mean nothing less than the extinction of much of the earth's biosphere, very possibly involving the Southern Hemisphere as well as the Northern.

Taken together, the two papers change everything in the world about the prospect of thermonuclear warfare. They have already received a careful and critical review by scientists representing the disciplines concerned, here and abroad, and there already appears to be an unprecedented degree of concurrence with the technical details as well as the conclusions drawn . . .

It is a new world, demanding a new kind of diplomacy and a new logic.[9]

There are numerous other sources, equally chilling in their conclusions, that suggest that nuclear war is not survivable for an individual, national community, or for the earth itself. Such a conclusion should destroy any complacency Bahá'ís might have about their role. The failure of the Bahá'í Community to respond aggressively to the issue of nuclear war could well mean the loss of their opportunity to assist in the spiritualization of the planet—for the earth and the meaning of physical existence would have ceased to be.

There is another aspect to the illusion of survivability. Once the recognition comes that our species faces the real possibility of the end of its existence—extinction in a nuclear Armageddon—the foundation of religious activity and belief is undermined.

Concerning the nuclear impact on the theological mode, I can draw upon a certain amount of experience with Hiroshima survivors. Many tried to invoke Buddhist principles, and others Shinto, Christian or various spiritual combinations . . . But they consistently found that such religious imagery . . . helped relatively little in their psychological struggle as survivors and rarely enabled them to give form or meaning to the experience. The magnitude of the experience seemed to defy the religious precepts that were accessible to them.

The general principle operating for them—and now for us—may well be that as death imagery comes to take the shape of total annihilation or extinction, religious symbolism becomes both more sought after and more inadequate.[10]

The challenge to those who pose spiritual solutions to nu-clear problems is to offer solutions that provide both a vi-sion of a future world that transcends the nuclear peril, as well as a functional political system capable of effecting the transition from nuclear nationalism to a global society that can manage and contain the power of the atom. The Bahá'í Community will find its role in the antinuclear movement lacking credibility unless it can combine its vision of a New World Order with the manifestation of a new political pro-cess capable of generating policy alternatives to such nu-clear issues as proliferation and disarmament. Otherwise, the imminent threat of human extinction will make the con-ceptual call to a New World Order seem to be merely an-other utopian religious appeal—cruelly divorced from real-ity and unable or unwilling to speak to the fears and anxie-ties of a generation living under the nuclear shadow.

Such considerations as those above suggest the import-ance of a study of the promise and perils of an organized and assertive initiative, sponsored by the local and national institutions of the Bahá'í Faith, on the nuclear arms issue. As Bahá'ís must refrain from involvement in partisan poli-tics, it is useful to briefly examine the nature of the anti-nuclear movement as that would be the political environ-ment into which Bahá'ís would move.[11]

While some aspects of the major organizations opposing nuclear weapons or the use of nuclear power tend to coin-cide with liberal or leftist politics in the West, it is instruc-tive to note the important divergence of this issue from such politics. For example, the personal identification of many establishment or conservative individuals with the move to ban nuclear weapons is unique among antiwar movements. At a series of twenty-seven national confer-ences starting in 1980 sponsored by the Physicians for So-cial Responsibility, featured speakers have included a former director of the CIA, retired American generals and admirals, scientists from Project Manhattan (which developed the first atomic bomb), assorted scientists, university presidents, deans and faculty from some of the nation's most prestigious medical schools and universities. The major purpose of the conferences was to show the true dimensions of a nuclear war and that there is no possible medical response. The American Council of Catholic Bishops issued in 1983, a strong statement condemning the use, deployment, and even the existence of nuclear weapons.

In short, the antinuclear movement counts as some of its most ardent supporters leaders from many of the conservative professional and scientific elite groups in America. They are grouped together with other, more partisan, groups who see the nuclear issue as part of the broader struggle against the oppression of modern superpowers. Yet even in terms of ideology, diversity prevails as both communist and capitalist nations are actively involved in stockpiling, testing and deploying nuclear arms.

Thus, this issue, almost alone of major social concerns, transcends the normal partisan and ideological quarrels that could ensnare and divide the Bahá'í Community. The possibilities for leadership are as manifold as the urgency for commitment is immediate. To quote a recently published and respected text in its section on the nature of the antinuclear movement in Europe, the U.S., and the U.S.S.R.:

This great struggle for global transformation encompasses normal politics, but it is far broader than any strictly political experience, resembling more the emergence of a new religion or civilization on a global scale than a change, however radical, in the personnel or orientation of political leaders.[12]

Our task therefore is to stimulate the thinking and activities of Bahá'ís and Bahá'í Communities in response to the unprecedented challenge posed by the issue of nuclear war.

It is one of the cardinal purposes of Bahá'í laws and institutions to become ". . . a supreme instrument for the establishment of the Most Great Peace. . ."[13] And, "It should also be borne in mind that the machinery of the Cause has been so fashioned that whatever is deemed necessary to incorporate into it in order to keep it in the forefront of all progressive movements, can, according to the provisions made by Bahá'u'lláh, be safely embodied therein."[14]

The issue of nuclear war offers an excellent opportunity for the Bahá'í Community to move to the forefront of the peace movement. This opportunity lies in the historic service that could be rendered to the many organizations and persons who have dedicated themselves, often at great personal sacrifice, to the cause of world peace. For, while the diversity of the peace movement is a strength that enables it to transcend petty partisan issues, that same diversity is also a source of fragmentation and disunity that diffuse its impact on the popular consciousness and on public policy.

What is needed is the leadership of a spiritual consciousness that is unifying and animating, and that is manifested in an administrative system committed to peace and able to manage diversity. Such leadership could be taken up by the Bahá'í Community. Motivated by the spirit of service, ready to learn from those more versed in the issue than ourselves, now is the time to offer—perhaps initially as the sponsor of educational forums or as the coordinating body for public programs—the gift of Bahá'u'lláh's Administrative Order, the divine mechanism for the resolution of human conflict and the spiritualization of human affairs.

An initial step in this direction would be to educate oneself and one's community about nuclear war. This can be done by reading, starting perhaps with the books mentioned herein; viewing some of the excellent films and videotapes available for rent or purchase;[15] attending the meetings and conferences of such peace and antinuclear groups as the Women's International League for Peace and Freedom, the Fellowship of Reconciliation, Ground Zero, Physicians for

Social Responsibility, Creative Initiative, the Union of Concerned Scientists, and others.

At the same time, there must be an equal effort to turn to those passages in the Bahá'í Writings, many of which are mentioned in other chapters in this volume, which deal with war, peace, politics, collective security, spiritual transformation, and the special leadership roles of women and youth in the mobilization of the Bahá'í Community. Indeed, the study of the issues of war and peace is an excellent entry into the related topic of the equality of men and women. For it is important to note that:

> The psychological background to this nuclear madness is an overemphasis on self-assertion, control and power, excessive competition, and an obsession with "winning"—the typical traits of partriarchal culture. The aggressive threats that have been made by men throughout human history are now being made with nuclear weapons, without recognition of the enormous difference in violence and destructive potential. Nuclear weapons, then, are the most tragic case of people holding onto an old paradigm that has long lost its usefulness.[16]

Thus, Bahá'í men and women have the double task of exposing and eradicating the "faults, habits, and tendencies" relative to war and violence they have inherited from their culture, and also the sexist attitudes which often support and underlie those tendencies. Such a task can only be approached honestly and openly and requires the wholehearted support and sponsorship of Bahá'í institutions and schools. Just as the intense and effective involvement of the American Bahá'í Community, especially its youth, in the issues of racism and the Vietnam War in the 1960s and early 1970s provided the energy that sparked the growth of the Faith to dramatic new levels of enrollments and activity, so can an equally intense commitment to the antinuclear war movement touch off a renewed surge of growth. The

time has never been more propitious. As a major study
on nuclear weapons sponsored by Harvard University reported:

> Now, in many Western industrialized countries, the pub-
> lic is in a state of political arousal, due to a heightened
> sense of fear. Inevitably, a search for an escape or relief
> will follow. This search can take three directions: first, a
> return to denying that nuclear dangers exist; second,
> finding refuge in simplistic, unexamined solutions; third,
> a commitment to finding ways to more secure grounds
> that take into account the complexities of the situation,
> yet promise a less threatening future.[17]

The mandate is clear. The need unmistakable. In compelling contrast to the gloom and doom cast by the nuclear
specter, the Bahá'í Community can move joyously and in
unity to offer solutions and hope to a world near hopelessness and despair. To do so, however, will require a significant new commitment—based on lessons from past
victories with other social issues, inspired by the fearless
example of leadership 'Abdu'l-Bahá offered to the war
weary of His time, led by the Administrative Order erected
by Shoghi Effendi, guided by the messages and plans of the
Universal House of Justice, and secure in the knowledge
that "... *in this day there is no more important matter in
the world than that of Universal Peace.*"[18]

Notes

1. Ruth Sivard, *World Military and Social Expenditures 1983*,
World Policy Institute, New York City.

2. Danny Collum and Mernie King, "Freezing the Arms
Race," *A Mattter of Faith: A Study Guide for Churches on the
Nuclear Arms Race* (Washington, D.C.: Sojourners, 1982) p. 77.

3. Shoghi Effendi, *The Advent of Divine Justice* (Wilmette,
Ill.: Bahá'í Publishing Trust, 1939) p. 17.

4. Jonathan Schell, *The Fate of the Earth* (New York: Avon, 1982) p. 189.

5. 'Abdu'l-Bahá, *The Secret of Divine Civilization* (Wilmette, Ill.: Bahá'í Publishing Trust, 1957) pp. 64–65.

6. Ibid.

7. Edward Teller, *The Legacy of Hiroshima* (Garden City, NY: Doubleday, 1957) pp. 244.

8. Robert Jay Lifton and Richard Falk, *Indefensible Weapons* (New York: Basic Books, 1982) p. 21.

9. Lewis Thomas, M.D., "TTAPS for Earth," *Discovery Magazine* (February 1984) p. 30.

10. *Weapons*, p. 70.

11. "Let them refrain from associating themselves, whether by word or by deed, with the political pursuits of their respective nations, with the policies of their governments and the schemes and programs of parties and factions. In such controversies they should assign no blame, take no side, further no design and identify themselves with no system prejudicial to the best interests of that worldwide Fellowship which it is their aim to guard and foster."—Shoghi Effendi, *The World Order of Bahá'u'lláh* (Bahá'í Publishing Trust, 1938) p. 64.

12. *Weapons*, p. 264.

13. *World Order*, p. 19.

14. Ibid., pp. 22–23.

15. A film company called Educational Film and Video Project has produced several excellent documentaries for public education on nuclear war: "The Last Epidemic," "In the Nuclear Shadow," and "What About the Russians?" To rent or purchase contact: Educational Film and Video Project, 1725B Seabright Avenue, Santa Cruz, California 95062, (408) 427-2627. Prices: two day rentals—$35 for video or $50 for film: purchase—$55 for VHS and Beta tapes, $75 for ¾-inch tapes, $300 for film (California residents add 6% sales tax).

16. Fritjof Capra, *The Turning Point* (New York: Bantam Books, 1982) p. 242.

17. The Harvard Nuclear Study Group, *Living with Nuclear Weapons* (Cambridge, Mass.: Harvard University Press, 1983) p. 4.

18. 'Abdu'l-Bahá, quoted in *The Bahá'í Revelation* (London: Bahá'í Publishing Trust, 1955) p. 208.

A Long and Thorny Path: Race Relations in the American Bahá'í Community

by Richard W. Thomas, Ph.D.

F UTURE HISTORIANS OF AMERICAN relations who examine the positive influences of various personalities
and movements upon black/white interactions during the
twentieth century will find 'Abdu'l-Bahá and the American Bahá'í Community exceedingly interesting. Possessing
much broader and more comprehensive perspectives in race
relations than we can now imagine, these future scholars
will probably wonder what the racial fuss was all about.
Why, they will ask, was the color of skin or the shape and
texture of head and hair so important that people fought,
maimed and killed over them? What was it about being
white, they most certainly will wonder, that infused white
people in the past with such arrogance?

As these future scholars study the organizations and
movements which fought against racial discrimination and
for racial unity—such as the National Association for the
Advancement of Colored People, the socialist and communist parties, and the various labor and Civil Rights
movements—they will find all of them to have been unfortunately too limited in scope and vision. Future scholars
will agree that few, if any, succeeded in unifying black and

white Americans into an organic multiracial community, the vital first step in the long and thorny path toward the unity of humankind. Let us hope that the American Bahá'í Community will be spared this future judgment.

A New Solution to An Old Problem. American Bahá'ís have a rich legacy in the arena of race relations. It is not all rosey as some would like to believe, but it is instructive and inspirational. When it is embarrassing, for example when in 1914 some white Bahá'ís in Washington, D.C. considered integrated meetings "the one serious obstacle to the growth of the cause" in that city, it is enlightening, because in the end the Washington Bahá'ís decided to conform to the Bahá'í principle of racial unity. This part of American Bahá'í history is profoundly instructive. As Gayle Morrison points out in her excellent book, *To Move the World:*

> The racial problems in Washington, D.C., from 1914 to 1916 cannot be seen simply as an example of a religious community failing to live up to its ideals. Rather, these early Bahá'ís are revealed as having been immature, deprived of their accustomed leadership, on their own and groping toward the light of understanding. The decision to follow either the Bahá'í way or the way of the world was theirs to make, without even a further word of prompting from 'Abdu'l-Bahá. Thus—however many unresolved feelings may have remained on both sides for many years to come—the 1916 resolution to end the white-only meeting and demonstrably reunite their efforts proved the sincerity of their commitment to a changing order.[1]

The racial conflicts of the Washington Bahá'í Community were not much different from those of the rest of America. The only real difference was the ideals to which Bahá'ís aspired. No other multiracial organization or movement placed such high demands on its followers or provided such an imposing human model of its teachings for them to emulate. "Let them call to mind," Shoghi Effendi, Guardian of the Bahá'í Faith, reminded Bahá'ís in 1939, "fearlessly and determinedly, the example and conduct of 'Abdu'l-Bahá while in their midst. Let them remember His courage, His genuine love, His informal and indiscriminatory fellowship, His contempt for and impatience of criticism, tempered by His tact and wisdom." Shoghi Effendi encouraged American Bahá'ís to "revive and perpetuate the memory of those unforgettable and historic episodes and occasions on which He ['Abdu'l-Bahá] so strikingly demonstrated His keen sense of justice, His spontaneous sympathy, for the downtrodden, His ever-abiding sense of the oneness of the human race, His overflowing love for its members, and His displeasure with those who dared to flout His wishes, to deride His methods, to challenge His principles, or to nullify His acts."[2]

'Abdu'l-Bahá taught Bahá'ís to view diverse racial groups in a positive manner. *"Bahá'u'lláh hath said,"* 'Abdu'l-Bahá wrote, *"that the various races of human kind lend a composite harmony and beauty of color to the whole. Let all associate, therefore, in this great human garden even as flowers grow and blend together side by side without discord or disagreement between them."*[3] Here was a dynamic new way of viewing the human race, a positive approach based on an appreciation of the diversity of race and color within the human family.

'Abdu'l-Bahá elaborated on this theme time and time again, massaging its urgent message into the soul and heart of humankind. *"Consider the flowers of a garden: though differing in kind, colour, form and shape, yet, inasmuch as they are refreshed by the waters of one spring, revived by the breath of one wind, invigorated by the rays of one sun, this diversity increaseth their charm and addeth unto their beauty."*[4] Diversity of human color and form, according to

'Abdu'l-Bahá, enhanced the overall beauty of humankind. This Bahá'í approach to human beauty was in sharp contrast to the prevailing esthetic standards of the time which were based upon certain ideal European physical and cultural types.

'Abdu'l-Bahá saw the lack of human diversity as negative, lacking the power to enrich and influence human life and potential. *"How unpleasing to the eye if all the flowers and plants, the leaves and blossoms, the fruits, the branches and the trees of that garden were all of the of same.shape and colour! Diversity of hues, form and shape, enricheth and adorneth the garden, and heighteneth the effect thereof. In like manner, when divers shades of thought, temperament and character, are brought together under the power and influence of one central agency, the beauty and glory of human perfection will be revealed and made manifest."* And that central agency, according to 'Abdu'l-Bahá, is *"Naught but the celestial potency of the Word of God, which ruleth and transcendeth the realities of all things, is capable of harmonizing the divergent thoughts, sentiments, ideas, and convictions of the children of men."*[5]

In 1911, the Universal Races Congress was held in London to discuss problems of race in the world. It included such Americans as W. E. B. Dubois and Mary White Ovington, representing the NAACP; Franz Boas, the famous anthropologist; and Charles A. Eastman, an American Indian. Unable to attend Himself, 'Abdu'l-Bahá sent a message to the conference in which He explained the importance of diversity in the human family. He asked them to consider the varieties of flowers in a garden and how they *"seem but to enhance the loveliness of each other"*; and *"when differences of color, ideas, and character are found in the human Kingdom, and come under the control of the power of unity, they too show their essential beauty and perfection."* Rivalry between the different races of humankind while necessary in past history was no longer necessary. *"Nay, rather! interdependence and cooperation,"* 'Abdu'l-Bahá advised the conference, *"are seen to produce the highest welfare in nations. The struggle that man continues is caused by prejudice and bigotry."*[6]

Stressing the great importance of the Universal Races Congress, 'Abdu'l-Bahá implored the conferees not to allow it to be *"a thing of words, but of deeds." "Some congresses are held only to increase differences. Let it not be so with you. Let your effort be to find harmony. Let Brotherhood be felt and seen among you; and carry ye its quickening power throughout the world. It is my prayer that the work of the Congress will bear great fruit."*[7] Unfortunately, this was both the first and the last Universal Races Congress.

Wherever 'Abdu'l-Bahá witnessed racial diversity, He called attention to it. Maḥmúd-i Zarqání, who kept diaries of 'Abdu'l-Bahá's Western tours, observed in April 1912, when 'Abdu'l-Bahá gave a talk at Howard University: "Here, as elsewhere, when both white and colored people were present, 'Abdu'l-Bahá seemed happiest."[8] Looking out over the audience 'Abdu'l-Bahá said: *"Today I am most happy, for I see here a gathering of the servants of God. I see white and black sitting together."*[9]

The next day 'Abdu'l-Bahá lectured three times. As the time for the third meeting approached, He was very tired and was not planning to talk long. But he became inspired by the sight of blacks and whites in the audience.[10] *"A meeting such as this seems like a beautiful cluster of precious jewels—pearls, rubies, diamonds, sapphires. It is a source of joy and delight."* Explaining the significance of this harmony, 'Abdu'l-Bahá went on to say: *"Whatever is conducive to the unity of the world of mankind is most acceptable and praiseworthy. . . . Therefore, in the world of humanity it is wise and seemly that all the individual members should manifest unity and affinity. In the clustered jewels of the races may the blacks be as sapphires and rubies and the whites as diamonds and pearls. The composite beauty of humanity will be witnessed in their unity and blending."*[11]

'Abdu'l-Bahá called on both black and white Americans to see themselves in a new light, to raise themselves above the norms of a segregated society. His images of different colored flowers and jewels replaced the racist images so common and acceptable at the time. 'Abdu'l-Bahá knew instinctively that He had to counter these negative cultural tendencies so ingrained in the American national character with a flow of radiant images of racial diversity. *"As I stand here tonight and look upon this assembly,"* He told one audience, *"I am reminded curiously of a beautiful bouquet of violets gathered together in varying colors, dark and light."*[12] 'Abdu'l-Bahá repeatedly warned Americans about what would happen if they did not solve their racial problems, yet He also stressed the positive aspects of *what could happen* if they were unified in love and harmony. *"When the racial elements of the American nation unite in actual fellowship and accord, the lights of the oneness of humanity will shine, the day of eternal glory and bliss will dawn, the spirit of God encompass, and the divine favors descend."*[13]

For those who may not have fully understood 'Abdu'l-Bahá's talks on the significance of race, His actions left no doubts. On several occasions, in His gentle, unassuming way, 'Abdu'l-Bahá challenged the racial mores of white society by acting out the principles of racial unity. On one occasion, after His talk at Howard University, 'Abdu'l-Bahá was invited to a lunch in his honor by two Bahá'ís, Ali-Kuli Khan, the Persia Charge d'Affaires, and Madame Florence Breed Khan, his wife. Some of the guests were members of Washington's social and political elite. Before the luncheon 'Abdu'l-Bahá sent for Louis Gregory, a well-known Bahá'í. They chatted for a while and when lunch was ready and the guests were seated, Louis Gregory was suddenly invited to the banquet by 'Abdu'l-Bahá. The assembled guests, including the Bahá'ís, were no doubt surprised when 'Abdu'l-Bahá gave Gregory the seat of honor on his right. Morrison points out how 'Abdu'l-Bahá "Gently yet unmistakenly . . . had assaulted the customs of a city that had been scandalized only a decade earlier by President Roosevelt's dinner invitation to Booker T. Washington." The fact that the Khans had not invited Gregory to the luncheon suggests that perhaps the Persian Bahá'ís had also come under the influence of American racism. Therefore, 'Abdu'l-Bahá's actions may have assaulted the customs of both non-Bahá'ís and Bahá'ís.[14]

The most far-reaching example of 'Abdu'l-Bahá's belief in racial unity was His suggestion that black and white Bahá'ís should intermarry. He encouraged Louisa Mathew, an English Bahá'í, to marry Louis Gregory as an example of Bahá'í racial unity. This action disturbed some white Bahá'ís who were still struggling with the idea of holding interracial meetings. By advocating interracial marriage 'Abdu'l-Bahá forced white and black Bahá'ís to face the fullest implications and ramifications of race unity.

'Abdu'l-Bahá never missed an opportunity to exemplifiy His deep concern for unity between black and white Americans. Even the very young were not exempt from His lessons of racial equality. In the story made famous by Howard Colby Ives in his book, *Portals to Freedom*, 'Abdu'l-Bahá was visited by some poor boys from the Bowery Mission area in New York. As the boys filed into 'Abdu'l-Bahá's room each was greeted individually. The last boy to enter the room was very dark, and because he was the only Black in the group he probably felt that 'Abdu'l-Bahá and His host would not accept him. But as Ives reports:

When 'Abdu'l-Bahá saw him His face lighted up with a heavenly smile. He raised His hand with a gesture of princely welcome and exclaimed in a loud voice so that none could fail to hear; that here was a black rose.

The room fell into instant silence. The black face became illumined with a happiness and love hardly of this world. The other boys looked at him with new eyes. I venture to say that he had been called a black—many things, but never before a black rose.[15]

This story of the black rose stands as one of the best examples of 'Abdu'l-Bahá's contributions to American race relations and to Black identity and pride. It remains especially uplifting to black Bahá'ís like the writer, who still tells it to his children. 'Abdu'l-Bahá's sensitive attention to and appreciation of dark-skinned Blacks is all the more noteworthy since at the time most black leaders, and the vast majority of Blacks, looked down on dark skin. "Black black" was not considered beautiful in the America that 'Abdu'l-Bahá visited and would not be so considered for a long time afterward. Robert S. Abbot, who founded the famous Black newspaper, *The Chicago Defender*, and who accepted the Bahá'í Faith in 1934, was attracted to the Bahá'ís because of their lack of race discrimination. But color discrimination within the Black community, practiced by light-skinned blacks toward dark-skinned blacks, was also a factor in Abbot's decision to become a Bahá'í. As his biographer Roi Ottley tells the story, Abbott was not allowed to join the choir of Grace Presbyterian Church because of the dark-skin color bias of the "old settler" mulattoes in the congregation. Abbott then joined the Christian Scientists, but left when they instituted separate places of worship for blacks and whites. "The man's endless search for racial peace," Ottley claimed, "led him finally to the Baha'i faith."[16]

Color prejudice in the Black community was common, especially in Washington, D.C., where an exclusive light-skinned club called the Four Hundred held sway for decades. As one scholar commented, "Washington, D.C., long a place of opportunity for black people, had probably the largest and most snobbish elite of all." Langston Hughes, speaking of this group in the 1920s, said that they were "as unbearable and snobbish a group of people as I have ever come in contact with." They "drew rigid class and color lines within the race against Negroes who worked with their hands, or who were dark in complexion and had no degrees from colleges." Darker complexion Blacks fared similarly in Black communities throughout America. No wonder Abbott sought the Bahá'í Faith as a refuge from the racism of both whites and light complexion Blacks.[17]

Dark skin was on the bottom of everyone's beauty chart at the time of 'Abdu'l-Bahá's visit to America, yet He saw as much beauty in black skin as He did in all colors, even when many Blacks—including the darker ones—saw beauty only in whiteness. When scholars talk of the emergence of the Black Is Beautiful movement in the twentieth century, they will have to include 'Abdu'l-Bahá and the little black boy He called the black rose.

Race Amity Work: A Period of Struggle and Compromise. Between 1912 and 1957, the American Bahá'í Community was singularly blessed with the guidance it received from 'Abdu'l-Bahá and Shoghi Effendi in the sensitive and volatile area of race relations. Without their guidance, and at times their direct intervention, the American Bahá'í Community would have suffered immeasurable setbacks in race relations. In fact, race relations within the nation as a whole may have been worse had the guiding hands of 'Abdu'l-Bahá and Shoghi Effendi, working through various Bahá'í race amity conferences and activities, not been present. It is painfully clear that among Bahá'ís white racial attitudes and behavior, combined with a persistent tendency toward compromise and avoidance of the racial issue on the part of local and National Spiritual Assemblies, could have seriously harmed the Bahá'í Community in America, were it not for the influence of 'Abdu'l-Bahá and Shoghi Effendi.

The vehicle for the salvation of the American Bahá'í Community was the race amity conference, the brainchild of 'Abdu'l-Bahá who Himself took the issue outside the Bahá'í Administration and made it a matter of public commitment. In short, he took the American Bahá'í Community by the hand and placed it in a position to make major contributions to the solution of racial conflicts in America. His plan was to organize "a series of large, well-publicized interracial meetings, conducted not to protest any specific grievance or to seek improvement of the lot of American blacks in some particular way, but to proclaim the oneness of mankind and to promote 'racial amity' between black and white Americans."[18]

'Abdu'l-Bahá gave the responsibility of arranging the first race amity conference to Mrs. Agnes Parsons, a wealthy white Bahá'í in Washington, D.C. The conference was held in 1921 and included such impressive persons as Joseph Douglass, the grandson of Frederick Douglass, and Alain Locke, among others. 'Abdu'l-Bahá sent a special message to the convention: *"Say to this convention that never since the beginning of time has one more important been held. This convention stands for the oneness of humanity; it will become the cause of enlightenment of America. It will, if wisely managed and continued, check the deadly struggle between these races which otherwise will inevitably break out."*[19]

A second race amity convention was held later that year in Springfield, Massachusetts. 'Abdu'l-Bahá's passing a month earlier imbued this convention with special meaning and provided Bahá'ís with their first opportunity to follow 'Abdu'l-Bahá's lead. A third convention followed in 1924 in New York which included the NAACP, the Urban League, and the League of Women Voters. That same year the National Spiritual Assembly of the Bahá'ís of the United States and Canada established an Amity Convention Committee and a fourth convention was convened. And then the spirit began to lag. The majority of white Bahá'ís were growing tired of the race issue. So the race amity work was deemphasized in favor of the World Unity Conferences, which had the advantage of being much less disturbing than race amity.[20]

These white Bahá'ís were sincerely perplexed by the racial issue and torn between following Bahá'í teachings and living in a racist society. There were also a few white Bahá'ís who remained prisoners of their own prejudices and sought any opportunity to frustrate the aims of 'Abdu'l-Bahá. They believed in world unity, but only on their terms —which were white and racially exclusive. These whites had little concern for what the race amity conferences had meant to black Bahá'ís—like Louis G. Gregory, who suffered much frustration and pain trying to be tactful and loving in an atmosphere of insensitivity. Sadie Oglesby, a black Bahá'í from Boston, stated at the 1927 Bahá'í National Convention that the Bahá'ís were no longer attracting new black believers and were losing those Blacks who had been interested in the Faith.[21] We will probably never fully know how many Blacks were lost as a result of the racism of white Bahá'ís.

The National Spiritual Assembly offered little leadership in this area and seemed to reflect the benign neglect of the white majority. By late 1926, however, the National Assembly had moved away from this obvious departure from 'Abdu'l-Bahá's wishes, and in 1927 it appointed a National Bahá'í Committee on Racial Amity. Louis Gregory was appointed as Executive Secretary; he accepted the position but felt it should have gone to a white person in deference to 'Abdu'l-Bahá's example of appointing Mrs. Parsons to set up the first race amity conference. The establishment of the committee pleased Shoghi Effendi because he believed that the success of the Bahá'í Faith in America was closely tied to Bahá'í activities in the area of race relations. Even at a distance, he had developed a penetrating understanding of race relations in the American Bahá'í Community. He was not satisfied with the superficial social interactions so common between blacks and whites and emphasized the need for " 'close and intimate social intercourse' beyond the confines of the official activities of the community."[22]

The year 1927 began the second stage of race amity work, but by late 1928 the work had slowed. Race amity activities took off once again in 1929; but they would continue to ebb and flow for the next two decades, to the frustration of those Bahá'ís who felt that the Bahá'í Faith needed a more consistent racial policy. In 1939, the term racial unity replaced racial amity and the National Assembly reappointed a special committee, but the ebb and flow of interest continued.[23]

The Most Challenging Issue. In 1938, Shoghi Effendi addressed the issue of race in the section entitled "The Most Challenging Issue" as part of *The Advent of Divine Justice*. Such intervention and guidance seemed to have emanated from the Bahá'í World Center just when the American Bahá'í Community most needed assistance. Boldly and without equivocation Shoghi Effendi reemphasized the racial issue "as the most vital and challenging issue confronting the Bahá'í Community at the present stage of its evolution." The resolution of the racial problem was inextricably linked to "the spiritual triumph of the American believers." Those Bahá'ís, therefore, who wanted to subordinate the race problem to the problem of world unity, could no longer avoid the obvious linkage between the two. According to Shoghi Effendi, the racial problem in America was an issue of "paramount importance" which the American believers were "far from having satisfactorily resolved." If American Bahá'ís could not solve their racial problems, how then could they build a new World Order?[24]

Shoghi Effendi expected both black and white Bahá'ís to do their respective parts in solving the racial problem. White Bahá'ís were to:

make a supreme effort in their resolve to contribute their share to the solution of this problem, to abandon once for all their usually inherent and at times subconscious sense of superiority, to correct their tendency towards reveal-ing a partronizing attitude towards the members of the other race, to persuade them through their intimate, spon-taneous and informal association with them of the gen-uineness of their friendship and the sincerity of their intentions, and to master their impatience of any lack of responsiveness on the part of a people who have received, for so long a period, such grievous and slow-healing wounds.[25]

Shoghi Effendi advised black Bahá'ís to "show by every means in their power the warmth of their response, their readiness to forget the past, and their ability to wipe out every trace of suspicion that may still linger in their hearts and minds."[26]

While there could be little doubt that white racism consti-tuted the core of the problem in America, Shoghi Effendi wisely delegated to each race equal responsibility in the solution. Neither race should think, he counseled, "that the solution of so vast a problem is a matter that exclusively concerns the other." Nor should they think, "that such a problem can either easily or immediately be resolved." Nor should Bahá'ís wait "confidently for the solution of this problem until the initiative has been taken, and the favorable circumstances created, by agencies that stand outside the orbit of their Faith."[27] In short, Shoghi Effendi told American Bahá'ís that they could count only on them-selves in solving the racial problem.

Shoghi Effendi's message provided the catalyst that set in motion the next stage of racial concerns within the Bahá'í Community. The National Spiritual Assembly in Morrison's apt phrase, "showed its willingness to assume a more active role in the struggle against prejudice, as Shoghi Effendi had directed, rather than simply to reflect the mixed values of the community." The spirit of the message pervaded the 1939 National Convention and the race issue assumed priority during consultation. Louis Gregory was again elected to the NSA. According to Morrison, "Attitudes toward minority representation on the National Spiritual Assembly seem to have changed permanently in 1939." Her reasoning is that since 1939, barring several years in the mid-1950s, at least one black has served annually. More noteworthy is her point that throughout most of this period two or three blacks were members of the National Institution at the same time, representing 20 to 30 percent of the National Spiritual Assembly. Since 1968 this high percentage of blacks on the NSA has remained stable.[28]

The spirit released by Shoghi Effendi became a fireball in the hearts of many Bahá'ís. The Race Unity Committee, under the leadership of Dorothy Baker, held and supported race unity activities throughout the country. The committee published books, articles, and a survey of community reports which focused on local race unity activities. The National Assembly visited Atlanta, where it held interracial meetings, much to the chagrin of some white Bahá'ís. In the fall of 1943, the National Assembly further endorsed the racial unity work by making it the theme of a two month nationwide proclamation campaign culminating the last year of the Seven Year Plan. This race unity work in 1943 and 1944 was so impressive that Louis Gregory was moved to call it "the banner year." In his report on the thirty-sixth National Convention, Gregory praised the year's work stating that it had "recorded the most progress in race unity since the movement began."[29]

This "banner year" of racial progress, however, was part of a cycle of Bahá'í race relations in which intense activities have followed admonitions and encouragement from 'Abdu'l-Bahá and Shoghi Effendi. After 1944, this cycle turned down once again as the race issue was gradually eclipsed by other concerns. By 1953, a new cycle had begun in the form of a new committee called the Interracial Teaching Committee. This cycle would also bring some progress and not a little frustration.[30]

Trying Times: Black Bahá'ís and the Black Movement During the Turbulent 1960s.[31] By the 1960s race relations both within and outside the American Bahá'í Community were undergoing radical changes. The Civil Rights and Black Power movements, influenced in part by revolutionary movements among nonwhites around the world, greatly enhanced the views black Americans held of themselves. Being black was no longer something to be ashamed of, but rather something to be proud of. "Black Is Beautiful" and "Black Power" became rallying cries for an entire generation.[32]

Many Blacks who joined the Bahá'í Faith in the 1960s brought with them certain expectations of whites, as well as a sense of Black consciousness. Unlike earlier black Bahá'ís who were more tolerant of racist attitudes and behavior, the new black Bahá'ís were much less tolerant and forgiving. Having read the Bahá'í Writings on racial unity, especially Shoghi Effendi's section on "the most challenging issue," they demanded to know why white Bahá'ís were dragging their feet on the racial issue. It did not help to be told that the Bahá'í Community had far more Blacks in decision-making positions than most secular and religious organizations. Instead, highly placed black Bahá'ís were often perceived as mere tokens, or even as "Uncle Toms," by the radical fringe of these emerging groups. The more established, older black Bahá'ís tended to reflect the same moderate social values and outlooks as their counterparts in society—in stark contrast to the values and outlook of the younger, more radical black Bahá'ís who identified with such black radicals as Malcolm X, Stokley Carmichael, and Huey Newton.

Some of the Black generation which had received inspiration and guidance from the magnanimous leadership of Louis Gregory had little patience with the black radicals of the 1960s. In fact, a few of these black Bahá'ís, who with endless patience and hard work had finally earned acceptance from white Bahá'ís, prided themselves on being free of race consciousness. Discussions of Black consciousness bored and irritated them. They were not "Black" but "Bahá'í," as if the two were mutually exclusive. They felt threatened by all the discussion of race, even though such discussion centered on the unfinished business of race relations within the Faith. They tended to be more interested in ending what they preceived to be a Black rebellion in the community, rather than understanding the anguish of the young radicals who loved thè Faith no less than they, and were merely attempting to reconcile the conflicting forces within and without the Bahá'í Community.

One source of conflict was the emphasis that young radical black Bahá'ís placed on "the most challenging issue." They could see that racism and paternalism still existed in the Bahá'í Community, that most white and Persian Bahá'ís lived in segregated suburbs, and that many shared the racial attitudes of their non-Bahá'í counterparts. They resented the reluctance and embarrassment of the more established black Bahá'ís who strained to maintain the fragile appearance of racial unity at the expense of discussing the more volatile issues of white racism. Since these young radicals, like their counterparts in the non-Bahá'í world, were not distinguished by their diplomacy, they sometimes drifted to extremes in their frustrated eagerness to force the issue.

Most of the black radicals eventually reconciled their differences with the more moderate elements within the Faith. This reconciliation, at least in the case of Detroit, came about mainly because a few of the older black Bahá'ís could command the respect of the young radicals. White

Bahá'ís active in the Civil Rights movement and in various white radical student movements, such as the Students for a Democratic Society (SDS), sided with their black coreligionists in demanding a more open approach to the racial issue. Both groups pursued the issue of racism and contributed to a much-heightened social awareness within the larger Bahá'í Community. A few radical black Bahá'ís, finding the community too cautious on racial issues, became inactive.

Those who eventually reconciled their differences with the moderate elements, however, did not have to compromise their principles. Rather, their views were expanded to embrace the goals of a new World Order. Although the community seemed at the time to be dominated by upper-class whites supported by black moderates, they saw that change was inevitable. However, such change would never occur if they as "radicals" left the Faith.

An article written by Hand of the Cause Ruḥíyyih Khánum, and published in the June 1961 *Bahá'í News*, was brought to the attention of several radical black Bahá'ís. It confirmed their views on race and positive social change within the Faith. Commenting on a conversation between Shoghi Effendi and the first Japanese pilgrim, Ruḥíyyih Khánum said, "Shoghi Effendi said to him that the majority of the human race was not white and that the majority of Bahá'ís would not be white in the future." Elaborating on this theme she went on to say:

As up until very recently the Bahá'ís of the world were almost exclusively white it is only natural that their virtues and their faults should have colored the Faith and its community life. It is illogical to suppose that what we have now is either mature or right; it is a phase in that development of the Cause; when peoples of different races are incorporated in the worldwide community (and in local communities) who can doubt that it will possess far greater power and perfection and be something quite different from what we have now? And yet let us ask ourselves frankly if we do not believe that what we North American Bahá'ís have, what we Western white Bahá'ís have is the real thing, practically a finished product, and it is up to the rest of the world to accept it? I think this is our mentality; it was mine up until a few years ago.[33]

Ruḥíyyih Khánum's letter predated the emergence of Black radicalism by several years and would have prevented much conflict and misunderstanding had black and white moderates been willing to discuss its implications. She had put her finger on one of the main issues that concerned black radicals, the thing that in effect forced them into radical positions: the assumption of many Bahá'ís that what they had was "the real thing, practically a finished product, and it is up to the rest of the world to accept it." If Ruḥíyyih Khánum, as a Hand of the Cause, could admit her assumptions on race, other whites could do no less, some black radicals reasoned.

Discussing Bahá'u'lláh's statement describing black people as like the pupil of the eye, Ruḥíyyih Khánum again elaborated on a theme dear to the hearts of the young radicals: "When Bahá'u'lláh likens the Negro race to the faculty of sight in the human body—the act of perception with all it implies—it is a pretty terrific statement. He never said this of anyone else." Pointing to the cultural link between Blacks in America and Africa, Ruḥíyyih Khánum continued: "I thought the American Negroes' humility, his kindness, friendliness, courtesy and hospitableness were something to do with his oppression and the background of slavery. But after spending weeks, day after day, in the villages of Africa, seeing literally thousands of Bahá'ís and non-Bahá'ís, I have wakened up to the fact that the American Negro has these beautiful qualities not because he was enslaved but because he has the characteristics of his race.

I learned why the Guardian so constantly spoke of the 'pure-hearted' African."[34]

The young black Bahá'í radicals who read these words were thrilled. Here was a white Hand of the Cause discussing with passion the very topics so dear to their hearts, reinforcing their beliefs in their African background. Ruḥíyyih Khánúm could not have said anything more appropriate for the times; and only she could have said it in such a bold manner. Such opinions voiced by anyone of lesser stature may have caused an uproar in the American Bahá'í Community. We will probably never know how many angry young black Bahá'ís, after having read and discussed this letter during the 1960s and even later, turned back toward the Faith, confirmed in the belief that the Bahá'í Community was more than just a social club where black and white moderates could insulate themselves from the turbulence transforming the larger society.

Other white Bahá'ís, such as Daniel Jordan, were also favorites of the young black radicals. During the 1960s, Jordan was one of the few members on the National Spiritual Assembly who reached out to young radical Bahá'ís. He did not sanction all their beliefs and actions, but he empathized with and understood the tempest swirling in their souls as they frantically tried to reconcile Black consciousness with the demands of an evolving universal Faith.

On the local level, Mrs. Naomi Oden of Highland Park, Michigan, a Bahá'í since the late 1940s, worked day and night to convince the angry radicals that the Bahá'í Faith was capable of meeting their needs and fulfilling their expectations of a just society. Affectionately known as "Mama Naomi," Mrs. Oden was one of the first upper middle-class black Bahá'ís in the Detroit area to take the Bahá'í Faith into the Black slums. She befriended dope addicts, prostitutes, welfare mothers, drunks, unemployed people, among others. But more than just teaching in their environment, she invited them to her home to attend social affairs, often to the surprise and discomfort of her black friends and associates. She was the single most important link between the Bahá'í Community and the angry young black radicals —both Bahá'í and non-Bahá'í. The majority of Detroit Blacks who embraced the Faith in the 1960s did so as the result of Mama Naomi's love and affection.

Mass Teaching Among Blacks in the Rural South. The most dramatic influence on race relations in the American Bahá'í Community in the last two decades has been mass teaching among Blacks in the rural South. In the early 1970s, glowing reports appeared in *The American Bahá'í* reporting the groundswell of new conversions: "SOUTH LEADS THE WAY IN TEACHING THE MASSES." "SOUTH RESPONDS TO DIVINE SUMMONS." "OVER 8,000 SOULS RESPOND TO THE HEALING MESSAGE OF BAHÁ'U'LLÁH IN THE CAROLINAS, HUNDREDS MORE IN ARKANSAS, KENTUCKY, MISSISSIPPI, OKLAHOMA AND TENNESSEE." "6,000 NEW BELIEVERS IN CAROLINAS."

The American Bahá'í called 1971, "a year of victories" and stressed the fact that the expansion of the American Bahá'í Community had "encompassed every minority designated by the Universal House of Justice." But the single most striking development of the year of victories was that the membership of the Bahá'í Community had "more than doubled," largely as the result of some 20,000 new enrollments in the Deep South.[35]

The vast majority of those new enrollees were rural Blacks. The news of their conversion swept through the Bahá'í world. With the Civil Rights movements on the decline and riot-torn cities still lingering in the collective consciousness of the nation, such positive racial developments as occurred in the American Bahá'í Community were a bright light in a period rapidly sliding into darkness and despair. Black and white Bahá'ís, unlike their counterparts in the non-Bahá'í world who were set adrift by the count-less failures and frustrations of various social movements, had much to celebrate.

The next year, the National Spiritual Assembly in re-sponse to the conversions in the South, and particularly in South Carolina, established the Louis G. Gregory Institute in Hemingway, South Carolina. The institute was dedicated on Sunday, October 22, 1972, to "the Memory of Hand of the Cause of God, Louis G. Gregory, himself a native of Charleston, South Carolina." The facility would become a focal point for the training of new believers.

Bahá'ís everywhere were so delighted by the dramatic events taking place throughout the rural Black South, that many of them found it difficult, even irreverent, to analyze the comlex social and cultural forces associated with what had come to be heralded throughout the Bahá'í world as "mass conversion." The Bahá'ís who were responsible for teaching and consolidating the Faith among the Blacks in the rural South, however, soon discovered that mass con-version was a complex phenomenon.

Dr. William Diehl, currently one of the directors of the Louelen Bahá'í School in Davison, Michigan, and his wife Beth, spent several years in Elloree, South Carolina during the period of mass conversion.[36] In this small rural town of seven hundred, seventy Blacks became Bahá'ís. "In some towns," Diehl explained "the reasons that people became Bahá'ís were very nebulous. Many people saw the Faith, not as a religon, but as a social action organization . . . that was following in the footsteps of Martin Luther King." This because the Bahá'ís teaching them stressed the ideal of the oneness of mankind. Much of the teaching was geared to that aspect of the Bahá'í Faith. Predictably, during the stage of consolidation, those Blacks who had become Bahá'ís thinking it was a social or political organi-zation soon lost interest and left the Faith.

According to Diehl, and contrary to popular belief throughout the Bahá'í world at the time, what occurred among Blacks in the rural South was not so much mass conversion as "the mass finding of seekers." Many of the rural Blacks who became Bahá'ís had not really understood the full significance of the religion, but "had an interest [and] . . . were spiritually attuned." Unfortunately, too much emphasis was placed on "card-signing."

The mass teaching of rural Southern Blacks was facilitated by aspects of Southern culture which went undetected by many sincere Bahá'ís. For example, Diehl points out that many elderly Southern Blacks had learned over time that they had to accommodate whites. So it was very easy to get these people to sign cards. Therefore, traditional Black accommodation to whites probably contributed to some degree to the mass conversion.

Dr. Diehl and his wife, Beth, (both white) discovered that once Blacks became Bahá'ís, they then had to force themselves to break out of the traditional roles that dominated their lives. The Diehls, who were living in a traditional small, rural Southern town discovered how difficult it was for black Bahá'ís to overcome racial traditions and norms. Every Sunday the Diehls visited the black Bahá'ís in their homes, said prayers, and invited them to their home the following Thursday. Every Sunday the black Bahá'ís would say they were coming, but they would not show up. Finally, and unexpectedly, a group of about thirty came to the Diehls' home. Several of the black Bahá'ís had gone around and gathered all the other Bahá'ís together. They explained to the Diehls that they had never been to a white person's house except to collect wages—and then only to the back door. "To them," Diehl commented, "it was an act of courage to enter a white person's house through the front door."

And yet this was not all. After that racial obstacle was overcome, resulting in more meetings and a stronger community, another problem rooted in rural Southern life surfaced. Suddenly, all the black male Bahá'ís stopped attending meetings at the Diehls. They had been warned that they would lose their jobs if they attended any more Bahá'í meetings. In addition, even though these Bahá'ís knew Mrs. Diehl, when they encountered her walking down the street they avoided eye contact. Black males did not look at white females. Yet the Bahá'í Faith enabled these white and black Bahá'ís to gradually break down these racial barriers, at least within their homes, which required much courage and dedication.

After braving various difficulties, this group of black Bahá'ís, now down to about twenty active members, was beginning to find a new understanding of the Bahá'í Faith and they wanted to build a Bahá'í Center. The National Spiritual Assembly, however, did not think that the time was ripe.

Perhaps one of the most difficult problems the Bahá'í Community experienced throughout the rural Black South was that it could not meet the variety of needs traditionally met by the Black church. Once the Louis Gregory Institute was established, however, it became obvious how important such an institution was to the social needs of the Black Bahá'í Community. As Diehl commented, "to see the transformation that that local community went through was just incredible."

The Louis Gregory Institute proved particularly helpful to black Bahá'ís in the neighborhood of the institute by providing them with social activities and a place with which they could identify. The need to identify with some tangible social institution was crucial because many of them still belonged to churches which provided such social functions as marriage and burial. To become a Bahá'í, for rural Blacks steeped in a tradition and culture where the church constituted the core of the Black community, was often to be set socially adrift. Thus, the establishment of the Louis Gregory Institute, with its Bahá'í burial ground, went a long way toward anchoring the spiritual and social life of rural black Bahá'ís in the area to the larger Bahá'í Community.

Because in the Bahá'í Faith most community functions, as well as personal deepening in the Sacred Writings, are based on literacy, the lack of literacy skills among many of the elderly black Bahá'ís in the rural South created additional problems. This lack of literacy, Diehl points out, of necessity forced traveling teachers into ministerial roles since there was a need for anyone who could read and write to carry on the deepening and administrative functions of the Bahá'í Community. Over time, the more deepened black Bahá'ís began focusing on children's classes which should produce a more literate and consolidated Bahá'í Community in the future. Few whites entered the Faith in the rural South. According to Diehl, the reason was that the emphasis was on teaching rural Blacks. While there were commendable aspects of this emphasis, such as the attitude that "the Blacks in the South were bound to be more open and spiritually . . . much more attuned to the principles of the Faith," the Bahá'í teachers also felt that Blacks were simply easier to teach.

The rural South is much like a developing country with the usual "development problems," and should be approached in the same way. This has been a test for the American Bahá'í Community which has traditionally measured Bahá'í life by the standards of the more sophisticated urban Bahá'í Communities. Tutorial schools for both adults and children in these communities would make a major contribution to solving some of these development problems. The Louis Gregory Institute has made an excellent start.

The announcement by the Universal House of Justice of the creation of an Office of Social and Economic Development "for extending the development of social and economic life both within and outside the Bahá'í Community, and to advise and encourage the assemblies and friends in their strivings'' comes just at the time when Blacks in rural and urban America are experiencing further setbacks in their overall quality of social and economic life. Concerned Bahá'ís will be inspired by this bold and timely initiative to apply Bahá'í principles to areas of grave human need.[37]

State of Race Relations in the Contemporary Bahá'í Community. How far have we come in race relations in the American Bahá'í Community? Without any systematic study of the topic, the best one can offer are some impressions and observations. Race relations within the community are closely related to the changes occurring in the larger society. The increasing suburbanization of the white population and the ghettoization of the Black population are having an impact on the quality of Bahá'í community life. In most large metropolitan areas, upper- and middle-class white, Persian and black Bahá'ís live in the more affluent suburbs, while the vast majority of lower-class black Bahá'ís in the United States live in the inner cities and in the rural South. One has only to visit Bahá'ís in areas such as Detroit, Cleveland or South Carolina to see these race and class factors operating.

Race and class divisions often exist within the Bahá'í Community. Bahá'ís of similar racial and class characteristics find themselves sharing similar social and professional activities in the non-Bahá'í world and carrying these social relations over into the Bahá'í Community. These social formations can be seen operating among Bahá'í youth also. Seldom are there Bahá'í School sessions where one does not observe Bahá'í youth forming cliques based upon class, race or geographical background. These youth cliques will develop into their adult counterparts unless the Bahá'í Community intervenes to foster social relationships that cross race, class and geographical barriers. Ideal Bahá'í social relationships will not develop without some deliberate effort on the part of the Bahá'í Community.

Race amity and race unity conferences have been the

Bahá'í Community's greatest contributions to American race relations. The latest one was held in October 1983 in Charleston, South Carolina. Such conferences build bridges between the races during periods of general insensitivity to racial issues. Yet, as valuable as these race amity conferences are, they are insufficient in meeting the challenges of race relations in advanced industrial America. These conferences were probably most effective in the period prior to the rapid demographic changes which took place during the last two decades and which increasingly separated Black and white communities. If race amity conferences are ever to achieve the lasting effect 'Abdu'l-Bahá envisioned for them, they will have to radically change their format to address more complicated racial problems.

Bahá'ís must stop acting as if racial problems remain static. Racial problems, like other social problems, become more complex as time goes on. Traditional formats are insufficient. Future race unity conferences should address such issues as the implications of the expanding Black underclass for racial and class stability in American cities; Black inner cities and white suburb; race and poverty in the Bahá'í Community; and the new racial conflict in inner cities between Blacks and Arab store owners.

An exciting new development in Bahá'í race relations is the race unity section in *The American Bahá'í*, which includes a column entitled "Your Turn." Started several years ago by the Race Unity Committee, this section has helped many Bahá'ís express views and elicit responses that have enhanced interracial communication and understanding within the American Bahá'í Community. The publication of Gayle Morrison's book *To Move the World* by the Bahá'í Publishing Trust in 1982, represented a quantum leap in Bahá'í race-related research and publication. The first critical study of race relations in the American Bahá'í Community, it has paved the way for other scholars to address issues and topics heretofore considered off limits, such as the racial attitudes, practices and policies of Bahá'í individuals and Bahá'í institutions.

To Move the World demonstrated that Bahá'í scholars in the field of race relations are capable of critical self-analysis, no matter how embarrassing and painful. The book is a bold and encouraging sign that the American Bahá'í Community is intellectually coming of age. Like most first generation studies *To Move the World* has shortcomings, such as inadequate treatment of the range of Black responses to shifts in Bahá'í policies. Notwithstanding, it is a great book.

The present racial situation in America demands the best we can offer if racial unity is to become a reality. We Bahá'ís cannot hope to address serious racial problems with traditional approaches. We must understand the problem of race and poverty in the rural South and the urban North through sensitive and comprehensive research and consultation with those who have firsthand knowledge of these problems and who deal with them every day.

Planners and organizers of race-related conferences and activities must listen more to the black poor, instead of limiting themselves to the middle and upper classes. Bahá'ís interested in understanding race and poverty in urban areas would do well to visit longtime Bahá'í advocates of the black poor whose long years of dedication and work among the poor and disowned have given them important insights.

Some middle-class and upper-class black Bahá'ís, much like their counterparts in other organizations, have lost touch with all but the more affluent segments of the Black community. This severely limits their ability to build bridges between all segments of the black and white communities. This shortcoming can be remedied by a conscious effort on the part of these Bahá'ís to develop and nurture contacts between themselves and more neglected elements of the Black community.

Black and white Bahá'ís must never make the mistake of becoming so satisfied with the high quality of interracial fellowship within their own community that they stop working toward a similar goal in the non-Bahá'í world. While Bahá'ís should be on constant guard against feelings of superiority because of their achievement of interracial fellowship, they should not, on the other hand, hide their light under a basket. The fact is that, in contemporary American society, the American Bahá'í Community has achieved a level of interracial fellowship unparalleled in the history of most religious or secular organizations. This is one of the community's greatest legacies. We should never forget it; America and the world desperately need to learn from it.

Notes

1. Gayle Morrison, *To Move the World: Louis G. Gregory and the Advancement of Racial Unity in America* (Wilmette, Ill.: Bahá'í Publishing Trust, 1982) p. 81.

2. Shoghi Effendi, *The Advent of Divine Justice* (Wilmette, Ill.: Bahá'í Publishing Trust, 1939) p. 29.

3. Quoted in ibid., p. 31.

4. 'Abdu'l-Bahá, *Selections from the Writings of 'Abdu'l-Bahá* (Haifa: Bahá'í World Centre, 1978) p. 291.

5. Ibid., p. 291–92.

6. G. Spiller, ed., *Papers on Inter-Racial Problems* (Boston: The World's Peace Foundation, New ed., 1911) pp. 156–87, 159.

7. Ibid., p. 159.

8. Quoted in Allen L. Ward, *239 Days: 'Abdu'l-Bahá's Journey in America* (Wilmette, Ill.: Bahá'í Publishing Trust, 1977) p. 40.

9. 'Abdu'l-Bahá, *The Promulgation of Universal Peace* (Wilmette, Ill.: Bahá'í Publishing Trust, Second Edition, 1982) p. 44.

10. H. M. Balyuzi, *'Abdu'l-Bahá: The Center of the Covenant of Bahá'u'lláh* (London: George Ronald, 1971) p. 181–82.

11. *Promulgation*, pp. 56–57.

12. Ibid., p. 49.

13. Ibid., p. 57.

14. *World*, p. 53.

15. Howard Colby Ives, *Portals to Freedom* (London: George Ronald, 1943) p. 65.

16. Roi Ottley, *The Lonely Warrior: The Life and Times of Robert S. Abbott* (Chicago: Henry Regnery Company, 1955) pp. 13–14.

17. Florette Henri, *Black Migration* (New York: Anchor Books, 1976) p. 188; *World,* p. 132.

18. *World,* p. 132.

19. Quoted in *World,* p. 141.

20. Ibid., pp. 155–60.

21. Ibid., p. 161.

22. Ibid., pp. 164–67, 174.

23. Ibid., pp. 275–96.

24. *Advent,* pp. 28–29.

25. Ibid., p. 34.

26. Ibid., pp. 33–34.

27. Ibid., p. 34.

28. *World,* pp. 269, 273.

29. Ibid., pp. 275–85.

30. Ibid., p. 293.

31. This section on black radicals is based on my personal experiences and my discussions with other black Bahá'ís. As a result, there is a certain lack of objectivity which I hope will be remedied by further work on the topic. There is a need for an oral history project to document this period and the views of the participants on all sides of the burning issues which often set Bahá'í against Bahá'í.

32. Harold R. Isaacs, *The New World of Negro Americans* (New York: The Viking Press, 1963) pp. 288–323 passim; Benjamin Muse, *The American Negro Revolution: From Nonviolence to Power* (New York: The Citadel Press, 1970).

33. *Bahá'í News,* U.S. Supplement (June 1961) p. 1.

34. Ibid.

35. *The American Bahá'í* (October 1970) p. 1; ibid. (January 1971) p. 1; ibid. (February 1971) p. 1.

36. The section of this paper dealing with conversion of Blacks to the Bahá'í Faith in the rural South is based on a taped interview of Dr. William Diehl, March 3, 1984, Louhelen Bahá'í School, Davison, Michigan.

37. *The American Bahá'í* (November 1983)

The Continuing Struggle Against Racial Injustice in the United States

by Carlton E. Brown

S INCE BAHÁ'U'LLÁH PROCLAIMED his earth-shaking revelation—the great call to the unity of all people—its
vibrating influence has increased the capacity of human
beings to seek positive change in the world and set in motion the major upheavals necessary to disrupt old, bankrupt
modes of human interaction and organization, to cast out
the destructive beliefs and ideals of a seriously wayward
world—all to clear the way for a new World Order. The
United States has been given the great, yet ominous duty
of playing a major role in this process.

Bahá'u'lláh declared that: *"The fundamental purpose
animating the Faith of God and His Religion is to safeguard
the interests and promote the unity of the human race, and
to foster the spirit of love and fellowship amongst men."*[1] Further, in His Most Holy Book, the Kitáb-i Aqdas, Bahá-
u'lláh admonished the rulers of America to *"bind ye the
broken with the hands of justice, and crush the oppressor
who flourisheth with the rod of the commandments of your
Lord."*[2] Shoghi Effendi, Guardian of the Bahá'í Faith, has
elaborated Bahá'u'lláh's charge in the important communication to the American Bahá'í Community entitled *The*

Advent of Divine Justice. In this work, he charged the American Bahá'í Community with a double crusade: "first to regenerate the inward life of their own community, and next to assail the long-standing evils that have entrenched themselves in the life of their nation."[3] Among the long-standing evils named by Shoghi Effendi are moral laxity, a deceitful and corrupt political life, racism, and an "excessive and binding materialism."[4] It is precisely due to the depth to which their nation has allowed these dispositions to embed themselves in its consciousness and in its social fabric that the American Bahá'í Community has been charged with the responsiblility of pioneering major aspects of the new World Order of Bahá'u'lláh, the very pursuit of which requires a complete eradication of these evils. And of these several evils, the Guardian has singled out racism as the most challenging issue facing the Bahá'í Community of the United States and the nation at large.

Racism has indeed been the most challenging issue facing the United States since prior to its beginning as a nation. America is the victim of one of the most virulent forms of racism the world has ever known. It began with wars of genocide against the aboriginal inhabitants of this land; it continued with the most destructive forms of slavery; the violent and deceptive seizure of Mexican lands; severe legal and social discrimination against Asian-Americans that culminated in the internment of Japanese-Americans in concentration camps during World War II; the legal, social and economic oppression of black Americans; the colonization of Caribbean peoples; and the destruction of peoples, cultures and nations in Asia.

Racism is deep and ubiquitous in the cultural and psychological fabric of the nation. Even its many well-meaning citizens cannot see the presence of some forms of racism before their very eyes, or understand their own involvement in its continuation. Many indeed believe that since the Civil Rights and Black Power movements of the 1960s, the problems of racism and prejudice have largely been resolved.

Yet, Bahá'ís believe that the United States is the crucible for the development of a new world civilization based on peace and justice. This nation, more than any other, contains within its borders citizens from every race and nearly every nation and culture on the earth. Clearly, the achievement of peace, equity and justice along cultural, religious and racial lines in the United States would demonstrate concretely the same possibility for the world. 'Abdu'l-Bahá has pointed out that the emancipation of black Americans from slavery led European powers to eradicate slavery in their colonies in Asia and Africa.[5] The Civil Rights movement aided practically and spiritually the movements of colonial liberation in Africa and the Caribbean. The achievements of black Americans increase the availability of trained intelligence that might be applied to the social and economic problems of the African continent and the influence that can be brought to bear on the international polity. As 'Abdu'l-Bahá stated early in this century: "the accomplishment of unity between the colored and whites will be an assurance of the world's peace."[6]

This chapter will examine briefly the advances made during the period of the Civil Rights and Black Power movements and take a deeper look at our present circumstances in order to assess the distance remaining to be traveled if we are to achieve true racial justice.

The Civil Rights to Black Power Period. From 1954 through much of the 1970s, racially and culturally oppressed groups in American society achieved a great deal in the political and legal arenas. In 1954, in most states, black Americans were generally barred from participation in the political and mainstream economic processes. They were prevented the exercise of their constitutional rights to vote and to run for public office. In the Southern states, strict segregation in all public and private institutions was enforced by law. De facto segregation existed in all major institutions in the Northern states, creating undereducation, underemployment, and critically substandard living conditions for most Blacks. In Western states, Hispanic Americans were relegated to substandard conditions as migrant workers, household laborers, or unskilled and semiskilled workers.[7] Chinese and Japanese Americans were forced to create their own societies in so-called Chinatowns and Little Tokyos in most cities. Their legal, economic and social fortunes rose and fell with U.S. policy toward their native lands.[8] Mass media, including newspapers and television, generally portrayed negative images of most minorities.[9] Therefore, outside of their own cultural institutions and activities, children of minority groups generally received negative images of themselves. The larger society also received negative images and stereotyped images of non-white groups, and several white groups as well—notably, Italian Americans. The legal battle for equality had been engaged since the early post-Civil War period by agencies such as The National Convention of Colored Men, The Chinese Six Companies, Native American tribal organizations, the National Association for the Advancement of Colored People, the Urban League and many other organizations. But state and federal governments were unresponsive at best and frequently hostile to these efforts. In spite of much resistance, early efforts did result in the enactment of some federal civil rights statutes. These, however, either contained vague provisions or lacked appropriate enforcement provisions.

Beginning around 1954, the necessary spiritual and material forces finally began to coalesce into one of the greatest mass movements of the twentieth century. The NAACP's legal battles against segregation culminated in the Brown vs. Board of Education decision by the Supreme Court in 1954. Mrs. Rosa Parks' refusal to give up her seat to a white man on a city bus in Montgomery, Alabama in

1955 led to the Montgomery Bus Boycott, the national ascension of Dr. Martin Luther King and the establishment of the Southern Christian Leadership Conference in 1957. The desire of black students in the South to define their own role in the struggle led to sit-ins and to the development of the Student Nonviolent Coordinating Committee. The development of white support for civil rights in the North led to the birth of the freedom riders and the Congress for Racial Equality. Finally, police brutality and harrassment in California led to the development of the Black Panther Party.

The twenty years from 1954 to 1974 were momentous ones in the history of the nation. Through protest, demonstrations, civil disobedience, political and legal measures, and occasional violence, oppressed groups achieved massive changes in their fortunes. Aided by a significant army of white citizens who lent their physical, monetary, political, legal, and moral support, the movement secured a decision in the Brown vs. Board of Education case in 1954 that ordered the dismantling of legally segregated educational facilities; the passage of the Civil Rights Act of 1957 for the protection of voting rights; the Civil Rights Act of 1960 buttressing the act of 1957; the Civil Rights Act of 1964—the broadest act of all—protecting civil rights in voting, public accommodation, public facilities, education, and fair employment; and the Voting Rights Act of 1965.[11] At later dates, affirmative action and equal employment provisions were developed.

Many activists and scholars even during this time period perceived the limitations of these pieces of legislation, the difficulty of enforcement, and the continuous vigilance necessary to maintain the gains won. Blacks were still murdered without responsive justice, near-slavery conditions continued to exist on share-cropper plantations in the South and in migrant agriculture in other parts of the country. Others began to realize that, even if the legislative and judical gains of the period were enforceable, the fortunes of nonwhite peoples would continue to be dependent on appeals to the good graces of powerful whites. The necessity of establishing firm, formal political power became an obvious next step. Others, particularly black Americans, understood the extent to which racial oppression in America is not only physically oppressive, but culturally and psychologically oppressive. The denigration and destruction of the cultural and spiritual heritage of nonwhite citizens and the enforcement of unicultural social life, born of American individualism and industrial capitalism, are strong elements of the American scene.[12] An increased understanding of American economics grew out of this period also. It demonstrated the extent to which the economic ideals of free enterprise, competition, and individual initiative were mythologies. Many others subscribed to the spiritual concept that true freedom is not an individual phenomenon, that no member of an oppressed group can be truly free until all of its members are free. This notion was extended to include the ideal of securing the freedom of all people of color everywhere in the world.[13]

These several realizations created the Black Power movement.[14] This movement affirmed the necessity for the development of a formal Black political power through elected offices and organizations. In addition, Black cultural affirmation and rejuvenation became a vital part of the movement for freedom. These notions spread to other racial groups. Soon one could hear the cries of Chicano Power and Chicano Pride, Puerto Rican Power and Puerto Rican Pride, Asian Power and Asian Pride.[15] The cultural notions implicit in the movement also reached into many white European immigrant communities—particularly those of Southern- and Eastern-European ancestry whose cultural matrix was somewhat different from the Anglo-Saxon tradition and who had also experienced milder forms of discrimination.[16] New legislation was passed at both the state and federal levels to insure cultural relevance in school curricula. Private foundations began to fund minority cultural activities, and white college campuses reeled from student demands for Black, Puerto Rican, Chicano, and Asian studies programs.

None of the realizations that led to the development of the Black Power and Black Pride movements and their various offshoots were new or revolutionary. Many of the nation's best intellects had recognized the necessity for the broad based social and structural changes from as far back as the pre-Civil War period.[17] But the masses of the people had never before been so fully exposed to the defects in the national social, political, economic, and cultural systems. For many young, nonwhite Americans, the sense of pride and of collective power for good that came with the movement was overwhelming. They could never see themselves as inferior and powerless again.

During this period, the number of nonwhite students attending colleges and universities nearly tripled; the income of Black and Hispanic families began to slowly catch up with those of white families; a few neighborhoods that had previously been exclusively white were slowly integrated—sometimes with positive results, sometimes amid violence; minorities secured work in sectors and at levels previously closed to them.[18] Banks and the housing industry were forced to abandon many overt discriminatory practices.[19] Many social organizations and governmental units—including the military—initiated programs to eliminate prejudice in their institutions and to increase interracial understanding; the Small Business Administration of the federal government developed a program designed to enhance the development of minority businesses; and, the federal General Services Admininstration provided measures to ensure that certain percentages of government contracts were awarded to minority firms. In short, by 1974 billions of dollars, many dedicated lives, and the forces of the people and the government were invested in the struggle for freedom and justice in American society.

The View from 1984. The 1970s brought a new mood and direction to the United States. Political conservatism combined with a new narcissism to allow tradtional racism to rear its ugly head once again. Though racism had never departed the American scene, it at least was more submerged during the 1960s. The victories for racial justice of the 1950s and 1960s began to diminish in importance; other accomplishments began to appear as actual losses; and, yet others were slowly dismantled by entrenching conservatism and the beginning of a severe economic recession.

The economic arena reveals the problems quite clearly. The incomes of minority groups in American society were rising toward the level of white Americans during the 1960s largely due to the legislative removal of educational and employment barriers in conjunction with a general economic boom. However, by 1974 the average incomes of black families had declined to only fifty percent of average white family incomes, from a high of sixty-eight percent in 1968.[20] White high school graduates continued to earn an average income comparable to those of black college graduates.[21] From 1980 through 1982, Black youth unemployment exceeded sixty percent, as opposed to twenty-five percent for white youth. Black unemployment overall exceeded twenty-five percent as opposed to overall national rates ranging between seven percent and fifteen percent. Unemployment among Native Americans and Puerto Rican Americans was substantially worse.

It should also be pointed out that the majority of nonwhite people who are employed work in secondary areas of the national economy that are characterized by low wage scales and little opportunity for advancement—custodial, maintenance, food service, clerical, migrant labor, etc.[23] In addition, huge numbers are employed in professional areas that have in recent years suffered the most severe financial setback—teaching, social services, government employment. Finally, several very reliable researchers have shown that members of minority groups who have managed to reach middle levels of employment in the primary areas of the economy are promoted and advanced at a much slower rate than their white counterparts.[24]

Minority groups have also not been allowed to effectively participate in the economy of entrepreneurs and business owners. There are approximately 200,000 minority-owned businesses in the United States, representing about 2 percent of all American businesses.[25] But, 80 percent of these businesses do not have paid employees, with the remaining 20 percent employing approximately 180,000.[26] The 1983 sales figures for the top one hundred Black-owned corporations were $2.2 billion[27] as compared with $4.5 billion for the bottom ten corporations on the *Fortune 500* listing for the same year.[28] This sharp contrast is produced by a complex of factors, including undereducation, scarcity of financing alternatives for minority entrepreneurs, and collective decisions by the white business community to protect minority markets for themselves.[29] In addition, Black and other minority businesses that have been able to survive and grow have often been forced out of business, or bought up, by larger white concerns when they become large enough to become public stock companies. This has occurred recently with two Black financial institutions.[30] Obviously, such circumstances prevent the economic growth of minority communities and maintain their dependence on the larger white community.

The political arena is equally revealing of the plight of racial minorities. Well into the 1960s there were very few nonwhite elected officials or appointees to high office. Tremendous change has taken place since then. For example, the number of black elected officials has risen from sixty-two in 1962, to about two thousand in 1980.[31] The number of nonwhite mayors has risen from an estimated five to ten, Black and Hispanic included, to approximately two hundred fifty, two hundred twenty-three of those being black Americans.[32] Blacks and other nonwhites have become state and federal representatives, have held local offices, have achieved the mayoralties of many of the nation's larger cities, and held high appointment posts on the Supreme Court, presidential cabinets, ambassadorships, etc.

These massive statistical changes are deceptive however. The bulk of Black political power emanates from the nation's largest cities which are almost bankrupt due to poor state funding formulas, eroding tax bases, the rise of the middle class suburb and the consequent rise in the indigent, service-needy populations of the inner cities.[33] Thus, even mayors and city counselors with vision and commitment to change are severely handicapped. Additionally, there still exist only nineteen elected black officials for every one hundred thousand black people in America, as opposed to two hundred eighty-two for every one hundred thousand white people in America.[34] Racism is still a heavy factor in the American electoral process. In 1983, the campaigns of two black candidates for mayoral posts in two of the nation's largest cities were reduced to racial contests of national proportions. The 1984 presidential campaign offered much of the same as the only black candidate began to do well in the primaries.

Constitutional civil rights, the major focus of the earlier Civil Rights Movement, have been seriously eroded. Federal monitoring of electoral activities in the southern portion of the nation have been substantially reduced. It has become clear that discriminatory electoral tactics have changed very little since 1954. In several Southern states vote tampering, prohibitive qualifications, and district gerrymandering have reappeared to limit the power of the Black vote.[35] Enforcement provisions in support of affirmative action, equal emloyment, and equal education have had their strength removed through legislative policy changes, budget reductions, and administrative action. Major businesses and institutions under federal contract or using federal funds have invented marvelously intricate methods of policy evasion.[36]

Public schooling was, of course, another critical focus of both the Civil Rights and Black Power movements. Questionable gains can be recorded in this area also. Thirty years after the 1954 Supreme Court decision, fully sixty-seven percent of all Black and Hispanic children still attend segregated schools.[37] Many school systems are attempting to resegregate through the use of such notions as "neighborhood schooling," reducing the costs of transportation to financially pressed school systems. Most allegedly desegregated schools reproduced segregation within each school through such methods as tracking, which generally relegate poor and nonwhite students to lower level school programs that terminate with the high school diploma.[38] This results in higher dropout rates for nonwhite students, higher suspension and expulsion rates, and significantly lower promotion and completion rates.[39] As nearly as can be estimated, these rates are a product of desegregated school systems' tracking approaches and far exceed estimated rates for black students prior to desegregation.[40]

Further, American public schools are highly monocultural in that they provide an education and a value system that only responds to a white middle-class view of the world, and tend to honor primarily those traditions and accomplishments that are in the historical development of Europe and America, to the exclusion of those of Asia and Africa and other parts of the globe.[41] These factors, combined with the back-to-basics movement and the resurgence of a militaristic patriotism, have all but obliterated the many efforts to establish greater cultural democracy and racial justice in the public schools.[42] The ideal of democratic unity in the United States has again been robbed of a necessary subcomponent—unity in diversity. The current brand of American education only prepares some of us to participate in the mainstream of society, never considering or knowing the needs of those who have been forced to live on the periphery. It thereby becomes an additonal factor in the perpetuation of racism in the nation and abroad. Higher education also suffers from the ills that affect public school education.

Almost all of those institutions that made attempts during the 1960s and 1970s to improve interracial understanding and reduce prejudices among their employees and in the society generally have abandoned such efforts and returned to business as usual. The Ku Klux Klan and other organizations designed for racist ends, instead of suffering predicted declines, have actually grown in membership and spread to new areas of the country.[43] Their many clandestine and overt acts of racism continue. The evidences of racism and prejudice can be seen at every turn. Television, the broadest multiple media in existence, is a major perpetrator. Witness the presentation of negative racial imagery, the glorification of base values, and the images of the poor and the disenfranchised it presents. The news media promote provincial, middle-class perspectives on events and realities in the nation and in the world at large. Most nonwhite people only enter the news in negative ways. Efforts aimed at the enlightenment of all media and the encouragement of change have failed.

To summarize, while it can be seen that there have been very many notable improvements in race relations in the past thirty years, it is clear that the majority of these changes are cosmetic in nature. No fundamental change in American racism has as yet occurred. Present conditions demonstrate that the America of 1954 is still, in essence, the America of 1984.

The True Nature of the Struggle. Ultimately perhaps, the least important result of the struggle for racial justice in the United States will be the liberation of black and other nonwhite Americans. The previous discussion of the international implications of this struggle indicate that the most important result may lie in its role in the establishment of international peace and justice. The end of war and exploitation on earth will, in turn, open the door for the reconciliation of the tremendous diversity of peoples and cultures. Only then will mankind begin to approach the establishment of the Kingdom of God on earth foretold by all the Prophets of the past. First, however, comes the necessary cleansing process that must involve the eradication of all forms of human exploitation and degradation. This process is necessarily evolutionary, however, and depends on our ability to constantly modify dysfunctional systems and human institutions. The United States is an ideal crucible for such a process.

Alterations in the political process must continue to take place before racial minorities will be able to participate as full partners. These alterations, as well as the addition of new minority voices from the diverse cultural perspectives of Americans, will create new and more human political agendas. Changes in our views of other nations and cultural systems will follow as reconciliations with the many motherlands of American citizens are explored. Diversity of perspective, opinion, cultural value, and experience cannot help but enhance and complete the whole. 'Abdu'l-Bahá stated to the Universal Races Congress of 1911: *"When differences of color, ideas, and character are found in the human kingdom, and come under the control of the power of unity, they too show their essential beauty and perfection."*[44]

There can be no justice until the tremendous economic inequalities that oppress minorities are removed from this society. Even among white citizens, a very small number control the overwhelming majority of economic resources and power. This conflict will exist in American society until the mass of the people realize it is detrimental to the entire nation. Elimination of extremes of wealth and poverty, as advocated by Bahá'u'lláh, is a necessary condition for the achievement of peace and justice. 'Abdu'l-Bahá explains: *"Rules and laws should be established to regulate the excessive fortunes of certain private individuals, and limit the misery of millions of the poor masses."*[45] Such, eventually, must be an important goal of this society.

Our national institutions, particularly education, must become more responsive to the needs of the poor and of minority groups in the society. Education must cease to be a means of carrying on the inequities of the past, and become a means of creating the equalities of the future. In this regard, the monoculturalism of schools, both in content and in process, must be replaced by multiculturalism and desire to address possibilities heretofore unattained. Education must also realistically address the economic needs of minority groups.[46]

Concomitant with the processes outlined above must be a constant effort to eradicate the feelings of inferiority, bitterness and hopelessness that have invaded the internal life of minority groups, and replace them with a sense of pride in self, culture and race. Racial oppression has many negative effects on the oppressed that serve to distort the positive spiritual and intellectual characteristics of culture. Aspirations and personal expectations often become severely limited, thereby serving to reduce effort toward improvement. Social and cultural structures and processes break down, aided by destructive messages of the dominant society.[47] But, as 'Abdu'l-Bahá so eloquently demonstrates in *The Secret of Divine Civilization*, the beginnings of the development of pride and renewed spiritual and cultural development are often found in the historical reawakening of a downtrodden group. *"Their pride must be aroused."*[48] For many nonwhite Americans, this process was well furthered during the 1960s.

Obviously, the eradication of the sense of inferiority, bitterness and hopelessness among nonwhite Americans must be accompanied by an eradication of the sense of superiority and monocultural rightness felt by most white Americans. This problem is pervasive and deep within the cultural, institutional, psychological fabric of American society and creates a sense of international righteousness, a belief in the near perfection of the culture, institutions, and lifestyles of the white citizenry.

Finally, a great deal of the racism that exists in the society is institutional in character. It is no longer necessary for institutional and business managers themselves to be bigots to aid in the perpetuation of racism. The ways in which institutions are structured, their accumulated policies, their decision methods, employee assessment methods, etc., are often racist in design or effect.

A few examples should suffice here: If a student is discriminated against in course placement in high school, he or she will not achieve the necessary scores on the Scholastic Achievement Tests to be admitted to certain colleges, and even to some majors within other colleges. The student is being discriminated against by one institution as a result of being discriminated against in another institution. Similarly, television news organizations are bureaucratic in nature and contemporary bureaucracies are conservative in outlook. Decisions about what to include in the news tend to reduce themselves to the lowest common denominator—what would the mass of Americans be interested in and consider inoffensive? On this basis, an enormous amount of news concerning nonwhite Americans goes unreported.

A few more examples: A bank representative denies a home improvement loan because according to company policy the home in question is in an area designated a high financial risk. The area is ninety-five percent Black; the combined effects of unemployment, discrimination, relegation to the secondary economy, and previous bank redlining have prevented residents form making home improvements. This banker participates in institutional racism by basing decisions in the present on the effects of racism in the past.

Or, a building contractor needs highly skilled pipefitters to complete a particular job. The contractor will use union workers or risk a strike and an unfilled contract. If the union has discriminatory policies, then the contractor inadvertently participates in institutional racism by hiring only union workers. It must be remembered that open advocacy of discrimination by union leaders did not end until the early 1960s. Employment patterns of unionized areas of labor have not changed substantially since that time.

Or, a skilled laborer is a union member and votes to continue the policy that dictates that new union members be sponsored by current members. Most intend to sponsor a son, nephew, or neighbor. Past policies of overt racial discrimination are in effect continued through this policy.

Cultural racism operates with institutional racism to create the effects observable in the society. Cultural racism is the general tendency to judge all ways of life, belief systems, and all behavior by the standard of European or American ideas—individualism, personal wealth, emotional restraint, competitiveness, and external motivation, to name a few. It is the tendency to view only the civilizations of Europe and America as the source of great works of art, literature, philosophy, and so forth.

Some examples will clarify: A trained counselor who thinks that it is rather silly that an Asian client won't discuss his problems in a group counseling session, being completely unaware that in most Asian cultures such self-disclosure is tantamount to bringing dishonor upon the family. Or, the music department at a high school that won't allow the use of contemporary Black music because it is popular music. Or, when a textbook publishing house won't include a section on African history and culture in its history textbook to correspond to precolonial European history and culture sections. Or, a store owner whose clientele is forty percent Puerto Rican but who refuses to post any signs or publish any advertisements in Spanish.

Of course, individual racism is still readily apparent to any casual observer of the American scene. This is an area that has been widely researched and no further elucidation is required here.

The importance of the American struggle for racial justice also lies in the manner in which it clarifies the limitations of contemporary human systems. After nearly one hundred years of massive change in the arenas of politics, employment, education, and law, the American people are still far from solving the problem of racial prejudice, their most challenging issue.

The major systems in the world today hold little ability to change the values, beliefs, and thinking of their citizens except in the areas of economics and general behavior. On this basis, negative ideals develop and so deeply embed themselves in the structures and cultures of nations that even major decision makers are powerless to discern certain problems or to act on them. Injustice in these nations will not cease until such time as the fundamental basis for constituting themselves is altered to a spiritual one instead of a material one. At such a point, all major institutions, subsystems, and laws will undergo changes that can help to achieve racial justice.

We must arrive at the understanding of human systems best explained by Shoghi Effendi in *The Promised Day is Come*. He declared that when human institutions cease to serve the general welfare of mankind, they should be discarded in accordance with the immutable law of change.[49] The struggle is ultimately spiritual in nature for in it lies much of the fate of the world. It is part of the process of the destruction of outworn systems and, at the same time, part of the process of building a new world based on fundamentally different principles. It cannot be won through material means, although the arenas of economics, education and international affairs are vitally involved.

The Bahá'í Faith and the Struggle for Racial Justice. How can racism be eliminated? How can unity be found between the white race and the nonwhite races? How can a permanent state of racial justice be achieved? These are important questions for the United States and its citizens to address in the waning years of the twentieth century. The Guardian of the Bahá'í Faith has issued this challenge to the American believers:

> Freedom from racial prejudice, in any of its forms, should, at such a time as this when an increasingly large section of the human race is falling a victim to its devastating ferocity, be adopted as the watchword of the entire body of the American believers. . . . It should be consistently demonstrated in every phase of their activity and life, whether in the Bahá'í community or outside it, in public or in private, formally as well as informally, individually as well as in their official capacity as organized groups, committees and Assemblies.[50]

Freedom from racial predice *in any of its forms*, given what has been discussed in these pages, involves a great deal more than feeling good will toward a race other than one's own. Cultural and institutional racism are a part of the problem, and their elimination must be part of the solution. Therefore, individuals must develop the capacity to systematically and continually examine themselves for the many manifestations of such racism and, with the aid of prayer and the Bahá'í teachings, remove these evils from their lives. Spiritual growth requires it.

In the same way, the cultural matrixes of some nonwhite groups in American society have grown to incorporate values and behaviors accommodative to and reactive to the many forms of racism. Individual members of these groups must also seek to remove the vestiges of these reactions to prejudice. These kinds of very personal activities may also be seen to constitute part of the necessary beginnings of the development of a new world culture based on the Bahá'í teachings. It should be understood that these kinds of cultural changes must be made openly manifest; in the words of the Guardian, they must be "deliberately cultivated."[51]

Concerning institutionalized forms of racism, it has already been explained that one does not need to be a prejudiced person to be involved in racist acts. The organizational structures, policies, and processes of the nation's social, cultural, educational, political, legal, and economic institutions and organizations are generally racist in design, intent or effect. Consequently, many individuals participate in acts of racism by this definition with no intent or foreknowledge. In fact, one can be a member of an oppressed racial group and carry out institutional racist acts.

To remove these forms of racism requires a full accounting of our obligation to respond to the Guardian's exhortations to consistently demonstrate our freedom from racial prejudice in any of its forms in all aspects and phases of our lives. Individuals in management, policy-making, supervisory, and professional positions must necessarily study their institutions and professions in order to discern the ways in which they perpetuate racism. Then they must seek to make appropriate changes. This is necessary for all individuals in such positions regardless of their race.

Most Americans encounter racist incidents in their everyday lives, but many fail to understand what is being observed. Many others accurately perceive what is occurring but fail to act in any way. Bahá'u'lláh has said that we should be *"an upholder and defender of the victim of*

oppression.''[52] We must act, but act in the spirit of
'Abdu'l-Bahá, as the Guardian admonishes, "through the
various and every-day opportunities, no matter how insignificant.''[53] To refrain from action in such situations
reinforces the perceptions of some members of minority
groups that all white Americans are racists.

Obviously, to carry out the obligations we have accepted
by becoming Bahá'ís requires risk—sometimes great, sometimes small. The actions being suggested are anxiety producing and require more of us to live our lives in totally new
ways. But, is this not precisely what the Revelation of
Bahá'u'lláh is about in its essence? Is this not a critical
aspect of becoming a new race of men and women? Is it not
clearly part of the process of establishing the Most Great
Peace? Is not the knowledge obtained through this revelation sufficiently advanced that it provides us with the
power necessary to become positive and creative leaders in
this struggle? If not the Bahá'ís, then who?

Notes

1. *Gleanings from the Writings of Bahá'u'lláh* (Wilmette, Ill.:
Bahá'í Publishing Trust, 1939) p. 215.
2. *Synopsis and Codification of the Laws and Ordinances of the
Kitáb-i-Aqdas* (Haifa: Bahá'í World Centre, 1973) p. 21.
3. Shoghi Effendi, *The Advent of Divine Justice* (Wilmette,
Ill.: Bahá'í Publishing Trust, 1971) p. 34.
4. Ibid., p. 16.
5. *Bahá'í World Faith* (Wilmette, Ill.: Bahá'í Publishing Trust,
1956) p. 269.
6. Ibid.
7. Paul Jacobs, Saul Landau and Eve Pell, *To Serve the Devil*,
Vol. I (New York: Random House, 1971) pp. 223–65.
8. Ibid., Vol. II, pp. 83–100, 166–220.
9. Ibid., Vols. I and II.
10. Albert P. Blaustein and Robert L. Zangrando, *Civil Rights*

and the Black American (New York: Washington Square Press, 1970) pp. 227–75.

11. Ibid., pp. 469–571.

12. Melville J. Herskovitts, *Myth of the Negro Past* (Boston: Beacon Press, 1958); James A. Banks, *Teaching Ethnic Studies: Concepts and Strategies* (43rd Yearbook of the National Council of the Social Studies, Washington, D.C., 1973); and B. N. Schwartz and Robert Disch, eds., *White Racism: Its History, Pathology and Practice* (New York: Dell, 1970); and Carl Grant and Milton Gold, *In Praise of Diversity* (Washington, D.C.: Teacher Corps, 1977).

13. Julius Lester, ed., *The Seventh Son: The Thought and Writings of W. E. B. DuBois* (New York: Vintage Books, 1971).

14. Stokely Carmichael and Charles V. Hamilton, *Black Power: The Politics of Liberation in America* (New York: Vintage Books, 1967).

15. *Devil*, Vols. I and II.

16. *Ethnic Studies*, p. 10.

17. Nathan I. Huggins, Martin Kilson and Daniel M. Fox, eds. *Key Issues in the Afro-American Experience*, Vol. I. (New York: Harcourt, Brace and Jovanovich, 1971) pp. 175–204.

18. U.S. Bureau of Labor Statistics, *Annual Report*, 1977.

19. *The Unfinished Business Twenty Years Later*, U.S. Commission on Civil Rights, September 1977.

20. Victor Perlo, *The Economics of Racism: U.S.A.* (New York: International Press, 1975), pp. 27–54.

21. Ibid., p. 40.

22. *Black Enterprise* (New York: Earl G. Graves Publishing Company, 1983) p. 39.

23. Calvin J. Larsen and Stan R. Nikkel, *Urban Problems* (Boston: Allyn and Bacon, 1979) pp. 119–124; John Ogbu, *Minority Education and Caste* (New York: Academic Press, 1978); and Victor Perlo, *Economics of Racism*.

24. John P. Fernandez, *Racism and Sexism in Corporate Life* (Lexington, Massachusetts: D. C. Heath Company, 1981).

25. *United States Bureau of the Census Statistical Report* (Washington, D.C.: U.S. Government Documents, 1980).

26. *Problems*, pp. 157–159.

27. *Black Enterprise*, June 1983.

28. *Fortune Magazine*, 500 Listing 1983.

29. Robert Allen, *Black Awakening in Capitalist America* (Garden City, New York: Doubleday and Company, 1969) pp. 150–155.

30. Joint Center for Political Studies (Washington, D.C., 1977).

32. Ibid.

33. Virginia Consortium of Urban Superintendents and Deans, *Report of the Legislative Committee* (Norfolk, Virginia: Old Dominion University, 1982).

34. Council on Interracial Books for Children, *Fact Sheets on Institutional Racism*, New York, October 1978.

35. *The National Leader* (Philadelphia: Publishers Enterprise National, Vol. 1, No. 29, November 25, 1982).

36. U.S. Commission on Civil Rights, 1978.

37. *Fact Sheets* p. 16.

38. John I. Goodland, "Access to Knowledge," *Teachers College Record* (New York: Columbia University, Vol. 84, No. 4, Summer 1983) pp. 787–800; Jeannie Oakes, "Tracking and Ability Grouping in American Schools: Some Constitutional Questions," *Teachers College Record* (New York: Columbia University, Vol. 84, No. 4, Summer 1983) pp. 801–820; and Carlton E. Brown, *Disciplinary Processes in Urban Public Schools* (Norfolk, Virginia: ESAS Special Student Concerns for Discipline Project, 1981).

39. *Disciplinary*, 1981.

40. Claton Braddock and David Hearne, *The Student Pushout* (Atlanta: Southern Regional Council, 1973).

41. Carlton E. Brown, *Implementing Multicultural Education in an Urban High School: Two Case Studies* (Amherst, Massachusetts: University of Massachusetts, unpublished dissertation, 1979), pp. 25–44.

42. "Knowledge", pp. 794–799.

43. *National Leader*, December 16, 1982; May 19, 1983.

44. G. Spiller, ed., *Inter-Racial Problems* (London: The World Peace Foundation, 1911), p. 156.

45. *Bahá'í World Faith*, p. 281.

46. Carter G. Woodson, *The Mis-Education of the Negro* (New York: AMS Press, 1977).

47. Frantz Fanon, *The Wretched of the Earth* (New York: Grove Press, 1966); Paulo Friere, *Pedagogy of the Oppressed* (New York: Continuum Press, 1970).

48. 'Abdu'l-Bahá, *The Secret of Divine Civilization* (Wilmette, Ill.: Bahá'í Publishing Trust, 1957) p. 10.

49. Shoghi Effendi, *The Promised Day Is Come* (Wilmette, Ill.: Bahá'í Publishing Trust, 1941).

50. *Advent*, p. 30.

51. Ibid.

52. *Bahá'i World Faith*, p. 136.

53. *Advent*, p. 30.

Poverty and Wealth in America:
A Bahá'í Perspective

by June Manning Thomas, Ph.D.

I N SOME COUNTRIES POVERTY IS a way of life for the majority of residents. Inhabitants of the countryside of India, the desert of Ethiopia, and the favela of Latin America live in true, abject poverty. To them, the lifestyle of the average American citizen is an unattainable dream. In nations that are predominately poor, it is not difficult to understand why poverty continues. To be sure, much of such poverty is a result of the unjust distribution of income: the wealthy elite are apt to live in great comfort oblivious to the needs of the masses. But much of the problem also lies in international factors, such as the domination of the world economy by industrialized nations.

Within those industrialized nations, such as the United States, reasons for the persistence of poverty are not so apparent. That the poor continue to exist is undeniable. Some try to ignore it—or they claim that poverty is only a temporary problem, rather like a troublesome child who will grow up, if only left alone. And, indeed, poverty has diminished greatly over the years. Possibly the majority of United States citizens were poor in the late nineteenth century. Although no official definition of poverty existed at that time, one author placed the subsistence population at anywhere from 30 to 50 million in 1904, in a nation of 82 million people.[1] During the Great Depression poverty overwhelmed the nation. A Brookings Institute study published in 1934, using a family poverty line comparable to that of the 1904 study, estimated that at least 70 million people—or 60 percent of American families—received less than an income "sufficient to supply only basic necessities."[2]

While life has improved dramatically since those days, a certain fraction of the population in America remains poor. The government has established an official measure of poverty to provide a rough idea of the nature and extent of the problem.[3] In 1981, according to this measure, approximately 13 percent of all families in the United States fell below the poverty level. This was an improvement over 1959, when the poverty rate was over 17 percent, but it showed an increase in poverty since 1974, when only 8.8 percent of all families fell below the poverty line.

Further evidence of our failure to eliminate poverty is the fact that the distribution of earned income has not changed significantly since 1947. In 1981, if one lined up the entire population of the United States, ranked according to family income and divided it into five equal parts (or quintiles), the fifth—the quintile with those of lowest income—would have only 5.0 percent of the income. Those in the highest or wealthiest quintile would receive 41.9 percent of the income. This is hardly an improvement over 1947, when the lowest quintile also received 5.0 percent of the income and the share of the highest quintile was 43.9 percent. The proportion of national income received by the lowest quintile has not improved at all.[4]

A sad fact of life in America is that poverty is concentrated in certain areas and among certain vulnerable subpopulations. For example, the incidence of poverty is higher for families in rural areas and families in central cities than it is for suburban families. Within central cities,

27.8 percent of all residents under eighteen years of age —nearly 4.5 million children—lived in families below the poverty level in 1981. The incidence of poverty is consistently higher among black people than among whites, a fact that significantly hinders the social and economic advancement of Blacks. In central cities, the rate of Black poverty among families with children is so high that close to one-half (46 percent in 1981) of black children live in poverty families. Others who suffer unduly include the elderly and families headed by women. The linkage between poverty and the sex of the household head is strong enough for some to regard poverty as a feminist issue: nearly one-third of all U.S. familes with female heads are poor.[5]

Because the United States is an affluent nation, it has the physical resources to insure that every man, woman, and child has adequate food, decent shelter, clothing, medical care, and the basics of a good education. Although many of these needs are provided, others are not. Government income maintenance programs tend to be inconsistent and inequitable, and benefits vary greatly from state to state and from person to person.

Although we have advanced to the point where public education is available to all, the quality of that education varies drastically. Large proportions of the poor do not receive government benefits because of chronic shortages (such as insufficient numbers of subsidized housing units), or because administrative red tape discourages eligible applicants from applying for and receiving benefits, or simply because money is not available.[6] Popular attitudes thwart positive action.

This country has made great strides in many directions —government, economics, technology, social welfare—and has served as a leader among nations; but all of its problems have not been solved. The problem of maldistribution of income is one that remains to be conquered. If the United States were to do so, it would serve as an example to the world and lay a path toward solution to problems of global income inequity. The Bahá'í Writings suggest definite steps that both society and the individual should take to conquer poverty and regulate wealth. They also suggest that America must play a special role in creating a better world. If all were to follow these guidelines and understand this role, the problem could be solved.

The first task is to examine the nature and limitations of material wealth in order to understand the extent to which modern society's emphasis upon money and material goods is misplaced. The special role of the United States is also important to discuss. In these times America is an important political, social, and economic leader in the world—and in future times it may become an important spiritual leader as well.

Material Wealth. All the world's great religions and philosophies recognize that material wealth is ephemeral. In the Bahá'í Faith also detachment from material concerns is highly praised. As Bahá'u'lláh wrote: "*The essence of wealth is love for Me. Whoso loveth Me is the possessor of all things, and he that loveth Me not is, indeed, of the poor and needy.*"[7] This passage and others written by Bahá'u'lláh's son, 'Abdu'l-Bahá, reveal that true wealth is the acquisition of spiritual qualities, and true poverty is the absence of the love of God.

Unlike earlier religions which exalt asceticism, the Bahá'í Faith does acknowledge that wealth can be good. Specifically, wealth that has been acquired through the exercise of one's personal craft or profession is "*approvable and worthy of praise.*"[8] A person who works hard to develop high skills and expertise deserves monetary compensation for that effort and should have no qualms about receiving such compensation. Likewise, parents should encourage their children to strive to become the best that they can in whatever their chosen trade or profession and to accept whatever material rewards may flow from that occupation. But persons who acquire great financial rewards must be spiritually mature individuals who realize the limitations and obligations of wealth.

Although earned wealth can be laudable, it is also inherently dangerous. In the Bahá'í Faith, as in other major religions, the message is clear: those who possess great wealth have reason to fear for their very souls. Jesus claimed that it was easier for a camel to go through the eye of a needle than for a rich man to enter the kingdom of heaven. Centuries later, the Qur'án warned, "Woe unto those who malign and speak evil of their fellows; who hoard earthly goods and count their riches."[9] Centuries after that, Bahá'u'lláh said, *"O Ye that Pride Yourselves on Mortal Riches! Know ye in truth that wealth is a mighty barrier between the seeker and his desire, the lover and his beloved. The rich, but for a few, shall in no wise attain the court of His presence nor enter the city of content and resignation."*[10] Without careful countermeasures, 'Abdu'l-Bahá explained, the rich would be deprived of "eternal happiness," for such happiness is contingent upon selfless giving.[11] It is impossible to hoard greedily and give abundantly at the same time. But it is possible to give moderately of one's wealth. Therefore, under Bahá'í law, the rich are obligated to give a certain portion of their fortune each year to help maintain the poor and unfortunate. 'Abdu'l-Bahá suggested that one path to salvation for a wealthy man would be for him to bequeath gifts to the poor in his will and to donate to the poor annually, so that *"perhaps this action may be the cause of his pardon and forgiveness, and of his progress in the Divine Kingdom."*[12]

These ideas, although they clearly echo Christian teachings, are not widely accepted in the industrial West. Of course, the United States has adopted a progressive income tax which requires that those with the highest annual income give about one-half of their taxable earnings to the federal government. But it is relatively easy for rich people to hire tax lawyers to shelter their incomes so that they need pay little or nothing. The government taxes income rather than wealth. It has gradually deemphasized older taxation systems which did tax wealth, such as the property tax, because they were cumbersome and unfair for other reasons. But under the modern income tax system the very wealthy can accumulate huge amounts of money without having to transfer much of it into income and so face taxation. It would be more appropriate to tax real wealth, but it would be even more laudable if the well-to-do were to voluntarily donate portions of their fortunes to assure the health and well-being of other citizens. This would help them fulfill their personal moral obligations as well as promote the welfare of the poor.

Many of the responsibilities of the rich also fall upon the middle class in modern industrialized nations such as the United States. The average American citizen is far wealthier than most inhabitants of the world. Yet even though Americans have more than enough money to meet their basic needs, most feel no obligation to share their incomes with those less fortunate. Charity is fairly common among both the wealthy and middle classes, but such giving is not viewed as a moral obligation. It is, in most cases, sporadic and modest in magnitude.

Modern society adores wealth, with no understanding of the spiritual handicaps that cripple the wealthy, their obligations to their fellow human beings, or the dangers of excessive love of things. In America materialism also affects the middle and lower classes. One of the manifestations of materialism is the widespread envy of, and curiosity about, the country's fabulously wealthy individuals and families. People admire those who are wealthy—even though their money may have come from grandfathers or great-grandfathers who earned it dishonestly. People mimic the lifestyles, clothing, and materialism of the prosperous. Acquisition of more and better material goods becomes the new salvation; and skillful advertising and merchandising nurture this lucrative desire. True happiness is, such advertising would have us believe, a newer, better car parked in front of a new, expensive house outfitted with all the gadgets one can buy. These things do not bring true happiness, of course, because true happiness is spiritual and emotional happiness.[13]

Excessive love of wealth and envy of the wealthy coexist with an almost palpable distaste for the poor. The beautiful people are those of great wealth, youth, and health. The poor, on the other hand, are subject to derogatory labels such as "welfare mothers," "leeches," and "bums." That the poor are largely children, the sick, the aged, and the infirm can be proven by statistics—over eighteen million of the twenty-nine million poor in 1980 were old people, invalids, or children. But statistics do not always change social attitudes or negative stereotypes.[14]

The Obligations of Society. It is one of the major principles of Bahá'u'lláh that *"Nobody should die of hunger; everybody should have sufficient clothing; one man should not live in excess while another has no possible means of existence."*[15] Both He and 'Abdu'l-Bahá after Him offered guidelines to limit private wealth and to provide for the needs of the poor. The idea of progressive taxation is one of these guidelines; another is the provision of social welfare. In addition, they specified that Bahá'í institutions have certain obligations to fulfill, apart from those of secular governments.

The guidelines that Bahá'u'lláh gave to Bahá'í institutions are modest in number but powerful in impact. Upon Spiritual Assemblies He placed the responsibility of consulting upon several matters, including *"the instruction of children, the relief of the poor, the help of the feeble throughout all classes in the world."*[16] The directive for Assemblies to consult upon the relief of the poor and the feeble is not one that is commonly carried out in North American Bahá'í Communities. But interest in social and economic development has increased since the October 1983 letter of the Universal House of Justice requested Assemblies to consult on these matters. (See Gregory Dahl's article in this volume.)

The Bahá'í Writings have always stated that these issues are important, although full attention to them may only come some time in the future. For example 'Abdu'l-Bahá urged that a community should, as soon as possible, establish other institutions next to its House of Worship or Mashriqu'l-Adhkár—a university, a hospital, and a school for orphans.[17] Shoghi Effendi predicted that such social institutions would come "in the fulness of time," and include facilities to "afford relief to the suffering, sustenance to the poor, shelter to the wayfarer, solace to the bereaved, and education to the ignorant."[18] Along with Bahá'u'lláh's directive to every father to educate his sons and daughters came His instructions to the Houses of Justice (now known as Assemblies) to supervise the education of any children whose parents could not afford schooling for them.[19]

Bahá'u'lláh addressed most of His specific guidelines for the mitigation of poverty and the regulation of wealth to *society*. The term presumably refers to secular governments in the present, but could very well refer to Bahá'í societies in the future. A village or nation composed of Bahá'ís would have much more flexibility to function as a society than do our currently small Bahá'í communities. At some point, Bahá'í institutions will have to implement rules and regulations similar to, and superior to, those of secular governments.

In this light, Bahá'u'lláh's suggestions to political commonwealths take on new meaning. One of the major principles of Bahá'u'lláh is that the members of society—and the leaders of a polity—must feel an obligation to assist the poor. He elaborated upon this concept in a series of letters written to the kings and rulers of the nineteenth-century world. In one letter He wrote, *"Fear the sighs of the poor and of the upright in heart who, at every break of day, bewail their plight, and be unto them a benignant sovereign. They, verily, are thy treasures on earth."*[20] He also told the kings: *"Know ye that the poor are the trust of God in your midst. Watch that ye betray not His trust, that ye deal not unjustly with them and that ye walk not in the ways of the treacherous."*[21] These passages admonish rulers to heed the needs of the poor and treasure them above worldly treasures—a far different perspective than one that perceives them as a burden. At the time Bahá'u'lláh wrote these letters monarchy prevailed in the world, but there is every reason to believe that the admonitions are for those who govern regardless of the structure of the government.

Fundamental to this concept is the importance of justice: it is simply unjust to allow some to wallow in excessive wealth while others go hungry. It is far better to insure a basic standard of living for all citizens and to regulate wealth to help provide for the needs of all.

To simply state that society should regulate wealth is not sufficient: How should this be done? One way to accomplish such regulation would be through progressive taxation of wealth instead of income. 'Abdu'l-Bahá announced in a speech delivered in New York City in 1912, that neither millionaires nor extremely poor people would exist in a community where the laws of Bahá'u'lláh were implemented. His statement clearly revealed His opinion that extreme wealth should not exist. Expanding the concept to show how such a society would function, 'Abdu'l-Bahá suggested in the same speech that society not tax a person whose need equaled his income. If a person's resources were greater than his needs, however, he should be required to pay a tax. Conversely, if his needs exceeded his production, he should receive money as an adjustment. Therefore, taxation would be proportional to production and need.[22] Alternative versions of this proposal, which might be called negative income tax, have been advanced at various times in various countries, but no society has implemented them in pure form.[23]

In another passage 'Abdu'l-Bahá illustrated the direct connection between progressive taxation and social welfare. He offered the example of a village inhabited by farmers as a simple prototype of the body of mankind in general. In this hypothetical village, a public storehouse would have several sources of revenue: taxes from the income of the populace; income from the animals; revenues from any minerals that have been prospected; inheritances from any who have died without personal heirs; and treasures that have been found on the land. All of these revenues would flow into the storehouse. Taxes would not be taken from any farmer whose needs matched his income. From most farmers a tenth of income surplus would be taken, but from those with a high surplus of income over needs, a higher proportion would be appropriated. The storehouse would provide income to any farmer facing financial emergency. It would also take care of all of the expenses of orphans, cripples, the blind, the old, and the deaf. All of these expenditures would be regulated by trustees elected by the villagers. All of the members of the body politic would live comfortably, and no one would be destitute.[24]

While this passage was not meant to be a literal blueprint, it clearly established the spirit of social welfare. Society, according to this perspective, should design an automatic system for taxing excess wealth and distributing necessary funds to all of those in need. Of special concern would be the aged, the infirm and orphans.

In spite of the importance of eliminating extremes of wealth and poverty, redistribution should not go so far as to mandate absolute equality for all citizens. Such equality is impossible because equality does not exist in intellect or natural ability. To strive for such equality would only result in *"want of comfort, in discouragement, in disorganization."*[25] The ideal is to find a balance between absolute equality and rampant extremes of wealth.

Modern governments are attempting to find this balance. The modern welfare state is legions ahead of its predecessors. As recently as sixty years ago in the United States, no national system existed for unemployment compensation, welfare, or the needs of the aged. Social Security, workman's compensation, food stamps, and Aid for Families with Dependent Children represent tremendous gains. But Social Security does not insure against the elderly dying from malnutrition; not everyone receives food stamps who needs them; and health care is not always available. Some countries have made greater advances: Great Britain provides a national system of health care and Scandinavian countries insure that all are well housed. But within the United States such ideas meet stiff resistance. And the idea of extending ourselves to the family of man that makes up the rest of the globe, to those desperate poor in other nations, receives only lukewarm, palliative support. One reason for this state of affairs is that we do not understand that not only society has certain obligations; so does the individual.

The Obligations of the Individual. When most people think of the obligations of the individual and of poverty, they think only of the moral problems of the poor. For generations it has beeen a popular myth that people are poor because of moral shortcomings. The truth of the matter, however, is that the moral shortcomings are in large part those of the rest of the population.

This is not to deny that personal morality affects poverty. But society cannot expect more from its low-income citizens than it expects from the middle and upper classes. Most cities have alcoholic derelicts, but these people make up a very small percentage of the poor. The habits that lead some to skid row permeate society from the bottom up. Well-to-do professionals also suffer from alcoholism and, in some circles, abuse drugs. We cannot expect the poor to abstain while others do not; and, we certainly cannot blame most poverty on alcoholism and drugs.

The same is true of premarital and extramarital sex. Teenage pregnancies do contribute to continuing problems of poverty; general lax attitudes toward marital vows lead to abandonment and increase the number of female-headed households. More widespread adherence to basic standards of morality would help alleviate this problem. But again, there can be no double standard: moral standards are low in all of modern society. Chastity and abstinence from harmful sustances such as alcohol and drugs should be adopted by all. The well-to-do are only able to shield themselves from the economic consequences of unwise actions better than others are able to. The entire population must develop higher moral standards, not just the poor.

The issue of work is an especially sensitive one. In the Bahá'í view, every person is obligated to work. 'Abdu'l-Bahá wrote, *"Every person must have a profession, whether it be literary or manual, and must live a clean, manly, honest life, an example of purity to be imitated by others. It is more kingly to be satisfied with the crust of stale bread than to enjoy a sumptuous dinner of many courses, the money for which comes out of the pockets of others."*[26] This perspective is basically in harmony with the Protestant work ethic. If at all possible, all are obligated to lead useful, productive lives and to have a career or occupation. Poor people should strive, as should everyone else, to work and somehow manage to earn a means of livelihood.[27] This is one reason for the importance of educating children even if their parents are not able to pay. Among Bahá'ís, the responsibility for making sure that this is the case rests squarely upon the Spiritual Assemblies. It is the individual, however, who has the responsibility to work.

The problem is that in the popular mind the linkage between poverty and the refusal to work has grown out of proportion. The idea that the poor are all loafers who prefer the dole to honest work is simply not accurate. Some, such as migrant workers and others in the lower levels of the service economy known as the working poor, often work harder than the rest of the population, and under appalling conditions, but still cannot climb out of their poverty. Some are physically or emotionally incapable of work, while others are children or single parents with very young dependent children and no access to child care. Many people cannot find full-time work because none is available. This last category includes those who live in central cities which have steadily lost jobs. In some cases jobs have moved to the suburbs, but accessibility to those jobs is hindered by insufficient public transportation, or by racial or class prejudice.

When prejudice is the problem, minorities or low income people are unable to move close to available jobs because of discrimination in the sale or rental of housing or the refusal of a municipality to build low income housing.[28] In other cases of lack of access, manufacturing plants have simply closed and left a region or a country. Workers who once would have had employment in such plants do not have the skills to compete for new service-sector jobs requiring high levels of training and education.[29]

Many continue to live with the misconception that most poverty is caused by the poor themselves, in spite of evidence to the contrary. The idea that the poor should be helped as little as possible (to discourage their ingrained laziness) is an outdated misconception that dates from eighteenth- and nineteenth-century industrializing Europe. The predominate inclination in those days was to punish the poor, who the rest of the populace viewed as dirty, undeserving and immoral. Attitudes had scarcely improved by the time of the Great Depression; the unemployed blamed themselves for their plight. Polls taken during the late 1930s showed that the majority of middle-class white

Americans believed that poor people could get off relief if they tried hard enough.[30] By the 1960s an updated version of this attempt to blame the victim arose in the academic community as the concept of the "culture of poverty."[31] Theorists speculated that the poor were hopelessly mired in a culture that discouraged ambition and permanently handicapped them. Enlightened writers and thinkers now recognize that the poor are no different from anyone else; they simply adjust to their lives in ways that are often unfamiliar.

It is unfortunate that race and poverty are also closely intertwined. That the poor are lazy is one popular misconception; that they are black is another. Most of the poor people in the United States are white. Blacks suffer disproportionately from poverty, just as do Hispanics. But racial minorities make up only a small percentage of the poor residents of America.[32] These facts are ignored by those who persist in viewing poverty as only a Black problem, or who conversely feel that Blacks are typically poor because they are inferior, lazy, disadvantaged, or for whatever reason happens to hold sway at the moment.

This is a country which, just over one hundred years ago, held its black resident as slaves; which, just over eighty years ago, subjected them to a reign of terror following the end of Reconstruction; and which, just over twenty years ago, legally abrogated their rights to equal access to quality education as well as free access to employment. Unlike foreign immigrants who have also faced problems of chronic poverty and discrimination, Blacks have had no automatic protection of skin color. Racism so pervaded American culture that for generations the system of color stratification was taken for granted. Some argue that class prejudice has now replaced racial prejudice as the barrier to socio-economic advancement. But race and class are closely connected. One's race is a good predictor, though not a determinant, of one's class.

This does not mean that Blacks are hopelessly mired in poverty. Nor does it mean that whites must always feel guilty about high rates of Black poverty, that white Hispanics will inevitably advance beyond the status of Blacks, or that Blacks should be given automatic economic security because their race has suffered so. But it does mean that Americans must be especially careful to insure that the effects of racism which still limit Black advancement are abolished. Such effects might include lack of access to housing in prosperous suburbs or other regions where jobs may be available, lack of quality education in ghetto school systems, and lack of mobility into unions and employment because of race. Blacks and other racial minorities, for their part, will have to strive to overcome the effects of racism and to build better lives in a new society characterized by harmonious interracial relations. The Bahá'í Faith offers an excellent model for such a society. (See the article by Richard Thomas in this volume.)[33]

In sum, the problem of poverty in America is not due to lack of motivation or to the inherent inferiority of the poor. It is caused by the acccumlated effects of racism, by chronic unemployment caused by shifts in the regional or national economy, and by old age or physical infirmity. The obligation rests on society to mitigate the effects of these conditions as much as possible. This obligation includes the responsibility to insure that traces of racial prejudice are erased, that work at decent wages is available for as many people as possible, and that the needs of the aged, the infirm, the children are met.

The Bahá'í Writings say that everyone must strive to be free of racial prejudice. They also state unequivocally that everyone has a moral obligation to help those less fortunate. This charge is directed not only to the wealthy, but also to those of modest means.

Bahá'u'lláh, in a list of individual spiritual obligations —including prayer, meditation, kindness to animals—said that the righteous one "*should succor the dispossessed, and never withhold his favour from the destitute.*"[34] 'Abdu'l-Bahá declared that "*The highest righteousness of all is for blessed souls to take hold of the hands of the helpless and deliver them out of their ignorance and abasement and poverty, and with pure motives, and only for the sake of God, to arise and energetically devote themselves to the service of the masses, forgetting their own worldly advantage and working only to serve the general good.*"[35] In another passage He urged everyone to "*Be a helper of every oppressed one, the protector of every destitute one, be ye ever mindful to serve any soul of mankind.*"[36]

It is not surprising, therefore, that the voluntary sharing of one's property with others is an important principle of the Bahá'í Faith. This sharing is just as much for the sake of the donor as the recipients.[37] It is, in effect, an attempt to overcome the bonds of materialism that fetter not only the very rich but even the average citizen in a country as affluent as the United States. And it is this very attitude that seems so foreign to most people. Our giving is desultory, formalized, reluctant. Few indeed are those who truly devote themselves to protecting the destitute and helping the oppressed. The poor are estranged from everyone else by walls of prejudice, insensitivity and plain apathy.

The obligations of the individual—exemplary personal conduct, freedom from racial prejudice, unselfish giving to those less fortunate—seem overwhelming. In fact, they are quite attainable; we need only look to the examples of Bahá'u'lláh and 'Abdu'l-Bahá.

Bahá'u'lláh was not aloof from the poor. Born to privilege and wealth, He shunned the sheltered life of the wealthy and associated with all levels of society. He often urged His followers to associate with the poor and remember their sorrows. He Himself never turned anyone from His door. His generosity astounded those of His friends who knew the true limitations of His circumstances, but He never stinted on giving. He became "*a refuge for every weak one, a shelter for every fearing one, kind to every indigent one, lenient and loving to all creatures.''*[38] Bahá'u'lláh actually lived as a poor recluse for a time in Iraq when He left His family and the other followers of the Báb. During this period Bahá'u'lláh chose a life of poverty, solitude, and reflection; He lived in an isolated cave, referring to Himself as *darvísh* or poor one.[39]

Accounts of Westerners who managed to observe 'Abdu'l-Bahá, either in the prison city of 'Akká or during His trip to the United States in 1912, abound with tales of His selfless generosity. In late 1902, New York attorney Myron Phelps spent an entire month in 'Akká. He vividly described the crowds of poor Arabs that waited near the house of 'Abdu'l-Bahá every Friday morning for His appearance. The Master placed a coin into the hand of each, caressed their faces and shoulders, and asked about their health. As Phelps wrote:

This scene you may see almost any day of the year in the streets of Akka. There are other scenes like it, which come only at the beginning of the winter season. In the cold weather which is approaching, the poor will suffer, for, as in all cities, they are thinly clad. Some day at this season, if you are advised of the place and time, you may see the poor of Akka gathered at one of the shops where clothes are sold, receiving cloaks from the Master. Upon many, especially the most infirm or crippled, he himself places the garment, adjusts it with his own hands, and strokes it approvingly, as if to say, ''There! Now you will do well.'' There are five or six hundred poor in Akka, to all of whom he gives a warm garment each year.[40]

Phelps went on to note that 'Abdu'l-Bahá regularly visited the poor in their homes, mentioned by name those who He did not see, and left gifts for all. He secretly sent bread to those in dire straits who were too proud to stand in the street and beg.

All the people know him and love him—the rich and the poor, the young and the old—even the babe leaping in its mother's arms. If he hears of any one sick in the city— Moslem or Christian, or of any other sect, it matters not —he is each day at their bedside, or sends a trusty messenger. If a physician is needed, and the patient poor, he brings or sends one, and also the necessary medicine . . . He is the kind father of all the people.[41]

All of this was done by a man who had Himself been incarcerated within the walls of the prison-city for thirty-four years because of religious persecution. Many in the town reviled Him because He was a Bahá'í. But 'Abdu'l-Bahá simply returned love to their hate and extended charity to all—regardless of color or creed. That charity was so overwhelming, so all-encompassing, that hardened enemies grew to love Him and beg His forgiveness for their past rancor.

A good example is the Muslim from Afghanistan who spent a great deal of energy publicly denouncing 'Abdu'l-Bahá as a heretic. When the man passed 'Abdu'l-Bahá in the street, he held his robe before his face less the well-known Bahá'í defile his sight. But it happened that the Afghan was poor and in frequent need of food and clothing. These 'Abdu'l-Bahá sent him regularly, although He received no thanks. Likewise the Master sent a physician to assist the man when he fell ill, even though the Afghan, persisting in his enmity, covered his face from the sight of 'Abdu'l-Bahá with one hand as he simultaneously held out his other for the physician to take his pulse. Finally, after twenty-four years of hatred and calumny from the Afghan and love and generosity from 'Abdu'l-Bahá, the man came to the Master full of penitence, fell to his knees, and begged forgiveness. 'Abdu'l-Bahá forgave him, but of course His generosity had never stopped.[42] Unlike those who give to the poor only when the poor are properly grateful, 'Abdu'l-Bahá gave even in the face of outright hatred.

Unlike those who give to the poor only if they can do so without sacrificing their own comfort, 'Abdu'l-Bahá gave unstintingly. Whatever money He had He used for both His family and the needy. One of His daughters wore only an old dress when she was married. When asked why He had provided no bridal clothes for the happy occasion, 'Abdu'l-Baha replied, "My daughter is warmly clad and has all that she needs for her comfort. The poor have not. What my daughter does not need I will give to the poor rather than to her."[43]

During His trip to the United States, 'Abdu'l-Bahá continued to demonstrate His selflessness. Early one morning in Dublin, New Hampshire, He met an old tramp with dirt-crusted hands. 'Abdu'l-Bahá took the old man's hands into His own and spoke to Him with love and affection. He then wrapped His long cloak around Himself, removed His trousers and gave them to the old man.[44] In another incident, when He spoke to the destitute men who frequented the Bowery Mission in New York, He told them of their high station in life and of the Kingdom of God that was for the poor. But He also gave them practical evidence of His love by pressing silver coins into the hand of each of four or five hundred men.[45] Throughout His journey in America 'Abdu'l-Bahá made a special effort to seek out and comfort the poor and downhearted.

Such instances of selflessness are examples to the rest of humanity. To be sure, such standards of behavior are high, but they are not impossible. Bahá'ís are taught that it is possible to pattern their personal behavior after that of the Master, 'Abdu'l-Bahá. Furthermore, one does not have to look very far to find examples of people who do extend selfless generosity to the rest of humanity. These include people who generously adopt children who might otherwise have no home; people who dedicate many hours to charity and volunteer work for the good of the needy; others who devote themselves to teaching and service to the poor. If one carefully reads the newspapers, other examples appear.

There is Mother Waddles in Detroit, Michigan, an extraordinary woman who has fed the poor of the city of Detroit for decades through her Perpetual Mission; or the occasional restauranteur who opens his doors to offer free Christmas or Thanksgiving dinners every year. Among Bahá'ís, many are the examples of those who have taken up residence in central cities or rural areas and tried to make their lives like the life of 'Abdu'l-Bahá. Yet we can all give more than we do. We can all be of solace and assistance to the sick, the lonely, the destitute. To do so is to begin to meet our personal spiritual obligations.

A society composed of individuals who truly strive for selflessness and who truly love all humanity is a society which is willing to take the measures necessary to insure the needs of all citizens and eliminate extremes of wealth and poverty. In particular, American society has the capacity and ability to do this.

The Promise of America. The United States of America holds a special place in the Bahá'í teachings. 'Abdu'l-Bahá said that "*The American continent gives signs and evidences of very great advancement. Its future is even more promising, for its influence and illumination are far-reaching. It will lead all nations spiritually.*"[46] While chiding the Persian government in 1875, He held up America as a counter-example to its backwardness: "*Today throughout the five continents of the globe it is Europe and most sections of America that are renowned for law and order, government and commerce, art and industry, science, philosophy and education.*"[47]

During His trip to America 'Abdu'l-Bahá gave still another indication of the importance of this country: "*America,*" He stated, "*hath developed powers and capacities greater and more wonderful than other nations. The American nation is equipped and empowered to accomplish that which will adorn the pages of history, to become the envy of the world, and be blest in both the East and the West for the triumph of its people.*"[48]

In contrast with this positive view of America, Shoghi Effendi wrote a sobering assessment of the nation in the 1930s:

It is precisely by reason of the patent evils which, notwithstanding its other admittedly great characteristics and achievements, an excessive and binding materialism has unfortunately engendered within it that the Author of their Faith and the Center of His Covenant have singled it out to become the standard-bearer of the New World Order envisaged in their writings.[49]

The choice of America as standard-bearer of the future, therefore, was made in spite of the fact that it was a country "immersed in a sea of materialism, a prey to one of the most virulent and long-standing forms of racial prejudice, and notorious for its political corruption, lawlessness, and laxity in moral standards."[50]

The intent of these passages is clearly one of qualified praise. America may become a truly magnificent nation, but this depends, 'Abdu'l-Bahá says, on a steadily progressive system of lasting reform.

All must work toward a society characterized by justice, peace, and tranquility—a society in which racial equality prevails, the basic needs of all citizerns are provided for, and work is available for all. All must work for the development of clear goals for the improvement of society based on principles of justice and compassion, and for the spiritual transformation of the populace.

No one denies that the task of reducing income disparity is difficult. It requires both will and direction. The nation must operate within the framework of national goals that place social improvement above all else. Were America to aim to satisfy the basic needs of its citizens, whether by improved welfare or provision of minimum income, it could be done. Were it to aim to reduce income inequality, it could be done. Were it to aim to insure the availability of work, that too could be done. All of these measures are necessary components of the task of eliminating poverty. But America would have to lift itself above the squabbles that surround current welfare programs. Justice, equity, and the promulgation of individual nobility are some of the values that should be included in solutions to contemporary economic problems.

For example, in dealing with the problem of urban poverty, it is impossible to imagine any progress without a fundamental recognition of the role of racial and class prejudice and the need to eliminate the effects of such prejudice. A sense of justice requires that society at least attempt to undo the deleterious effects of the past and prepare for a future unhampered by these evils. To do so, however, requires considerable guidance concerning the proper way to alleviate remnants of past racial injustice. The Bahá'í Faith offers such guidance with its teachings on affirmative action (in the form of preference given to minorities under certain specific conditions) and with the explicit directions given both American blacks and whites in Shoghi Effendi's essay on "The Most Challenging Issue."[51] Likewise, a sense of equity requires that the needs of all of the poor be met, not just those in certain racial or age categories.

The importance of justice and equity is understood by most people, although they do not necessarily agree upon their definitions or practical implications. The importance of maintaining and enhancing the nobility of the individual is less clearly understood. The noble individual is one who is at harmony with spiritual and moral laws. This not so much a statement of moral judgment as of pragmatic truth. The noble individual must be respected for the basic intelligence that motivates all of mankind. A practical implication of this principle is the need to allow people to determine their own destinies. Society must give the poor the means as well as the ability to improve themselves as much as possible, and to make decisions about the best means for doing

so (a principle that Gregory Dahl elaborates on in his article). Furthemore, the rest of the populace, those not in
need, must understand the laws governing their behavior
and attitudes toward those less fortunate.

With the spiritual enlightenment of the populace will
come improvement in government. 'Abdu'l-Bahá has
explained that *"The primary purpose, the basic objective, in
laying down powerful laws and setting up great principles and
institutions dealing with every aspect of civilization, is human
happiness; and human happiness consists only in drawing
closer to the Threshold of Almighty God, and in securing the
peace and well-being of every individual member, high and low
alike, of the human race; and the supreme agencies for accomp-
lishing these two objectives are the excellent qualities with
which humanity has been endowed."*[52]

Notes

1. John Ryan's standard of $700 per year in 1904 money;
estimate applied by James T. Patterson, *America's Struggle
Against Poverty: 1900–1980* (Cambridge: Harvard University
Press, 1981) p. 11. Patterson points out that Robert Hunter,
author of *Poverty* (New York, 1904) used a much more modest
definition of poverty, and estimated that 20 percent of the
population in northern industrial areas was poor.

2. *America's Struggle*, p. 16. The Brookings "poverty line" of
$2,000 corresponded to about $700 to $800 1904 dollars.

3. In 1980 the poverty level for a family of four with two
children was $8,351 annual income, and for a single person over
sixty-five, $3,950. Noncash benefits, such as housing assistance,
are not included as income, although recently the federal government had considered counting such benefits as income, a move
that would significantly lower the number counted as poor. U.S.
Bureau of the Census, Current Population Reports, Series P-60,
No. 138, *Characteristics of the Population Below the Poverty Level:
1981* (U.S. Government Printing Office, Washington, D.C.,
1983).

114   *June Manning Thomas*

4. U.S. Department of Commerce, Bureau of the Census, *Money Income of Households, Families, and Persons in the U.S.: 1981* (U.S. Government Printing Office, Washington, D.C.).

5. *Characteristics of the Population: 1981.* In that year 16.7 percent of all central city residents were poor, as well as 28.2 percent of all unrelated single people over 65 years of age who lived in central cities, and 32.7 percent of all U.S. families headed by females with no husband in the home.

6. Robert H. Haverman, "Introduction: Poverty and Social Policy in the 1960s and 1970s—An Overview and Some Speculations," *A Decade of Federal Anti-Poverty Programs: Achievements, Failures and Lessons,* ed. by Robert H. Haveman (New York: Academic Press, 1977), pp. 10–15. In 1981 41.1 percent of all families received food stamps, and only 23.7 percent of all poor families who were renters were able to live in publicly owned or subsidized rental housing. U.S. Bureau of the Census, Current Population Reports Series P-60, No. 136, *Characteristics of Households and Persons Receiving Selected Non-Cash Benefits, 1981,* (U.S. Government Printing Office, Washington, D.C., 1983), p. 7.

7. *Bahá'í Revelation: A Selection from the Bahá'í Holy Writings* (London: Bahá'í Publishing Trust, 1955) p. 138–39.

8. *Bahá'í World Faith: Selected Writings of Bahá'u'lláh and 'Abdu'l-Bahá* (Wilmette, Ill.: Bahá'í Publishing Trust, 1956) p. 167.

9. *Bahá'í Revelation,* p. 161.

10. Ibid., pp. 114–115.

11. 'Abdu'l-Bahá, *The Promulgation of Universal Peace* (Wilmette, Ill.: Bahá'í Publishing Trust, Second Ed., 1982) p. 132.

12. 'Abdu'l-Bahá, *Some Answered Questions* (Wilmette, Ill.: Bahá'í Publishing Trust, 1981) p. 277.

13. Shoghi Effendi, *The Advent of Divine Justice* (Wilmette, Ill.: Bahá'í Publishing Turst, 3rd rev. ed., 1969) p. 16.

14. U.S. Bureau of the Census, Current Population Reports, Series P-60, No. 134, *Money Income and Poverty Status of Families and Persons in the United States, 1981* (U.S. Government Printing Office, Washington, D.C., 1982).

15. *Bahá'í Revelation,* pp. 291.

16. Quoted in Shoghi Effendi, *Bahá'í Administration: Selected Messages. 1922–1932* (Willmette: Ill.: Bahá'í Publishing Trust, 1974 p. 22.

17. *Bahá'í World Faith* p. 416.

18. *Bahá'í Administration* p. 184.

19. *Bahá'í World Faith*, p. 200.

20. *Bahá'í Revelation* p. 24.

21. Ibid., p. 8.

22. *Promulgation*, p. 216–17.

23. The negative income tax, advocated by several major economists would retain the graduated nature of the curent income tax but would also give graduated income (in a negative direction) to those who fell below a certain income line. This negative tax or grant system would take the place of categorical welfare and in-kind programs. See Haverman, "Introduction," pp. 15–18.

24. 'Abdu'l-Bahá, *Foundations of World Unity* (Wilmette: Ill.: Bahá'í Publishing Trust) 1945, pp. 40–41.

25. *Bahá'í Revelation*, p. 295.

26. *Bahá'í Scriptures*, quoted in J. E. Esslemont, *Bahá'u'lláh and the Era* (Wilmette, Ill.: Bahá'í Publishing Trust, 1980) p. 102.

27. Bahá'u'lláh, *Gleanings from the Writings of Bahá'u'lláh* (Wilmette, Ill.: Bahá'í Publishing Trust, 1939) p. 202.

28. Thomas A. Clark, *Blacks in Suburbs: A National Perspective* (New Brunswick, NJ: Center for Urban Policy Research, 1979.)

29. Barry Bluestone and Bennett Harrison, *The Deindustrialization of America: Plant Closings, Community Abandonment and the Dismantling of Basic Industry* (New York: Basic Books, 1982) pp. 35–40. For a special discussion of the black worker see William Julius Wilson, *The Declining Significance of Race: Blacks and Changing American Institutions* (Chicago University Press, 1978) especially pp. 92–99.

30. *America's Struggles*, p. 46.

31. See the works of Bettylou Valentine, *Hustling and Other Hard Work: Lifestyles in the Ghetto* (New York: The Free Press, 1978) and Charles Valentine, *Culture and Poverty: Critique and Counter-Proposal* (Chicago: University of Chicago Press, 1969).

32. *Characteristics of the Population, 1981.* 31,822,000 fell below poverty level of those 21,553,000 were white and 9,175,00 were black.

33. See Gregory Dahl's article in this volume. Ruḥíyyih Khánum, in comments addressed to pilgrims on February 24, 1984,

stressed the importance of allowing people to decide for themselves how to undertake economic development.

34. *Bahá'í Revelation*, p. 98.

35. 'Abdu'l-Bahá, *The Secret of Divine Civilization* (Wilmette, Ill.: Bahá'í Publishing Trust, 1957) p. 103.

36. *Bahá'í World Faith*, pp. 216–17.

37. *Bahá'í Revelation*, p. 212.

38. *Bahá'í World Faith*, pp. 220–221.

39. 'Abdu'l-Bahá, *Promulgation* p. 33.

40. Myron H. Phelps, *Life and Teachings of Abbas Effendi* (New York: G. P. Putnam's Sons, 1903) p. 5.

41. Ibid., p. 6.

42. Ibid. pp. 9–10.

43. Ibid., p. 103.

44. Howard Colby Ives, *Portals to Freedom* (London: George Ronald, 1948) pp. 128–29.

45. *Promulgation*, p. 34.

46. Quoted in *Advent*, p. 72.

47. *Divine Civilization*, p. 10.

48. Quoted in *Advent*, p. 72.

49. Ibid., p. 16.

50. Ibid.

51. Ibid., pp. 28–34.

52. *Divine Civilization*, p. 60.

Human Rights and the Bahá'í Faith

by Juan R. Cole, Ph. D.

T HE TWENTIETH CENTURY HAS WITNESSED the most
sophisticated thinking and legislation about human
rights in all of recorded human history. Yet since 1900,
more innocent people have been deprived of their basic
rights in more ingenious and horrible ways than ever before. The trench warfare, poison gas, and maiming of civilians that accompanied the First World War established a
major theme that was to sound again and again throughout
the world in the decades succeeding the armistice. War had
become total, had been wedded with new technologies to
produce piles of skulls that dwarfed the feeble efforts of
Genghis Khan or Tamerlane.

At the same time, the capitalist empires of the West
discovered their inability to coexist peacefully, or to accommodate the new demands for national independence beginning to sound from the Arab World and from India.
Europe's workers, many once attracted by socialist promises of peace, foolishly surrendered to the passions of nationalism, only to be mowed down by machine guns, dying
for ends that remain unclear. Europe and North America
suffered from gross maldistribution of wealth and income
at home, while abroad the Western Powers parlayed their

117

technological and military superiority into an acquisitive stranglehold on most of Asia and Africa. In Europe itself the inequities of the war settlement and the financial insecurity of the Depression years helped foster political movements of the Right and the Left that sacrificed individual rights on the altar of national advancement or military aggrandisement. In 1938 a survey of the world would have shown few places where the five criteria of human rights recently put forward by Richard Falk were met in any way.[1] In most of the world basic human needs, basic decencies, participatory rights, security rights, and humane governance were woefully absent.

The maelstrom of the second World War swept away, in many parts of the planet, even the little security and the few basic decencies that the earth's masses had managed to achieve. The atomic bombardments of Hiroshima and Nagasaki epitomized the utter negation of human rights, offering a gruesome but fitting finale to a dreadful global cataclysm that killed, maimed or displaced millions and saw the German National Socialist Party's attempt to murder an entire people—Europe's Jews. From that point on formulations of human rights had to forbid the novel crime of genocide.

Since 1945 the world's human rights situation has improved in some areas. Certainly basic human needs and decencies are met in most of Europe and North America, a stark contrast to the 1930s and 1940s. In the Soviet Union and the United States, the twin scourges of Stalinism and McCarthyism were faced and overcome by the late 1950s. But even a war-ravaged Europe proved reluctant to relinquish its former colonies. In much of the Third World the postwar years were taken up with protracted struggles against colonial powers for participatory rights in their own governance. The creation of the United Nations provided a new global perspective to human rights thinking even in the West. In the light of its ideals, however, the real situation in many respects remains dismal. The issuance of the Universal Declaration of Human Rights and the subsequent United Nations covenants on the subject set forth sublime goals forged in the consultative process among representatives of numerous countries. Yet the actual condition in the majority of the world's nations often seems a parody of such idealistic documents.

Even in the prosperous nations of the United States, Western Europe and Japan, millions of poor people remain who do not sufficiently share in national prosperity, who labor in dangerous or extremely fatiguing settings, and who face the ever present nightmare of joblessness. Indeed, in the United States an unemployment rate of nearly ten percent has come to be seen as entirely acceptable by the nation's leaders, who disregard its debilitating effects upon the marriages, mental health, and children of jobless workers.

However unsatisfactory the condition of the workers in the developed nations, their plight is far to be preferred to the life led by literally billions of people in the Third World. I am not here speaking of poverty and unemployment alone, but of a lack of all those basic standards suggested by Falk. Most of the world's people do not have participatory rights, either at the local or the national level; nor do they have security from arbitrary actions by their police or military, or from the military of neighboring countries.; and they seldom feel the touch of humane governance. Moreover, the developed nations that enjoy so many more of the human rights outlined in the Universal Declaration often find it in their national security or economic interests to support regimes and policies that continue to deprive most of the world's inhabitants of their rights.

Insofar as the Bahá'í Faith is a world religion, it must address the crucial issues in human rights throughout the globe. As it grows numerically, people increasingly will be concerned to know its stance, nor will they be satisfied with platitudes. Bahá'ís have a duty to investigate their own scriptures to discover their relevance to the question of human rights, and to employ their discoveries both to contribute to the global debate on the matter and to set policy for their own religious institutions.

That a religion might have something to add to thinking about human rights is entirely appropriate. Much of traditional human rights thinking was grounded in scriptural values. The Ten Commandments of the Hebrew Bible, the Vedas, and the Qur'an, the ethical teachings of Zoroaster, Gautama Buddha, Confucius, and Jesus have inspired countless laws bearing on human rights and influenced the behavior of governments and societies toward greater appreciation of individual human worth. One thinks of the ancient Indian emperor Ashoka who upon his conversion to Buddhism abandoned his expansionist territorial designs and promulgated edicts commanding interreligious tolerance and harmony throughout his vast dominions.

Of course, religion has also been responsible for some of the most horrifying abuses of human rights—be they the Spanish Inquisition, the Thirty Years War, or any number of other atrocities committed in the name of God or the Eternal Truth. Religion, like any other human institution, can be perverted to unnatural ends; but there can be no question of its supreme importance as a source of positive human values and meaning. Because it can be misused so easily, it is all the more important for the leaders and members of any religion to remain constantly aware of the enlightened principles ordained by the Founders of their faiths.

The Bahá'í Faith can play a valuable role in elaborating and promoting human rights in many ways. First, much human rights thinking has been developed in the West, often incorporating peculiarly Western values, such as extreme individualism and the absolute sanctity of private property.

As a religion that initially originated in the Third World (Iran, Iraq, Turkey, and Palestine) and went on to expand into Asia, Africa, Europe, and the Americas, the Bahá'í Faith can offer a perspective that is at once a Third World and a global one. Further, as a nongovernmental organization affiliated with the United Nations, the Bahá'í Faith often has the opportunity to present proposals and viewpoints that are heard in international councils.

Bahá'ís have recently put much energy into highlighting the human rights abuses being perpetrated upon their co-religionists in Iran by the ruling Islamic Republican Party. They know directly of circumstances where, on grounds of religious bigotry, a large group of people has been deprived of life, liberty and property. They have seen their children refused admission to schools because of their religous affiliation; they have been denied ration cards for the same reason; and have witnessed their most devoted and active friends, male and female, arbitrarily imprisoned and subsequently murdered or executed.

Their efforts to make the world aware of this travesty are admirable. But unless the Bahá'í Community consistently shows a similar zeal for the plight of the oppressed elsewhere, the sincerity of its overall concern with human rights as an issue will be questioned. Too often Bahá'ís feel that such concern might be misinterpreted as an interference in the sort of partisan politics they have been urged, at least at this stage of the religion's development, to eschew. In fact, there is no contradiction between an activist advocacy of human rights and a commitment to neutrality in regard to struggles between political parties. To the contrary, it is precisely so that Bahá'ís may witness in a nonpartisan manner to such values as the importance of human rights that they avoid narrow political entanglements. A nonpartisan policy may be, indeed must be, activist; otherwise it deteriorates into selfishness and complacency.

CLEARLY, THE BAHÁ'Í SCRIPTURES envisage a society in which the basic human needs of each of its members would be met. 'Abdu'l-Bahá detailed at length the duties of small communities toward their indigent members, explaining that the public treasury should be used to help those who fell on hard times get back on their feet.[2] Food, clothing, shelter, should be the birthright of every human being. On the other hand, the right carries with it a duty to strive to earn a living and to learn a trade.[3]

In today's complex world, such principles cannot be discussed merely on a local level. A certain amount of global resource management is necessary if widespread malnutrition, starvation and death from exposure and disease are to be extirpated. It is typical of the global-mindedness of the Bahá'í Faith that, not only have guidelines been suggested for the behavior of local communities toward the under-privileged in their midst, but the issue has been addressed at the international level as well. Shoghi Effendi, the Guardian of the Bahá'í Faith, wrote:

> The unity of the human race, as envisaged by Bahá'u'-lláh, implies the establishment of a world commonwealth in which all nations, races, creeds and classes are closely and permanently united. . . .The economic resources of the world will be organized, its sources of raw materials will be tapped and fully utilized, its markets will be coordinated and developed, and the distribution of its products will be equitably regulated. . . . Destitution on the one hand, and gross accumulation of ownership on the other, will disappear.[4]

In the current North-South dialogue between the rich and poor nations of the world, no more favorable outcome could be expected than that envisaged by Shoghi Effendi on March 11, 1936 in the Holy Land.

Although hundreds of millions of persons in Latin America, Asia and Africa are inadequately fed, clothed and housed—and such considerations must be the starting point for any human rights policy—there are further levels of rights owed by society to its individuals. Education is one such basic decency. Illiteracy plagues a majority of the world's inhabitants, particularly affecting the urban poor, rural dwellers, and women. Often Third World governments spend as much as fifty percent of their budgets on the military while failing to provide even the most elementary instruction to their millions of villagers. Even in some developed nations soaring defense budgets have recently caused reductions in spending on education.

The unambiguous Bahá'í commitment to universal education has resulted in a number of village tutorial schools in the Third World, and even given rise to ambitious projects like the Rabbani vocational agricultural school in Gwalior, central India. This is so in spite of the relatively few resources available to the Bahá'í Community in many less developed countries. In His book of laws, revealed around 1873, Bahá'u'lláh commanded every parent to ensure that both sons and daughters were instructed in reading and writing.[5] Where the parent fails in this duty, He added, the authorities should intervene to ensure that the children are educated. *"Knowledge,"* He wrote elsewhere, *"is as wings to man's life, and a ladder for his ascent. Its acquisition is incumbent upon everyone."*[6] In 1875 'Abdu'l-Bahá wrote that: "The primary, the most urgent requirement is the promotion of education. It is inconceivable that any nation should achieve prosperity and success unless this paramount, this fundamental concern is carried forward."[7]

THE MEANING OF basic human decencies is relative and constantly evolving. I would suggest that, increasingly, education in the benefits of humane and reliable birth control technology is a prerequisite for a decent human life in much of the Third World. For obscurantist and superstitious reasons some religious bodies have done the poor in the less-developed countries the supreme disservice of forbidding them the right to plan their families at a reasonable size. The leaders of the Bahá'í Faith might make a bold and timely statement encouraging birth control (which need not imply abortion) in our teeming, overpopulated world.

PARTICIPATORY RIGHTS imply, at a minimum, the ability to help shape government policy in one's own community, be it local or national. Too much of the world is governed by military dictatorships or totalitarian one-party regimes. Moreover, participatory rights should extend beyond the political horse race to economic issues as well. It is seldom in the capitalist democracies of the West that consumers and workers participate in the highest level of economic decisions which are made only by corporate leaders. Workers seldom enjoy the profits garnered by corporations, being paid instead simple wages. The inequities here go beyond issues of blue collar versus white collar. Some very white collar scientists working as employees of large corporations have made discoveries that would have earned them millions of dollars had they been working for themselves. But they simply received their normal salary and perhaps a bonus, while the company reaped the profits.

The two great camps into which the developed world is divided, the capitalist democracies and the communist dictatorships, both fall short in the area of participatory rights. Economic democracy is lacking in the West; a single-minded attention to greater equality in the distribution of income and wealth in the socialist nations has led to one-party rule from the top in which many political rights, including the simple one of freedom of speech, have been lost. The emerging world civilization promoted by the

Bahá'í Faith must find a way to foster both political and economic democracy.

The Bahá'í Faith developed in an extremely crucial period of modern history, beginning with the Bábí movement in 1844 and ending its heroic age with the death of 'Abdu'l-Bahá in 1921. During this period, the basic institutions of the world underwent profound changes as a result of the Industrial Revolution and the rise of a modern class of manufacturers. The race to colonize the world began in earnest on a foundaton not simply of mercantilism as in the past, but on the unequal exchange implied by a near monopoly of industry in Europe and North America and the reduction of most of the rest of the world to suppliers of raw materials and purchasers of finished goods. This was a time when entire classes were transformed; in much of the world, old institutions such as monarchy began falling because of the structural changes in society. In those parts of the world, such as the Ottoman Empire and Iran, that were encompassed by European power but not absorbed into the industrial empires, pressure grew upon indigenous elites to borrow from Europe in the areas of military reform, bureaucracy, science, and participatory democracy. Tunis adopted a constitution, Egypt's first parliament met, and a movement for both a constitution and a parliament began in the central Ottoman lands and, later, in Iran.

Bahá'u'lláh and 'Abdu'l-Bahá, in spite of the highly politicized nature of the debate, took firm stands on these issues. Bahá'u'lláh commended a constitutional monarchy with a democratically elected parliament or congress the best form of government. In that turbulent period, He approved of constitutionalism insofar as it combined the symbolic authority of kingship with the benefits of democracy and republicanism.[8] (This is also true of modern parliamentary governments with a more or less symbolic presidency which allows the prime minister to rule while the president attempts to keep the country united.) In 1875, when the debate over the propriety of governmental reform waxed fiercest both in the Ottoman Empire and Iran, 'Abdu'l-Bahá wrote,

> In the present writer's view it would be preferable if the election of non-permanent members of consultative assemblies in sovereign states should be dependent on the will and choice of the people. For elected representatives will on this account be somewhat inclined to exercise justice, lest their reputation suffer and they fall into disfavor with the public.[9]

While many of the world's great religious traditions recommend values that generally encourage consultation, the Bahá'í Faith embodies a straightforward commitment to political democracy. Within the Bahá'í religious institutions themselves—which are designed to coexist with secular governmental institutions—democratic elections are practiced. As the religion spreads in the Third World, it inevitably socializes its members toward more democratic methods of self-governance, thus helping spread an appreciation of participatory rights.

While the Bahá'í Faith rejects the possibility of an entirely classless society imposed by revolution and dictatorship, its Central Figures demonstrated a profound concern for the amelioration of the condition of the poor and the altering of the class structure throughout the world so as to be more egalitarian. 'Abdu'l-Bahá envisaged a world with no millionaires (much less billionaires) and no extremely poor, a world with steeply progressive taxes and a negative income tax to provide relief to the indigent.[10] He boldly advocated joint ownership of firms by employees and employers, with the workers enjoying part of the profits in addition to their salaries.[11]

'Abdu'l-Bahá's was a sort of populist democratic socialism that allowed for both a large public and a substantial private sector. The private sector might consist of owner-worker cooperatives that would reduce the alienation of workers from the profits of their labor. Such a program would be opposed by many on both the Right and the Left, but it is precisely the aim of the Bahá'í Faith to produce a new society with innovative solutions to the conflicts that now plague both the capitalist and the socialist worlds.

Internal political and economic democracy within nations cannot be attained without international arrangements as well. No less than authoritarian and totalitarian dictators, the intervention of superpowers in the affairs of their weaker neighbors detracts from the participatory rights of the world's people. Neocolonialism and neoimperialism have too often replaced the old direct rule of the nations of the southern hemisphere by those of the North. The Bahá'í system would replace as the world's policemen the great Powers (whether of East or West) with a new, more powerful United Nations whose intervention would be less self-interested.

Participatory rights imply freedom of speech, freedom of assembly, and freedom of the press, all of which are necessary for the creation of an informed public opinion. On this theme, 'Abdu'l-Bahá wrote:

It is therefore urgent that beneficial articles and books be written, clearly and definitely establishing what the present-day requirements of the people are, and what will conduce to the happiness and advancement of society. These should be published and spread throughout the nation, so that at least the leaders among the people should become, to some degree, awakened. . . .[12]

Shoghi Effendi delineated a world order in which: "The

press will . . . while giving full scope to the expression of the diversified views and convictions of mankind, cease to be mischievously manipulated by vested interests. . . .[13]

Religion and freedom of speech often seem incompatible. The religious sensibility frequently finds certain kinds of statements, no matter how civilly put, simply intolerable. It is all the more remarkable, then, when we read Shoghi Effendi's statement that "at the very root of the Cause lies the principle of the undoubted right of the individual to self-expression, his freedom to declare his conscience and set forth his views."[14] It is rare for any public institution in most of the world these days to defend freedom of speech so unequivocally. The degree to which the policy and practice of Bahá'í institutions move toward this lofty ideal will be a measure of their own faithfulness to Shoghi Effendi's vision. Unless they uphold the right to self-expression within their own communities, Bahá'í institutions will remain unable to act as exemplars for the rest of the world in regard to this essential right of human beings.

Participatory rights must extend to every member of the community equally, which in turn requires the avoidance of discrimination on any of the usual bases of race, color, class, religion, and so forth. The unity of mankind and the elimination of such prejudices form, of course, the bedrock of the Bahá'í Faith. Bahá'u'lláh spent a lifetime attacking bigotry in all its forms. Just before His passing He wrote against the wave of antisemitism then engulfing some European countries, the ugly forebearer of Hitler's Holocaust:

> At present the light of reconciliation is dimmed in most countries and its radiance extinguished while the fire of strife and disorder hath been kindled and is blazing fiercely. Two great powers who regard themselves as the founders and leaders of civilization and the framers of constitutions have risen up against the followers of

the Faith [Judaism] associated with Him Who conversed with God [Moses]. Be ye warned, O men of understanding. It ill beseemeth the station of man to commit tyranny.[15]

'Abdu'l-Bahá's frequent exhortations against racism during his trip to the United States followed in this tradition of a spiritual representative of the supposedly less civilized East pulling the curtain away from the moral shortcomings of the West. In Paris he declared: "All prejudices, whether of religion, race, politics or nation, must be renounced, for these prejudices have caused the world's sickness. . . . Every ruinous war, with its terrible bloodshed and misery, has been caused by one or other of these prejudices."[16]

THE ELIMINATION OF prejudices, and the wars they so often foster, also lies at the root of security rights. Every human being has the right to security of life and personal property, a right that can only be safeguarded in a world of peace and equality of personal status. There should be no mistake. The right to a peaceful world is constantly imperiled by the ambitions of the elites that control the world's most populous countries. Under the pretext that each of them is under siege by an external enemy with which it must compete in stockpiling arms (which in turn must be used· if they are not to become outmoded), these nations create a war psychosis. Neither of the world's superpowers is in any serious danger of being militarily attacked, yet the military and political leaders of both promote the idea of imminent hostilities as a means of convincing the public to support gargantuan expenditures on arms and military adventures overseas. In fact, politicians and generals wish to control as much of the world as they can, and under the guise of "defense" departments they establish a military presence throughout the Third World.

Only the public in each country can put an end to this hugely expensive and ultimately disastrous game, by demanding an end to it. As physicist Carl Sagan recently said in a television debate with former Secretary of State Henry Kissinger: "The way to reduce the number of nuclear arms is to reduce the number of nuclear arms." (See other articles in this volume on the possible Bahá'í contribution to the peace movement.)

In regard to world security and peace, Bahá'u'lláh wrote:

> The time must come when the imperative necessity for the holding of a vast, an all-embracing assemblage of men will be universally realized. . . . Such a peace demandeth that the Great Powers should resolve, for the sake of the tranquillity of the peoples of the earth, to be fully reconciled among themselves. Should any king take up arms against another, all should unitedly arise and prevent him.[17]

The principle of collective security, if taken seriously by the world's leaders (as indeed it sooner or later must be) could help to prevent or curtail war, which among the most developed nations has already become unthinkable. The continuing debacle in the Middle East, which could have early on been stopped by an effective and impartial United Nations military intervention, demonstrates the impotence of the current attempts of regional and global Powers to police the area unilaterally. For example, the United Nations Interim Forces in Lebanon were never given permission to actively employ their firepower, reducing them to immobility, and then to target status.

FALK'S FINAL CATEGORY, humane governance, is the one most people think of when the subject of human rights is broached. This is the most visible level of human rights and the one most easily addressed by publicity and diplomacy—

whence its prominence in the newspapers. Bahá'u'lláh extolled the ruler *"who marcheth with the ensign of wisdom unfurled before him, and the battalions of justice massed in his rear. He verily is the ornament that adorneth the brow of peace and the countenance of security."*[18]

Many modern states rule through terror, through death squads of revolutionary guards, arresting individuals simply for membership in opposition political parties or even only for criticisms of state policies, such as the kind every small-town editor in democratic nations routinely voices. Few are the modern states that enforce *habeas corpus*, require some positive proof of wrongdoing, for the long-term detention of those arbitrarily arrested. In some countries thousands of persons have simply been abducted by militias with ties to the state and subsequently executed and buried in mass graves, creating a modern kind of nonperson—"the disappeared." Bahá'ís should be particularly outraged at this technique since it has been applied to some Bahá'í leaders in Iran.

Given the numerically small size of the Bahá'í Community in most countries, there appears little the Bahá'í can do in a direct way to protest inhumane governance. I would argue that the development of Bahá'í institutions, participation in Bahá'í elections, and the teaching of children and friends the Bahá'í principles constitute in themselves long-term, organic contributions to the emergence of more humane governance in most of the world. At this point, public protests by Bahá'í officials of inhumane policies would, in most of the world, simply result in the religion being banned. Indeed, it often is banned by dictatorial regimes in any case because its progressive principles and democratic organization seem to pose a threat to them.

Still, Bahá'ís cannot ignore instances of inhumane governance. Bahá'í officials and laypersons should familiarize themselves with the annual reports of Amnesty International and similar nonpartisan monitoring groups. Since

Amnesty International rules do not allow individuals to investigate human rights abuses in their own country, Bahá'ís could support this organization and similar ones without imperiling the functioning and the safety of their local Bahá'í Communities. In the long term, Bahá'í institutions might themselves begin investigating and issuing policy papers on humans rights abuses, especially in countries where there are large numbers of Bahá'ís, and therefore ample resources in terms of local information. The effectiveness of small activist groups such as the Society of Friends in this regard should be instructive for Bahá'ís interested in such enterprises. The plight of the Bahá'ís in Iran should impel their coreligionists throughout the world to strive to improve conditions for prisoners of conscience, for oppressed minorities, and for those who might at any time "disappear." Only thus can they repay their debt to the human rights organizations that have so generously, so wholeheartedly, taken up the cause of the Bahá'ís, who are a relatively small group of scant political consequence.

Short of this, Bahá'ís should at least familiarize themselves with the human rights records of the regimes under which they live, from impartial and unbiased sources, so that they avoid any actions that might associate or identify the Bahá'í institutions with tyrannical governments. Such incidents have occurred, as in the Latin American country where the National Spiritual Assembly of the Bahá'ís and other high-ranking members of Bahá'í institutions met and were photographed with a military dictator indicted by the United Nations, Amnesty International, and other organizations as a mass murderer. Such incidents should never again be allowed to occur. Noninterference in party politics is hardly synonymous with the abdication of conscience.

The Bahá'í Faith is a beacon to the conscience of modern humankind, the principles enshrined in this religion's scriptures have promulgated some of the loftiest ideals for the rights of human beings. On all of the levels suggested by such analysts as Falk and already delineated by United Nations declarations and covenants, the Bahá'í Writings not only support essential human rights but offer new insights into the divine and inalienable nature of those rights. It is up to Bahá'í Communities worldwide to implement and exemplify these enlightened principles.

Notes

1. See Richard A. Falk, *Human Rights and State Sovereignty* (New York: Holmes and Meier, 1981). See also Marguerite Garling, *Human Rights Handbook* (New York: Facts on File, 1979).

2. 'Abdu'l-Bahá, *Foundations of World Unity* (Wilmette, Ill.: Bahá'í Publishing Trust, 1971) pp. 38–41.

3. Bahá'u'lláh, "Bishárát," *Tablets of Bahá'u'lláh*, trans. Habid Taherzadeh, et al. (Haifa: Bahá'í World Centre, 1978) p. 26.

4. Shoghi Effendi, *The World Order of Bahá'u'lláh* (Wilmette, Ill.: Bahá'í Publishing Trust, 1974) pp. 203–04.

5. *A Synopsis and Codification of the Kitáb-i-Aqdas: The Most Holy Book of Bahá'u'lláh* (Haifa: Bahá'í World Centre, 1973) pp. 15–16.

6. Bahá'u'lláh, "Tajallíyát," *Tablets*, p. 51.

7. 'Abdu'l-Bahá, *The Secret of Divine Civilization* (Wilmette, Ill.: Bahá'í Publishing Trust, 1957) p. 109.

8. Bahá'u'lláh, "Lawḥ-i-Dunyá," *Tablets*, p. 93.

9. *Divine Civilization*, p. 24.

10. *Foundations*, p. 37.

11. Ibid., pp. 43–44.

12. *Divine Civilization*, p. 109.

13. *World Order*, p. 204.

14. Shoghi Effendi, *Bahá'í Administration* (Wilmette, Ill.: Bahá'í Publishing Trust, 1928) p. 63

15. Bahá'u'lláh "Lawḥ-i-Maqṣúd," *Tablets*, p. 170.

16. 'Abdu'l-Bahá, *Paris Talks* (London: Bahá'í Publishing Trust, 1912) p. 146.

17. Bahá'u'lláh, "Lawḥ-i-Maqṣúd," *Tablets*, p. 165.

18. Ibid., p. 164–65.

Revisioning the Women's Movement

by Ann Schoonmaker, Ph.D.

T HE WOMEN'S MOVEMENT IN THE United States has
sailed a stormy course over the past few decades and
involved an incredible amount of pain, bitterness and anger.
The release of Betty Friedan's book *The Feminine Mystique* in the early 1960s became a catalyst for many women.
It named the sources of the frustration they had experienced and served as a focal point around which they could
gather. On one side, it stimulated consciousness-raising
groups and aroused social awareness of sexual injustice;
but, on the other side, these activities threatened many
women who felt their lifestyles were under attack and who
feared the loss of everything they valued.

After the National Organization for Women was formed
and the drive to ratify the Equal Rights Amendment gained
momentum, the polarization of these two camps intensified.
The tension may have peaked in 1975, the very year designated as the International Year of Women by the United
Nations.

Over the years, I had heard women on both sides dis-
agreeing with each other on television and had followed the

controversy in books and articles. I believed that part of the tension sprang from different developmental stages; the rest I discounted as exploitation of the media. The inadequacy of these naive explanations became apparent, however, when I encountered the direct, absolute bitterness and hostility face to face.

Imagine, if you will, a gymnasium filled with women. Most are sitting on the bleachers, listening to the speakers; others are moving around behind the scenes, intent on errands, or engaged in serious conversations in small groups. Suddenly, some in the audience call out, hissing and screaming as they attack a speaker. Others defend her, with equally angry words and voices.

Such was the scene in a Princeton University gymnasium near the beginning of the International Year of Women. I had set out eagerly that morning to attend the meeting of the New Jersey state caucus which was to elect delegates and prepare mandates for the national meeting preceding the world conference. My hopes had been high. Finally I would have an opportunity to be directly involved in an official function of the women's movement.

Those high hopes were shattered by seeing the absolute polarization of ideas, values and goals that divided various groups of women. I was dismayed to hear women screeching at one another. Where was their dignity? Where was their pride? How could the women's movement move ahead unless women were united, unless they worked together to achieve the same ends and supported each other? I could not deny the anger and frustration of both sides. They were acted out right in front of me. One side was shouting for equal rights, abortion, independence; the other for family, motherhood, and the right to life. Each thought its way was the only way; that everyone must agree unilaterally. There was no way I could take sides since I valued some aspects of both positions. I left the meeting bitterly disappointed and frustrated.

Since that time, both camps have faced disappointments.

One side fought valiantly for the ratification of the Equal Rights Amendment, only to miss by narrow margins as the deadline approached. The other side struggled equally hard and unsuccessfully to have Congress overturn the Supreme Court's ruling on abortion. Both sides also have faced challenging new realities. Economic conditions forced many women to enter the job market despite their preference to remain at home in more traditional roles; successful business women now question the competitive values which are the norm in the marketplace. Supermoms wonder if its worth all the time and energy to try to "have it all" simultaneously. Single women executives look wistfully at babies in young mother's arms.

Recently, a strange malaise has pervaded the women's movement. There is a curious sense of numbness and inactivity, a feeling of drift, without real direction or purpose. On the surface, this malaise has several causes. First, the pressing need for economic survival: working mothers have less time to attend organizational meetings. Second, burnout—with women on both sides feeling ineffective and impotent after failing to meet their previous goals.

On a deeper level, however, I believe that the women's movement has moved into this period of impasse and inertia because its leaders have never known its ultimate source and purpose. Without any transcendent vision of its meaning or goal, they have become lost in a maze of differing feelings and opinions. What is needed is a new perspective, a revisioning of the women's movement, which would offer guidelines and mutual support to all women and allow them to unite, while honoring their vast diversity of talents, perspectives and needs.

The only way out of this impasse will be for us women to discover the ultimate source, power, momentum, and purpose behind the women's movement, to see it as an integral part of the spiritual evolution of the planet and the beginning of a new era of human history. As a Bahá'í, this means for me that I must turn to the Bahá'í Sacred Writings for a deeper understanding of the principle of the equality of the sexes.

Unblocking the Impasse. As we investigate how women are still trapped within the limits of a Western male consciousness and reality, we realize how tragic it is that women are ignorant of the real source and purpose of the women's movement. There are moderates who focus on establishing legal means to eliminate injustice, oppression and inequality between the sexes, but the goals of radical feminists appear to be to achieve the same position and control within the power structure as men—to wipe out any distinction between the sexes, creating an androgynous or unisexual conformity.

These goals reveal that women are still unconscious of their own unique status and being in the world, that womankind has not yet reached her own maturity, that humanity has developed only one-half of its potential—the masculine. We have moved unwittingly from the frying pan into the fire, from the unconsciousness of the feminine mystique into another form of unconsciousness: the "feminist mystique." As we awoke from unconscious feminine patterns, we became trapped within the confines and limits of Western patriarchal patterns. The dreadful sense of being caught in the middle between these two impossible positons leaves us in limbo.

The male mystique continues to permeate both secular and religious traditions in the West, and women are trapped in a dialectical pattern between the oppressor and the oppressed. The superior male power (generally white, Anglo-Saxon, and Protestant) served as the oppressor to the oppressed and inferior (most often female, nonwwhite, and non-Protestant). This pattern of dominance and dependence was ingrained in the Western, male, hierarchical, linear world of consciousness and therefore accepted as reality. The most devasting effect of this assumption, however, has been that this "superior" male pattern has been considered the goal, the thing to be strived for and emulated, by women, and by nonwhite, minority persons. And, because the Western pattern has invaded Third World cultures, the male mystique has become the global pattern.

Even though this pattern is recognized by Bahá'ís as the framework of an old, worn-out paradigm of reality that is rapidly collapsing, it still possesses incredible power, vitality and momentum. Although this pattern may often be criticized and deplored, both men and women assume it to be an inevitable part of reality and so play out their social-cultural roles within it.

This irony became devastatingly clear to me one night several years ago as I was teaching a college course entitled *Introduction to Philosophy: Human Alienation*. During that first lecture I drew on the blackboard a diagram of five major forms of alienation which exist in the world today: 1) the alienation of man from his fellow man; 2) the alienation of man from his work; 3) the alienation of man from nature; 4) the alienation of man from his own true, inner, creative self—from his potential unity of mind, body and spirit; and finally, 5) the alienation of man from his Creator, in the loss of that transcendent vision, appreciation, and love that brings us all out of nothingness and gives meaning and purpose to our lives.

As I ended the lecture, the class and I were both stunned by the enormity of the global alienation which permeates our civilization. As no one moved in the eerie silence after the dismissal bell rang, it flashed through my heart and mind that these forms of alienation were a direct result of what *man* had indeed achieved. This was what *man*'s Western patriarchal view of the world had created over the centuries, and *his* megalithic monopoly of linear consciousness: this alienation, this pain.

Even more shocking, however, was the realization of how we women had accepted these patriarchal patterns, striving to become equal, and denying our own feminine perceptions of a more holistic, centered reality. We, as women, were equally alienated: from our sisters as well as from our fellow man, from our essential work, from nature, from our true selves, from our Creator.

As a consequence, a woman has had only four basic alternatives. First, to stay in her "place," in the inferior position of an oppressed and often mistreated woman, accepting that reality, denying that her world could be different, remaining unconscious of her potential and of her alternatives. This is still the only possibility for millions of starving, illiterate, poverty stricken women in the world. Their lives are endless drudgery; they barely survive at the most meager level of subsistence; they are caught in an endless cycle of childbirth and child-death, often while they themselves are mere children. Second, she may conform to male patriarchal assumptions—this time consciously, but still as a victim. She affirms the pattern as her own as well, voluntarily playing the classic feminine role. (This is known psychologically as identifying with the aggressor.) Third, she may fight to take an equal position with the male aggressor/oppressor, seeking equal status within the patriarchal model, demanding every prerogative of the male. (In reality, this is another form of identification with the oppressor.) Fourth, she may retreat backward in time, endeavoring to recapture a matriarchal reality, seeking to become one with the universe, seeking the time of witches, magic, and nature myths when women had all the power—a time before heroes began slaying dragons and masculine reality took over.

Each of these four modalities work within or against the patriarchal system of reality and identify positively with the male by either actively copying that role or passively serving him (either consciously or unconsciously), or rejecting the male and retreating into a world of women and nature.

As we consider these four alternatives, it would seem that they are the basis for the divisions within the women's movement. As women began awakening out of the first layer, becoming conscious for the first time, they chose one of the three other forms and fought against the other two. These were the only choices they knew possible. And so the women's movement became, not a joyful sisterhood celebrating the rich potentialities and diversities of all women, but a fragmented, disillusioned and bitter quarrel.

The idea that another choice might exist is just barely emerging in the recognition of what has been named the *gender gap* in American politics. This recogniton is still tangled up within the divisions and disunity of the women's movement. Yet the awareness is growing that women and men respond differently to political issues. Bella Abzug has recently written: "The gender gap has been established as a political fact of life. It is endlessly being measured, dissected, probed, analyzed, and debated by pollsters, academics, sociologists, politicians, the media, and by women themselves." And she notes specifically that: "Compassion, a yearning to peace, concern about the environment, the desire for economic security and equality are shared by most women, although the degree to which a particular factor motivates a particular woman or group of women may vary. But the important message of the gender gap is that women do join together across *all* racial, social, ethnic, religious and regional lines."[1]

Nowhere, however, has there been the recognition of the radical social change which Bahá'ís believe will emerge when the principle of equality of men and women becomes a reality—when the full talents and abilities of *womankind* complement those of *mankind* so that world civilization can fully mature. Nor has there been the recognition of the compelling spiritual forces which have set this process in motion and propel it forward.

Time for a Change. A new perspective is desperately needed in the women's movement to provide a new focus and a new sense of direction and purpose. Bahá'ís believe that this perspective will come from the Revelation of Bahá'u'lláh: the true message of hope which possesses the power of the Word of God to transform the planet into a new world of love, peace and unity; to address all forms of human alienation and oppression; and to provide the means for full social transformation.

Theologically, therefore, the Bahá'í Revelation is the proclamation of the most radical revolution of all. It does not propose cosmetic reform, but provides for a radical revisioning of our social structures. It does not call for remodeling society with patchwork or makeshift changes, nor does it tear down the old without knowing what shape and form the new structure will take. It is both a revisioning and a recreating of the very foundations of our being and becoming.

The force behind such momentous, radical change could never be drawn from human power. Such restructuring of the vast complex social-political realities of our present civilization could come only from the power of the Word of God itself. According to Bahá'u'lláh, the Word of God is the very generating force behind all of the creation: *"The Word of God is the king of words and its pervasive influence is incalculable. . . . The Word is the master key for the whole world, inasmuch as through its potency the doors of the hearts of men, which in reality are the doors of heaven, are unlocked. . . . It is an ocean inexhaustible in riches, comprehending all things."* [2]

The development of woman's full potential, which has been lying dormant since the beginning of creation, has now been called forth in this new religious dispensation: *"One of the potentialities hidden in the realm of humanity was the capability or capacity of womanhood. Through the effulgent rays of divine illumination the capacity of woman has become so awakened and manifest in this age that equality of man and woman is an established fact. . . . At last this century of light dawned, the realities shone forth, and the mysteries long hidden from human vision were revealed."*[3]

The message of the Bahá'í Faith strikes an amazing note of possibility for all women. First, the challenge for individual women to "recognize and realize" their own latent potential in every degree of human accomplishment; but, even more significantly, the emergence of womankind as a full coequal and complementary partner with mankind so that human civilization will take the next vital step forward. The proclamation of the equality of men and women, therefore, must be seen within a broad context and must include various parameters: theological, historical, sociological, and psychological.

The Theological Basis of the Women's Movement. In order to establish the reality of the equality of men and women, we have to eliminate the worn-out doctrines and shibboleths that emerged from earlier socio-religious conditions and which denied woman's equality by claiming she was created unequal by God.

Although the equality of men and women was revealed by Bahá'u'lláh as part of His religion, it was not until 1912, when 'Abdu'l-Bahá traveled throughout the United States and Canada, that this revolutionary principle was announced and discussed before large audiences of both men and women. 'Abdu'l-Bahá spoke of sexual equality briefly each time He explained the major teachings of Bahá'u'lláh. He also gave several major talks completely devoted to the topic, for example, in Chicago at the Federation of Women's Clubs, and in New York City at the Women's Suffrage Meeting.

In Philadelphia, 'Abdu'l-Bahá explained the theological basis for the equality of men and women: "*In proclaiming the oneness of mankind He* [Bahá'u'lláh] *taught that men and women are equal in the sight of God and that there is no*

*distinction to be made between them. . . . God is the Creator of
mankind. He has endowed both sexes with perfections and intelligence, given them physical members and organs of sense,
without differentiation or distinction as to superiority; therefore, why should woman be considered inferior? This is not according to the plan and justice of God. He has created them
equal; in His estimate there is no question of sex."*[4]

'Abdu'l-Bahá was explicit that man must not make distinctions which God did not make: "*The truth is that all
mankind are the creatures and servants of one God, and in His
estimate all are human. Man is a generic term applying to all
humanity. . . . To accept and observe a distinction which God
has not intended in creation is ignorance and superstition.*"
Equality is inherent in the framework of creation. "*When
we consider the kingdoms of existence below man, we find no
distinction or estimate of superiority and inferiority between
male and female. . . . Why should man, a higher and more in-
telligent creature, deny and deprive himself of this equality the
animals enjoy? His surest index and guide as to the creative intention concerning himself are the conditions and analogies of
the kingdoms below him where equality of the sexes is fundamental.*"[5]

When we envision the women's movement within this
context, we realize that it is an intrinsic part of a process
of worldwide recreation and regeneration, part of a new
World Order designed by God, and not by either radical or
conservative feminists. The universe is whole, free from
the divisions of previous man-made theologies. Woman is
different from man, but equal. There is no male-female
dualism in which man is the superior—representing mind,
reason and spirit—and woman the inferior—representing
body, sexuality and evil.

It has been of deep concern for me personally, therefore,
to view the convolutions and the pain which feminist theologians are undergoing to legitimize women's full equality
with men. The basic issues discussed by these theologians
have already been anticipated by 'Abdu'l-Bahá while He

was in America. For Bahá'ís, the intrinsic equality of women is taken for granted, with women taking an equal place within the elected arm of the Administrative Order, and as Hands of the Cause and Auxiliary Board members. With Bahá'u'lláh's abolition of clergy and monasticism, there is no need for women to seek ordination. Hence, there is no need to develop new religious structures from the various implications behind Biblical texts which were descriptive of social conditions of the early Christian era. Feminist theologians Elisabeth Fiorenza and Rosemary Reuther document most admirably how biblical texts function to perpetuate and justify the oppression of women, yet also hint at a deeper nonpatriarchal vision.[6]

How unnecessary to change the sex of God[7] when Bahá'u'lláh has provided the simplest, most complete description of God as unknowable and transcendent beyond any sexual limitation: *"Exalted, immeasuralbly exalted art Thou above any attempt to measure the greatness of Thy Cause, above any comparison that one may seek to make, above the efforts of the human tongue to utter its import! From everlasting Thou hast existed, alone with no one else beside Thee, and wilt, to everlasting, continue to remain the same, in the sublimity of Thine essence and the inaccessible heights of Thy glory."*[8]

Historical Perspective. For the first time in religious history, equality of the sexes stands as an inherent spiritual principle, part of the Word of God. Sexual equality, therefore, is not just an impossible ideal promoted by idealistic feminists, nor a pious hope proposed by theorists and subject to debate. It does not stand alone, but rather is joined with other basic teaching principles which aid and support it: the elimination of all forms of prejudice, a spiritual solution to the world's economic problems, the importance of universal compulsory education.

In previous times women were considered inferior, subjugated to men, confined to the household and to rearing children. 'Abdu'l-Bahá deplored such oppression and asserted that Bahá'u'lláh had "destroyed" the idea that women were to be kept "prisoners of the household."[9] He explained that: "*In past ages it was held that woman and man were not equal. . . . woman was considered inferior to man, even from the standpoint of her anatomy and creation. She was considerd especially inferior in intelligence, and the ideal prevailed universally that it was not allowable for her to step into the arena of important affairs. In some countries man went so far as to believe and teach that woman belonged to a sphere lower than human. . . .* [In this century] *of light and the revelation of mysteries, God is proving to the satisfaction of humanity that all this is ignorance and error; nay, rather, it is well established that mankind and womankind as parts of composite humanity are coequal and that no difference in estimate is allowable, for all are human.*[10]

The consequences of this discrimination have had devastating effects, not only for individual women, but also for civilization. This was true especially in the past: "*Again, it is well established in history that where woman has not participated in human affairs the outcomes have never attained a state of completion and perfection.*"[11] And it will hold true in the future as well: "*Until the reality of equality between man and woman is fully established and attained, the highest social development of mankind is not possible. . . . And let it be known once more that until woman and man recognize and realize equality, social and political progress here or anywhere will not be possible.*"[12]

In many of His talks, 'Abdu'l-Bahá developed the idea that teachings appropriate to human needs during the early history of the race can "*neither meet nor satisfy the demands of this day and period of newness and consummation.*" It is time for the maturation of the human race: "*Humanity has emerged from its former degrees of limitation and preliminary training. Man must now become imbued with new virtues and powers, new moralities, new capacities. New bounties, be-*

stowals and perfections are awaiting and already descending upon him."[13]

Sociological Understandings. The declaration by Bahá'u' lláh of the principle of the basic and fundamental equality of the sexes has profound implications for understanding the basic structure underlying society as a whole. 'Abdu'l-Bahá expanded upon this teaching by presenting the concept of complementary functions. He used several metaphors to explain how the happiness and progress of society depended upon this concept of complementarity: *"The world of humanity consists of two parts: male and female. Each is the complement of the other. Therefore, if one is defective, the other will necessarily be incomplete, and perfection cannot be attained. . . . Just as physical accomplishment is complete with two hands, so man and woman, the two parts of the social body, must be perfect. It is not natural that either should remain undeveloped; and until both are perfected, the happiness of the human world will not be realized."*[14]

He also compared society to a bird with two wings: *"The world of humanity is possessed of two wings: the male and the female. So long as these two wings are not equivalent in strength, the bird will not fly. Until womankind reaches the same degree as man, until she enjoys the same arena of activity, extraordinary attainment for humanity will not be realized; humanity cannot wing its way to heights of real attainment. When the two wings or parts become equivalent in strength, enjoying the same prerogatives, the flight of man will be exceedingly lofty and extraordinary."*[15]

The concept of complementarity then becomes the basis for 'Abdu'l-Bahá's insistence upon equal opportunity for women in all areas, and especially education: *"The only difference between them now is due to lack of education and training. If woman is given equal opportunity of education, distinction and estimate of inferiority will disappear."*[16] And:

"Therefore, woman must receive the same education as man and all inequality be adjusted. Thus, imbued with the same virtues as man, rising through all the degrees of human attainment, women will become the peers of men, and until this equality is established, true progress and attainment for the human race will not be facilitated."[17]

Equal education will mean that women will be able to take an equal place in all spheres of human endeavor: *"There must be no difference in the education of male and female in order that womankind may develop equal capacity and importance with man in the social and economic equation. Then the world will attain unity and harmony. In past ages humanity has been defective and inefficient because it has been incomplete."*[18]

Psychological Challenge. 'Abdu'l-Bahá set the stage for the advancement of womankind with His explanations of sexual equality, within nature, as part of a divine, "creative intention"; and within society on a complementary, functional basis. In doing so, He removed the previous theological obstacles which kept women in an inferior position. He also gave women an amazing challenge: *"The purpose, in brief, is this: that if woman be fully educated and granted her rights, she will attain the capacity for wonderful accomplishments and prove herself the equal of man. . . . Both are human; both are endowed with potentialities of intelligence and embody the virtues of humanity. In all human powers and functions they are partners and coequals. At present in spheres of human activity woman does not manifest her natal prerogatives, owing to lack of education and opportunity. Without doubt education will establish her equality with men."*[19]

True equality is therefore possible, but latent. There are still psychological obstacles which must be recognized. Women need to be encouraged in order to develop out of their latent condition; they need to be educated to know that they have capabilities. *"Equality means equal qualification. In brief, the assumption of superiority by man will con-*

tinue to be depressing to the ambition of woman, as if her attainment to equality was creationally impossible; woman's aspiration toward advancement will be checked by it, and she will gradually become hopeless."[20]

'Abdu'l-Bahá was completely honest and forthright in explaining that women would need to be especially encouraged and even taught that they could achieve: "*We must declare that her capacity is equal, even greater than man's. This will inspire her with hope and ambition, and her susceptibilities for advancement will continually increase. She must not be told and taught that she is weaker and inferior in capacity and qualification.*"[21]

Near the close of the twentieth century we can see the devastating consequences of how the lack of opportunity and education for women has perpetuated human misery when we view the faces of starving, illiterate women and their children in Third World countries. 'Abdu'l-Bahá warned of these consequences more than seventy years ago. He explained that an uneducated mother would not only perpetuate ignorance in her children, but also in society as a whole: "*Futhermore, the education of woman is more necessary and important that that of man, for woman is the trainer of the child from its infancy. If she be defective and imperfect herself, the child will necessarily be deficient; therefore, imperfection of woman implies a condition of imperfection in all mankind, for it is the mother who rears, nurtures and guides the growth of the child. . . . If the educator be incompetent, the educated will be correspondingly lacking. . . . Could the student be brilliant and accomplished if the teacher is illiterate and ignorant? The mothers are the first educators of mankind; if they be imperfect, alas for the condition and future of the race.*"[22]

The converse is also true, for once women achieve their potential, 'Abdu'l-Bahá predicted that they would be the key factor in achieving world peace: "*In truth, she will be the greatest factor in establishing universal peace and international arbitration. Assuredly, woman will abolish warfare among mankind.*"[23] He explained that the "*most momentous question of this day is international peace and arbitration, and universal peace is impossible without universal suffrage.*" Once women become educated, He declared, they will use their whole influence against war. Because women rear children, they will refuse to allow them to be sacrificed in battle. They will not "*sanction war nor be satisfied with it. So it will come to pass that when women participate fully and equally in the affairs of the world, when they enter confidently and capably the great arena of laws and politics, war will cease; for woman will be the obstacle and hindrance to it. This is true and without doubt.*"[24]

It is in this arena that women's innate differences result in women's superiority, and where their complementary function will be most valuable. 'Abdu'l-Bahá posed the greatest challenge of all to women in Boston on August 26, 1912: "*Therefore, strive to show in the human world that women are most capable and efficient, that their hearts are more tender and susceptible than the hearts of men, that they are more philanthropic and responsive toward the needy and suffering, that they are inflexibly opposed to war and are lovers of peace. Strive that the ideal of international peace may become realized through the efforts of womankind, for man is more inclined to war than woman, and a real evidence of woman's superiority will be her service and efficiency in the establishment of universal peace.*"[25]

The Ultimate Challenge for the Women's Movement. We turn then to the implications behind these statements by 'Abdu'l-Bahá and raise the question of how they might enable a revisioning of the women's movement today. What has He set before women as their greatest challenge and opportunity? I believe that He has laid out two essential tasks for those women in this country who have had the benefits of equal opportunities and education: first, to reach out our hands to those women who still remain in illiterate, inferior conditions; and second, to take up the cause of achieving world peace. Each woman must make individual choices based on her circumstances and priorities. But, it occurs to me that beyond our own individual decisions about how we develop our talents and abilities, beyond how we choose to balance the questions of motherhood and career, beyond how we deepen in and teach the Cause of God, 'Abdu'l-Bahá has delineated these two collective tasks for womankind in the future.

The first arena will be that of education all around this world. We must begin the momentous task of educating other women wherever they live so that they may develop their own potential capacities. Think of Ṭáhirih sitting behind her screen. What if she had been left uneducated? Where are the next dynamic, vital young Ṭáhirihs waiting to be educated? Who will find and educate them?[26]

The second arena will be for women to assume direct responsibility for achieving world peace. Who will be the Martha Roots of world peace?[27] Who will travel the world giving the message of peace today? What more important focus, direction, or purpose could there be for the women's movement to assume? Do we really have any alternative? Do we really have any choice? Bahá'u'lláh declared that: "*The All-Knowing Physician hath His finger on the pulse of mankind. He perceiveth the disease, and prescribeth, in His unerring wisdom, the remedy.* . . . *Be anxiously concerned with the needs of the age ye live in, and center your deliberations on its exigencies and requirements.*"[28] The needs and exigencies of our time demand that we undertake these tasks which are uniquely woman's assignment.

Notes

One contribution of the women's movement has been the encouragement to present one's own personal perspective as just that. Designing this article, I have tried to maintain a balance between an academic objectivity and the subjectivity of my personal experiences. I hope, however, that my personal limitations will not affect the clear message of hope contained within the quotations from the Sacred Writings of the Bahá'í Faith, but serve merely as a setting from which they may shine.

1. Bella Abzug, "3 Scenarios for the '84 Election," *Ms.* (March 1984) p. 40, an excerpt from *Gender Gap: Bella Abzug's Guide to Political Power for American Women* (Houghton Mifflin, 1984).

2. Bahá'u'lláh, *Tablets of Bahá'u'lláh* (Bahá'í World Centre, 1978) p. 173.

3. 'Abdu'l-Bahá, *The Promulgation of Universal Peace* (Bahá'í Publishing Trust, Second Edition, 1982) p. 74. *Peace* is the most complete collection of 'Abdu'l-Bahá's talks in the United States and Canada. See also, *Paris Talks* (London: Bahá'í Publishing Trust, Eleventh Edition, 1971).

4. *Peace*, p. 174.

5. Ibid., p. 76, 75–76. See also, ibid., pp. 108, 137 and 182.

6. Their books are substantial: Rosemary Radford Reuther, *Sexism and God-Talk: Toward a Feminist Theology* (Boston: Beacon Press, 1983); Elisabeth Schüssler Fiorenza, *In Memory of Her: A Feminist Theological Reconstruction of Christian Origins* (New York: Crossroad, 1983). See also an excellent review article by June O'Connor, "Toward an Inclusive Theology," *Christian Century* (November 30, 1983), pp. 1114–1117.

7. For example, Naoime Goldenberg's assertion, "We women are going to change the sex of God." See also, Mary Daly's now classic book, *Beyond God the Father: Toward a Philosophy of Women's Liberation* (Boston: Beacon Press, 1973).

8. Bahá'u'lláh, *Prayers and Meditations of Bahá'u'lláh* (Wilmette, Ill.: Bahá'í Publishing Trust, 1938) p. 128.

9. *Peace*, p. 166.

10. Ibid., p. 133.

11. Ibid., p. 134.

12. Ibid., pp. 76–77.

13. Ibid., p. 438.

14. Ibid., p. 134.

15. Ibid., p. 375.

16. Ibid., p. 174.
17. Ibid., p. 375.
18. Ibid., p. 108.
19. Ibid., p. 136–37.
20. Ibid., p. 76.
21. Ibid.
22. Ibid., p. 133–34.
23. Ibid., p. 108.
24. Ibid., p. 134.
25. Ibid., p. 204.
26. For a description of Ṭáhirih's relationship to the women's movement, please see "Women: Attaining Their Birthright" by Constance Conrader, *World Order* (Summer 1972) pp. 43–59.
27. M. R. Garis has written a biography of Martha Root, *Martha Root: Lioness at the Threshold* (Wilmette, Ill.: Bahá'í Publishing Trust, 1983).
28. Bahá'u'lláh, *Gleanings from the Writings of Bahá'u'lláh* (Wilmette, Ill.: Bahá'í Publishing Trust, 4th edition, 1969) p. 213.

A Bahá'í Perspective on Economic and Social Development

by Gregory C. Dahl

A S WE DISCUSS QUESTIONS OF economic and social development, we soon find ourselves making comparisons between countries at different stages of development, or between different classes and categories of people, such as the "advantaged" and "disadvantaged." Such comparisons necessarily rely on a body of preconceived notions and conventional wisdom which we have unconsciously acquired from the society in which we live. Most of us have little or no direct experience in even one less-industrialized country, let alone many. Unknown to us, our world view is largely composed of prejudices and biases which are themselves major reasons for the current inequalities and injustices in the world. Often when we think we are acting logically and fairly, in reality we are only perpetuating a social system which is cruel and unjust. But we are too close to the system to properly evaluate its weaknesses or visualize alternatives.

For example, we are all comfortable with the notion that there are developed, advanced, or industrialized nations and

155

there are underdeveloped, developing, or poor nations. When we hear the term *economic development,* we visualize a struggling "backward" nation and deplore the economic inequalities in the world. Our next thought usually concerns the need for the rich to share their wealth with the poor in the form of aid or development programs. These concepts are firmly rooted in the consciousness of people at all social levels, including our leaders and the great mass of our countrymen. They are prevalent in all countries, both rich and poor. Since this view of the world as basically divided into haves and have-nots—with the rich having what the poor want—is so pervasive and fundamental to any development effort, I would like to discuss in some detail exactly how the Bahá'í teachings offer a radically different way of viewing the situation.

The Spiritual Foundations. To approach this question, it is necessary to begin with a discussion of man's true spiritual nature and the purpose of human life. Only in this way can we hope to obtain a clearer and fresher view of those aspects of human existence which we call social and economic. Our approach will be to summarize briefly certain major themes in the Bahá'í teachings which bear on development and then examine a few implications of our findings.

First, we are taught as Bahá'ís that the fundamental purpose of human life is to develop divine attributes, to become more godly and spiritual, in preparation for other worlds of God into which we will pass at death. Material development is seen as a useful tool in the process of spiritualization, but not an end in itself. Our world today, however, is strongly materialistic: both capitalist and communist systems hold material advancement to be the highest good. Development is generally viewed in entirely material terms. The Bahá'í view, on the other hand, is that development must be seen in a much broader perspective. The development of attitudes, abilities, spiritual and moral qualities, intellect, and higher aspirations all must parallel material attainments. Material things are not seen as intrinsically evil or sinful, as they are in some religious traditions, but they are not emphasized.

Bahá'u'lláh wrote: *"How sad if any man were, in this Day, to rest his heart on the transitory things of this world! The world is but a show, vain and empty, a mere nothing, bearing the semblance of reality. Set not your affections upon it. The civilization, so often vaunted by the learned exponents of arts and sciences, will, if allowed to overleap the bounds of moderation, bring great evil upon men. . . . If carried to excess, civilization will prove as prolific a source of evil as it had been of goodness when kept within the restraints of moderation. O friends! Help ye the one true God, exalted be His glory, by your goodly deeds, by such conduct and character as shall be acceptable in His sight. He that seeketh to be a helper of God in this Day, let him close his eyes to whatever he may possess, and open them to the things of God."*[1]

Next, we have the central Bahá'í principle of the oneness of mankind. Bahá'u'lláh has likened mankind to one body. *"He Who is your Lord, the All-Merciful, cherisheth in His heart the desire of beholding the entire human race as one soul and one body."* And again, *"Be ye as the fingers of one hand, the members of one body."*[2] Within a body there is great diversity of form and function, and some parts are of more value than others. We treasure our eyes and our heart, for example, more than our fingers or feet. But despite this diversity, all parts of the body have an equal right to, and receive, the full support and assistance of the whole. If we close a finger in a drawer, we do not (and cannot!) simply walk away and leave the problem for later; the whole body rushes to the aid of the finger and rescues it from the drawer. If this attitude were applied, even to a small extent, in people's dealings with each other, we would soon no longer live in a world in which we routinely ignore the difficulties and suffering of others.

We see the same principle in Bahá'u'lláh's injunction to

see God's qualities and attributes in all things. As Bahá'ís we are exhorted to appreciate and love God's creation. And of all God's creation, man has the greatest capacity to reflect divine attributes. Thus we must treat our fellow man with courtesy and respect. Since our divine qualities are often latent and potential rather than fully developed, we are exhorted to look to the good and overlook shortcomings, to encourage and assist each other. In this way we can help each other mature.

Another related element of the Bahá'í view is that education and science are essential to improving the human condition. Bahá'u'lláh has written: *"Knowledge is as wings to man's life, and a ladder for his ascent. Its acquisition is incumbent upon everyone."*[3] Bahá'u'lláh also saw education as part of a larger purpose for man, transcending individual and local interests. He wrote: *"All men have been created to carry forward an ever-advancing civilization."* And again, *"The knowledge of such sciences, however, should be acquired as can profit the peoples of the earth, and not those which begin with words and end with words."*[4] Thus Bahá'ís have a strong tendency to enter service-oriented and humanitarian professions.

A specific application of these attitudes is found in the Bahá'í procedure for decision making known as *consultation*. As Bahá'ís, we are told to seek the advice of others in our personal and business lives and to reach decisions affecting our communities through consultation in a group. 'Abdu'l-Bahá has written: *"Settle all things, both great and small, by consultation."*[5] In many passages, he has elaborated on the spirit and method of Bahá'í consultation, emphasizing that love and fellowship are the foundation.

Bahá'í consultation is not only a procedure for arriving at good decisions, but perhaps even more importantly it is a method for teaching people to work together and to establish strong and effective human relationships. No number of social gatherings or worship services can produce a true sense of unity as effectively as working together. This process of working together forces us to face (and eventually appreciate) the fact that we are different, but that each has an important and unique contribution to make to the whole. In a Bahá'í consultative group, all present have an equal voice. Bahá'ís are taught to recognize that the best ideas may come from the most humble speakers. These groups are thus a powerful forum for exposing Bahá'ís in a practical, concrete way to the spirit of equality and brotherhood which is central to the Bahá'í teachings.

Finally, in Bahá'u'lláh's teachings, work performed in the spirit of service to mankind is elevated to the rank of worship of God. Spiritual attainment for Bahá'ís must be expressed in acts of service to others. Bahá'u'lláh prohibited monasticism and asceticism. He extolled a life of good works, advising: "*Let deeds, not words, be your adorning.*"[6]

Bahá'ís are exhorted to place a high value on spiritual qualities and good character, including detachment from the material temptations of a transient world. But spiritual development, for Bahá'ís, can and must be reinforced by material means in a social context. There is no inherent conflict between the spiritual and the material in the Bahá'í view. The challenge is to utilize material means for spiritual ends. Bahá'u'lláh has given clear guidelines for material progress in this age, centering around the principle of the oneness of mankind and the need for the diverse peoples of the world to learn to live and work together in harmony.

Now, if we review this brief survey of some of the major themes in the Bahá'í teachings which bear on the question of economic and social development, we find that they apply *equally* to both the rich and poor societies in today's world, the educated and uneducated, the haves and have-nots. Bahá'ís the world over are struggling to master the art of consultation, to learn to work together on equal terms with Bahá'ís often very different than themselves, to grow in spiritual qualities, to sharpen their intellect and realize their potential, to overcome prejudices, to learn arts and sciences, to serve mankind. Each individual, and each society, has a different blend of these elements of human growth. But, despite our obvious diversity, we are all pursuing much the same path.

There are thus no grounds whatsoever for an individual Bahá'í, or the Bahá'ís collectively in a particular country or society, to feel they are more advanced or developed than others. We do not know enough about the spiritual advancement of others to be able to make such a judgment. Nor is it in the spirit of Bahá'u'lláh's teachings for us to think of ourselves as better than others. Bahá'u'lláh writes, for example: *"Know ye not why We created you all from the same dust? That no one should exalt himself over the other. Ponder at all times in your hearts how ye were created."*[7]

In fact, the tendency of citizens of the industrialized countries to regard themselves as advanced is probably the reverse of the true spiritual situation. Bahá'u'lláh, like Christ before Him, has clearly indicated that wealth is usually an obstacle to spiritual advancement: *"The rich, but for a few, shall in no wise attain the court of His presence nor enter the city of content and resignation."*[8] If the purpose of human life is the development of spiritual qualities and a noble character, then we must compare countries and cultures on this basis, if at all. And I dare say that on this basis many a less-industrialized country would win handsomely in a competition with an industrialized country. What, we must ask ourselves, are the major conditions for the development of higher human qualities? Surely among them would be a loving, supportive family and community, especially during childhood; an emphasis of hospitality, generosity, integrity and service; and the inspiration and guidance of religion. My own observations, and those of others who live and work in the less-industrialized countries, are that these conditions are more prevalent in these countries than in industrialized countries.

It is true that a large number of children in materially poor countries face disease, physical hardship, and low social status, but they usually have warm supportive families, and often (particularly in the countryside) a relatively stable social structure in which to mature. The majority of children in materially rich countries have an abundance of toys, sophisticated and well-equipped schools, and excellent food and health care. But a large and growing proportion live in fractured families, among adults who have difficulty relating to each other, and in a hostile and competitive society frantically pursuing empty material goals. Although neither type of society offers a very good prospect for its children, the poor may well have the spiritual and human advantage.

In addition to these cultural and religious differences between materially rich and poor countries, there is also increasingly a question of the survivability of whole societies in the face of the threat of military or economic confrontation between nations. It is the rich, by virture of their ample resources and technical development, who have created the weapons of destruction now threatening the very existence of life on the planet. And they have pointed their weapons principally at each other. Even if these weapons are never used, the sophisticated technical and economic systems of the industrialized countries are exceedingly vulnerable to even minor disruptions which could immobilize activity and threaten life itself. Villagers in less-industrialized countries, on the other hand, are still relatively accustomed to physical hardship, are close to their sources of food and shelter, and remain far less dependent on external resources and sophisticated machines. They are likely to be much less affected by any kind of crisis or conflict in the world, whether military or economic.

The purpose of these arguments is not to belittle economic development, advanced education, or modern technology. The benefits of technical wizardry are too obvious to be denied. The point is that we must view material development as a means, not an end—a potential, not a realization. There is no doubt that material wealth and education increase our capacities for good. But our spiritual worth presumably is judged by God against these capacities. From him to whom much is given, much is expected. It is here that the rich have fallen short, largely squandering their advantages in the pursuit of trivial pleasures and ignoring the hardships of others. Given this realization, those of us who come from wealthy countries should look on those from less-industrialized countries in a new light and from a more humble perspective, willing to learn as well as to share and give. We must all, both materially well-off and not, work to ennoble each other through our attitudes and actions.

These fundamental principles and attitudes find practical expression in the Bahá'í approaches to social and economic conditions, to which we will now turn.

Local Initiative. Bahá'í work at the local level can best be appreciated in the context of current trends in the field of economic development as practiced by governments and aid agencies. In these circles there is a new emphasis on the importance of participation and self-reliance. For example, the Secretary General of the Society for International Development, in the foreword to the volume summarizing the Society's 1983 world conference on development, refers to "a major new trend—development by people and experiments in people's participation and self-reliance."[9] In the preface to the same volume, the editor stresses the need for "human-centered development." One also reads in current development literature about "development as if people mattered."

This new emphasis follows the disappointing experience of more than two official United Nations development decades during which the majority of aid resources was poured into large scale aid and investment programs. The unexpected result of this approach has been that poverty in the receiving countries was hardly affected at all. In many countries the rich grew richer, with little aid reaching the poor. Furthermore, many investment schemes were poorly conceived. Often insufficient allowance was made for maintenance (for example, for roads and irrigation works), so that not much remained of the projects after a few years. After this generally bitter experience, a new interest has been generated in smaller scale efforts which take into account the need to involve and win the support of the local people.

Continued political and social unrest after so much development effort, despite real gains in total production, have also drawn attention to the importance of nonmaterial aspects of the development process. In words of Soedjatmoko, the rector of the United Nations University:

> Both the successes and failures of twenty-five years of development experience have shown that the organized pursuit of material improvement does not automatically bring in its wake freedom, human dignity, justice, and civility. These values have in fact often fallen victim to the development endeavor, even when the provision of basic services includes access to education and legal protection.[10]

We see, then, that development experts are finally coming to understand that development must be *people*-centered and that it must address questions of values and social justice. Contrary to the previous widely held belief, it is now being realized that the single-minded pursuit of material development does not itself resolve human problems, and material progress does not even necessarily make such problems easier to solve.

This is easy to say, but it flies in the face of established and traditional ways of thinking. The underlying notion of economic development for many years has been the approach which is taught in elementary economics classes: 1) production results from the coming together of labor and capital; 2) in poor countries labor is abundant and capital scarce; so, 3) for development to take place, all that is needed is to increase the supply of capital. The question of knowledge, skills and human capabilities was not part of this view. When investments didn't work in developing countries because of lack of technical know-how or management skills, theories were proposed about the need for managerial and technical inputs in addition to raw capital and labor. More recently, however, it has become apparent that urban and industrial development has not brought about an improvement in the living standards of the poor—that prosperity has not "trickled down" as it was expected to do—and more consideration is being given to problems of community development and education in the countryside.

However, the large development agencies are not ideally suited to promoting rural development programs because such programs require large numbers of dedicated workers familiar with local languages and customs. Dedicated workers are hard to find, even in small numbers. Such programs are also hard to administer, and they absorb too little money to satisfy central administrators who measure the worth of programs by their monetary cost.

Against this background, Bahá'ís have been patiently working on community development at the grass roots level for many years. At one time our work was considered insignificant, and we had little to say when people concerned about poverty and inequality asked us what we were doing. Now, however, the fruits of our endeavors are becoming apparent. With Bahá'í Communities in over 113,000 communities around the world (as of January 1983), most of these in rural areas of the less-industrialized countries, Bahá'ís are recognized as being in the forefront of the community development effort at the village level in many countries. Furthermore, the corps of several thousand Bahá'í *pioneers*—Bahá'ís who have left their home countries to live and work in other lands, learning the language and customs of the people in their adopted homes —represent an unparalleled resource for development. While the Bahá'í approach has seemed slow, it is now coming to be recognized as far more effective in the long run than the grand schemes which have been so popular in official aid circles. The tortoise is overtaking the hare.

Let us examine more closely the nature of the Bahá'í effort in the 113,000 communities where Bahá'ís reside. We have seen that the Bahá'í teachings emphasize the development in the individual of good character traits and a spiritual attitude toward life. This aspect of development cannot be overemphasized, though it is not often discussed. The performance of any institution depends on the quality of the individuals who compose it. Anyone who has worked in the development field will agree that dishonesty and corruption are at least as important as other factors in retarding economic development. Often they are the single most important factors. Trust and cooperation cannot be built if the individuals involved are dishonest and interested only in self-enrichment. Thus Bahá'ís begin with moral and ethical education for both adults and children.

Then, as has already been mentioned, schools are sometimes organized in those areas where the civil authorities are not able to provide adequate facilities. Because the Bahá'í Communities usually have only very limited resources, the Bahá'í schools are often humble, constructed by the villagers of local materials. The teacher is usually locally supported. There are at least one hundred-fifty schools of varying degrees of sophistication directly sponsored by Bahá'í Communities around the world. And, more importantly, the number is growing rapidly, as a direct expression of the priority given in the Bahá'í teachings to education and knowledge for self-improvement and the advancement of society.

Another aspect of the Bahá'í approach is the emphasis on

effort. Work performed in the spirit of service to mankind is elevated by Bahá'u'lláh to the rank of worship, while begging is forbidden and idleness discouraged. Bahá'u'lláh wrote *"Waste not your time in idleness and sloth. Occupy yourselves with that which profiteth yourselves and others."* And again: *"Please God, the poor may exert themselves and strive to earn the means of livelihood. This is a duty which, in this most great Revelation, hath been prescribed unto every one, and is accounted in the sight of God as a goodly deed. Whoso observeth this duty, the help of the invisible One shall most certainly aid him."* [11]

The idea that God will come to the assistance of anyone making a sincere effort—that God helps those who help themselves—is important. There are many passages in the Bahá'í Writings that encourage us to overlook our weaknesses and trust in God when we undertake challenges we think are beyond our capacity. Such an attitude of reliance on God and on His assistance to strengthen our own inner capacities is conducive to improved self-confidence and motivation. Most of the materially poor people of the world are at the lowest status levels in their society and, as a result, are lacking in self-esteem and have little motivation. It is no accident that the vast majority of Bahá'ís in the world are drawn from oppressed minorities and the rural poor—those who respond most readily to the Bahá'í concepts of the worth and dignity of each human being and the potential for self-improvement. Of course, all of us, no matter how materially well-off, can benefit from these attitudes. In the rich countries too we find many proponents of the power of positive thinking.

As individuals become more sure of themselves and more self-reliant, they paradoxically find their relationships with others improving and can learn to cooperate more fruitfully. Thus there is an important distinction to be made between interdependence and dependency. As individuals grow and mature, interdependence increases and dependency decreases. Interdependent people have a sense of dignity and self-worth, while dependency undermines these essential human qualities. The Bahá'í effort around the world is to encourage strongly a sense of human worth in the matrix of a global family, thus cultivating a spirit of interdependence while discouraging dependency.

As an expression of this attitude, Bahá'í Communities and individuals are encouraged to seek solutions to local or individual problems at the local or individual level. If an individual has a problem, his first question must be, "How can *I* change so that my problem will be resolved?" And in Bahá'í Communities where there are at least nine adult Bahá'ís, they must form a Spiritual Assembly. This Assembly of nine elected members is enjoined to consult together on all questions of concern to their community, and to reach their decisions by consensus in a spirit of love. This is a purely local process, drawing on local resources, without direct reference to outside assistance.

Whenever an individual or Assembly feels that external assistance is required, however, it is free to request help from the national or even the international level of Bahá'í Administration. Such assistance is forthcoming within the limits of available resources. In fact, a major responsibility of Bahá'í National Assemblies is to assist and encourage the development of the local Assemblies under their jurisdiction. This task is not much different from that of raising a child: initially, the senior institutions must give great attention and care, guidance, and even protection to the junior local institutions. But this must be done in such a way that they develop their own maturity and become strong and independent—not in a way that encourages permanent dependence, as much current development assistance does.

Bahá'u'lláh's injunction to the poor to "*strive to earn the means of livelihood*" is balanced by his admonition to the rich to share of their wealth with the poor. "*They who are possessed of riches, however, must have the utmost regard for the poor ... Tell the rich of the midnight sighing of the poor... To give and to be generous are attributes of Mine; well is it with him that adorneth himself with My virtues."*[12] As already mentioned, this teaching has been reflected in a proportionately large number of Bahá'ís from affluent backgrounds who have chosen to move to and settle in the less-industrialized countries in order to further the spread of their Faith and be of greater service to mankind. A large proportion of Bahá'ís, at the time of choosing a career, select a service-oriented profession. Increasingly, young Bahá'ís in affluent countries are obtaining training in professions directly useful in the Third World, such as medicine, agriculture, development economics, and so forth. Because the Bahá'í sense of community cuts across class and other barriers, the human resources of each national community are more widely available to all than is the case in most groups, and the pioneers, once settled in a foreign country, find many ways to be of service. The sense of sharing and working together for common ends is very strong.

These principles of dignity, self-reliance, cooperation and interdependence are emphasized and elaborated in an important message from the world governing body of the Faith, the Universal House of Justice, to the Bahá'ís of the world on the subject of economic and social development, dated 20 October 1983. Because of its importance in defining current Bahá'í objectives and methods of approach in this field, we shall quote from this message at length:

From the beginning of His stupendous mission, Bahá'-u'lláh urged upon the attention of nations the necessity of ordering human affairs in such a way as to bring into being a world unified in all the essential aspects of its life. In unnumbered verses and tablets He repeatedly and variously declared the 'progress of the world' and the 'development of nations' as being among the ordinances of God for this Day. . . .

The steps to be taken must necessarily begin in the

Bahá'í Community itself, with the friends endeavoring, through their application of spiritual principles, their rectitude of conduct and the practice of the art of consultation, to uplift themselves and thus become self-sufficient and self-reliant. Moreover, these exertions will conduce to the preservation of human honor, so desired by Bahá'u'lláh. . . .

Progress in the development field will largely depend on natural stirrings at the grassroots, and it should receive its driving force from those sources rather than from an imposition of plans and programs from the top. The major task of National Assemblies, therefore, is to increase the local communities' awareness of needs and possibilities, and to guide and coordinate the efforts resulting from such awareness. . . .

This challenge evokes the resourcefulness, flexibility and cohesivesness of the many communities composing the Bahá'í world. Different communities will, of course, perceive different approaches and different solutions to similar needs. Some can offer assistance abroad, while, at the outset, others must of necessity receive assistance; but all, irrespective of circumstances or resources, are endowed with the capacity to respond in some measure; all can share; all can participate in the joint enterprise of applying more systematically the principles of the Faith to upraising the quality of human life. The key to success is unity in spirit and in action.

This is indeed an unusual approach to economic and social development—preserving human honor, seeking the driving force for development from "natural stirrings at the grassroots," and yet drawing on the resources of a vast worldwide community.

Some Working Examples. Those who have not had direct experience with Bahá'í Communities may have difficulty visualizing exactly how such an approach can work in practice.

So it may be useful to illustrate the themes developed above by reference to specific current activities.

One project which reflects Bahá'í concerns and priorities is a Bahá'í-admininstered rural development project underway at the time of this writing in Haiti. It is receiving financial support from the Canadian Government through their International Development Agency (CIDA) and from the Universal House of Justice through the National Spiritual Assembly of the Bahá'ís of Canada. The project is centered at, and uses the physical facilities of, a modern Bahá'í primary school in a rural area not far from the Haitian capital city of Port-au-Prince. The school, known as the Anís Zunúzí Bahá'í School, was constructed with generous donations from European Bahá'ís.

In an earlier rural development project also supported with Canadian government funds, local Bahá'ís, with the help of a Canadian Bahá'í pioneer fluent in the local Creole language, conducted a course at the school to train preschool teachers for surrounding villages. The training included a range of subjects relevant to rural life, such as community health, nutrition, family life, basic science, agriculture, and early childhood education. These teachers were well received in the villages. Villagers helped construct small education centers for their new teachers, receiving modest financial assistance for the construction work from project funds (about $50 per structure), and sturdy furniture. The villagers assumed part of the responsibility for the ongoing support of the teachers and, most importantly, a new community spirit and willingness to cooperate was evident.

The new and somewhat larger project was designed to build on the success of the first project. It was recognized, however, that the first step would be to identify needs, leading to the design of practical projects utilizing available resources which would both fill these needs and receive the wholehearted support of the local people. Thus this second project is devoted almost entirely to bringing together the rural people and their needs, on one hand, and available human and financial resources for development, on the other. The objective is to encourage the formation of active self-help groups in the villages to serve as the focus and center of the development effort. The project personnel divide their time between interviews, discussions, and statistical studies to define needs *as perceived by the local population* in the villages, and the development of contacts with many groups and individuals who are ready to offer technical and educational assistance to receptive communities. The project is developing a resource center at the Bahá'í school containing literature and, to the extent possible, equipment and facilities relevant to rural life in that area. Small-scale demonstrations of particular technologies, such as beekeeping and the use of new seed strains, are being undertaken. In addition, it is hoped that personnel connected with the project will acquire a unique body of experience in the application of technology to specific rural needs in Haiti. These needs could include, for example, animal husbandry, poultry farming, irrigation, various aspects of agriculture, and construction techniques appropriate in the countryside, in addition to basic education. It is a tribute to the vision of CIDA, and evidence for the rising awareness of the need for this type of comprehensive approach to development, that they have agreed to contribute to the financial cost of this project.

The Haiti project represents a small beginning for the Bahá'ís in that country in the field of economic and social development. It is necessarily limited in scope because of human and financial constraints. But the Bahá'í schools and projects in Haiti and in other countries illustrate the emphasis placed by Bahá'ís on the development by young people in rural areas of broad intellectual skills, as distinguished from manual training. Economic development is the development of people. It will not be accomplished through superficial programs of distributing goods or training in manual skills. People must develop in all their capacities until they become the major actors in determining their own destiny. This can only be done through education which teaches methods of thought, problem solving and the application of scientific principles to practical situations.

Many educational systems in the Third World perpetuate the existing class structure by teaching the privileged few to be leaders and thinkers, while giving the rest a rudimentary education "appropriate to their social station." Bahá'í schools can, must be, and often are, centers for human development that win support of the people because they are of and for the people. They reflect Bahá'u'lláh's advice: *"Regard man as a mine rich in gems of inestimable value. Education can, alone, cause it to reveal its treasures . . .*[13]

Another Bahá'í project affecting the welfare of whole populations is a series of radio stations in South America directed at the needs of the indigenous rural people. The first such station was established in Otavalo, Ecuador, in 1977. Situated in the heart of mountainous country populated by Quechua-speaking people, the staff of Radio Bahá'í pioneered the concept of a radio station that serves as a tool of the local listeners themselves. Quechua-speaking local staff were trained in the use of the station's equipment, an almost unthinkable break with traditional attitudes in the region. Soon the station claimed over 80 percent of the local listenership. In 1978, the station sponsored the first in a series of annual music festivals featuring local Quechua musicians. These events, which are broadcast on the station, are attended by five to seven thousand people and receive wide publicity. Annual Children's Festivals, begun in 1979, also attract thousands of participants and spectators; they feature drama, poetry and folk dancing as well as music. The two annual festivals are generally credited with having dramatically encouraged a sense of pride among the Quechua people in their Quechua culture and traditions.

In addition to cultural and musical programming, the station has carried programs about the Bahá'í teachings and programs directed toward practical concerns of the rural farmers, such as agriculture and hygiene. CIDA has provided funding for some of the rural development and cultural activities of the station, including the acquisition of a jeep to enhance two way communication with the population of the region and encourage participation in the programming of the station. The Canadian government has also generously provided a series of radio programs created in Canada for use in rural areas. As a result of the great success of this endeavor, a similar station has now been built in Peru, and others are under construction in Bolivia, Chile, and the state of South Carolina in the United States.

Bahá'í efforts in social and economic development have not been confined to the Western Hemisphere. In fact, some of the oldest and most successful programs and institutions are on other continents. Mention should be made, for example, of the New Era School in India, which has been offering high quality primary and secondary education since its establishment in 1945. It has recently expanded to include a Rural Development Institute providing vocational courses, as well as a Junior College and a Youth Academy. Plans are being developed for a Teacher's College to complement existing programs. Mention should also be made of the Rabbani School, likewise in India, which is providing secondary education specifically designed to equip its students to serve their home village communities, using agricultural and animal husbandry techniques learned at the school.

Aside from educational institutions—schools and radio stations—another and even more important area of Bahá'í endeavor around the world is in the training of Bahá'ís in the skills of consultation and cooperation. I have already mentioned that every community where at least nine adult Bahá'ís reside forms a local Spiritual Assembly consisting of nine members elected by secret ballot, without campaigning or nominations, from the community at large. There are more than 25,000 of these Assemblies around the world, involving nearly a quarter of a million people in a vast experiment in community development. These Assemblies are the fruit of many years of difficult and sacrificial work by pioneers to establish the Bahá'í Faith in all corners of the globe. They reflect the emphasis in the Bahá'í teachings on the establishing of local administrative institutions which, as they mature, will increasingly be able to resolve problems and provide guidance not only for the Bahá'í Communities they serve, but the broader non-Bahá'í community as well.

These Assemblies address the heart of many otherwise intractable problems of development that involve entrenched divisions and animosities at the village level. It is not uncommon for Bahá'í Assemblies to include black and white, high caste and low caste, employers and their employees, rich and poor, educated and uneducatd. Often the initial challenge of physically coming together in equality, in defiance of deeply ingrained and habitual racial or class divisions, is the greatest hurdle, and its achievement truly heroic. In this crucible of exposure to each other's views, while maintaining a prayerful, courteous and loving atmosphere, the members of the Assembly learn to appreciate what each has to offer.

By contrast, many community development efforts by official agencies founder because of the lack of cooperative spirit at the local level. In Pakistan, I was taken to see a "model" biogas electric plant in a village outside Islamabad. The government had constructed this plant with the latest "appropriate technology" as a demonstration plant in an effort to duplicate the successful experience in India with the use of methane gas given off by cow manure. Unfortunately, the plant was not operating because the village had two rival leading families who could not agree regarding the use of the generated electricity. The government was powerless in this situation; they could build electric plants, but had no means to address local feuds and rivalries. It is at this level, however, that the Bahá'í effort begins. From a foundation of greater harmony and willingness to work together new development efforts can spring.

For many years the principle emphasis in Bahá'í development activities has been on the strengthening of Bahá'í administrative institutions such as the local and national Spiritual Assemblies, and on a limited number of educational and other projects directed primarily at the urgent needs of Bahá'í populations. These priorities were dictated by the small size and extremely limited resources of the Bahá'í Community. Now, however, the number of followers of Bahá'u'lláh and the number of communities which have already reached a certain level of administrative competence have grown to the point that Bahá'í Communities can, and must, begin to consider ways in which they can contribute directly to the amelioration of social and economic problems in the larger, primarily non-Bahá'í society around them.

This change in emphasis was signalled by the Universal House of Justice in their important message to the Bahá'ís of the world dated April 1983, in which they refer to "the oncoming challenges of assisting, as maturity and resources allow, the development of the social and economic life of peoples, of collaborating with the forces leading towards the establishment of order in the world, of influencing the exploitation and constructive uses of modern technology, and in all these ways enhancing the prestige and progress of the Faith and uplifting the conditions of the generality of mankind."

This new field for service by individual Bahá'ís and Bahá'í institutions, implying an increasing involvement with issues and movements outside the Bahá'í Community itself, presents new challenges. It will necessarily require that Bahá'ís inform themselves more thoroughly of the activities and experiences of other groups striving for similar goals, and find ways of both learning from and assisting those activities—all that is implied in the word *collaboraton*. In many specific aspects of development work Bahá'ís are relatively inexperienced and will benefit greatly from warm relations with other organizations having years of service in the field. On the other hand, Bahá'ís bring to this task significant human resources and a reservoir of constructive attitudes which cannot fail to make an important contribution when applied in the context of practical, well conceived projects.

To assist in this process, new Bahá'í organizations have been formed to collect information, coordinate resources, and promote activities in the development field. Of greatest importance is the new Office of Social and Economic Development at the Bahá'í World Center, formed in 1983. Also of interest is the Canadian Bahá'í International Development Service (CBIDS), which since 1983 has been compiling an index of Bahá'í human resources available for development work and advising the Canadian Bahá'í National Spiritual Assembly in their collaboration with CIDA. The Canadian Bahá'í Community is also host to the Association for Bahá'í Studies which devoted its annual meeting in 1983 primarily to the subject of social and economic development.[14] The new Bahá'í International Health Agency, also in Canada, is examining possibilities for health-related projects in less-industrialized countries and sponsoring international gatherings of Bahá'ís in the health professions.

Global Reforms. While local efforts are essential to any lasting progress in development and are viewed by Bahá'ís as the foundation and starting point for such endeavor, ultimately peoples and nations will only prosper if the injustices and inequities of our present world system can be corrected.

Before turning to Bahá'í teachings on this subject, it may be useful to gain some perspective on the magnitude of the economic imbalance in the world—an imbalance which reflects profound injustice and reveals the inadequacy of our political institutions. Statistics published by the World Bank on income distribution allow us to make some rough calculations of income distribution worldwide. If we arbitrarily choose a cutoff figure of $500 per capita income at 1981 prices, we would find about half of mankind—over two billion people—with incomes less than this level. This half of mankind would have an *average* per capita income of only about $200. The incomes of all of these people combined would amount to about $435 billion.

By contrast, the world spent about $660 billion on arms in 1983, or almost $1.3 million per minute. These expenditures, if distributed to the poorer half of mankind, would have increased their income by one-and-a-half times. In other words, more than two billion people could be more than twice as well off in material terms if military spending were redistributed to the poor.

This analysis is simplistic, of course. It is intended only to give an idea of the magnitudes involved. In actual practice, a large portion of funds for development go into education and other forms of investment rather than into direct consumption, leading to improved welfare in the future more than in the present. Nevertheless, the fact remains that we live in a world with vast resources being squandered on endangering the survival of the species when the same resources could dramatically improve the welfare of the majority of people on the planet. Put another way, we are throwing away (putting to a totally unproductive, and even dangerous, use) human skills and work equivalent in money terms to one and one-half times the daily toil and sweat of two billion people. For this half of mankind, who struggle so hard each day to earn a pittance (an average of fifty-five cents a day for each man, woman and child), it is exceedingly discouraging to see the profligate waste of the rich.

We should also note that this imbalance in the use of public resources is not improving, nor is it confined to the wealthy countries. World military expenditures are rising more rapidly in percentage terms than total production and are thus consuming an ever larger share of total world output. In both rich and poor countries, defense expenditures exceed central government expenditures on either education or health, and in the poorest countries defense spending is as large as central government spending on education and health combined.

The United States and the Soviet Union, accounting between them for about one-third of total global production, are world leaders in misdirecting resources. The American government spent close to $250 billion on arms in 1983. In that same year Americans poured $5 billion into gambling in casinos. By contrast, official development assistance from all wealthy non-communist countries to poor countries was $36 billion, and from the United States was $8 billion. The United States was ranked fifteenth out of seventeen OECD countries (a grouping of the industrialized, non communist countries) in the percentage of GNP devoted to official development assistance.[15] The United States was contributing less than $200 million to support the United Nations, and was in the process of reducing these contributions.[16] Figures for the Soviet Union are not as readily available, but their record is no better.

Another important problem facing the world economy— one which is related to the problem of military expenditures —is the dramatic increase in the debts of less-industrialized countries and the resultant strain on their economies and the world financial system. Third World countries had a combined foreign debt at the end of 1983 of over $800 billion dollars—and this figure represented an increase of 33 per cent in one year.[17] For many debtor countries, the interest payments alone on their foreign debt consume a quarter or more of their export earnings. They are, therefore, obliged to borrow further in order to obtain the cash with which to make their debt service payments. Thus the volume of outstanding debt balloons. The situation is aggravated by high interest rates which result in large measure from the deficit spending of the industrialized countries and particularly of the United States. This precarious and worsening situation cannot continue indefinitely, but comprehensive solutions are beyond the scope of present institutions and agreements.

The fact is that international financial flows consist mostly of banking transactions. Banking, in turn, is built on a slippery foundation called confidence. Depositors must always believe that their bank will provide them their cash on demand, knowing full well that it is the function of banks to lend the larger part of their depositors' money for investment or commerce. Any evidence of mismanagement can cause a collapse of confidence, which once lost is hard to recover. The widespread banking crisis of the 1930s gives a taste of the effects of loss of confidence in banks. While modern countries have provisions designed to prevent runs on their domestic banking system, the world has no similar institutional safeguard against an international banking crisis. The massive strains on the banking system resulting from unwise lending to governments are thus a source of serious concern—not only for the welfare of the debtor countries, but also for the stability of the world's economic relationships and for world peace.

It is a dangerous situation, both from the perspective of

the confrontation between the superpowers and because of the increasing tension between the less-industrialized countries and the industrialized countries. History has shown that wherever injustice is perceived and not remedied, conflict follows and institutions eventually are forced to change. With our technological advances in the weapons of war, however, the threat of conflict as a means of resolving injustices is far more serious, and far less likely to have a constructive outcome, than has been the case in the past. A new awareness of injustice and a new approach to its elimination in international affairs is desperately needed.

The Bahá'í teachings make a two pronged attack on these global problems. First, Bahá'u'lláh has clearly indicated that injustice and tyranny stem from the fundamental spiritual crisis of the time and that any lasting solution must be sought first in the spiritual regeneration of men. He has written, for example:

> Behold the disturbances which, for many a long year, have afflicted the earth. . . .Though the world is encompassed with misery and distress, yet no man hath paused to reflect what the cause or source of that may be. . . . How bewildering, how confusing is such behavior! No two men can be found who may be said to be outwardly and inwardly united. The evidences of discord and malice are apparent everywhere, though all were made for harmony and union. . . . Regard ye not one another as strangers. Ye are the fruits of one tree, and the leaves of one branch. We cherish the hope that the light of justice may shine upon the world and sanctify it from tyranny.[18]

As a result of this fundamental Bahá'í view that the root cause of war and other social problems is spiritual and moral, Bahá'ís generally have refrained from political action, pouring their effort and resources instead into the propagation of the spiritual ideals and verities of their Faith.

As mentioned above, the resulting development of tens of thousands of Spiritual Assemblies working together in a prayerful, cooperative and loving atmosphere is the practical fruit of this endeavor. As these Assemblies grow in their abilities and experience, they will be able to acquire more and more responsibility for local affairs in their areas of jurisdiction. Eventually it may be that Bahá'í values and methods, having demonstrated their efficacy on the local level, will be endorsed by nations for application within their national governments.

The second prong of the Bahá'í approach is to promote the formation of a world government and to support those institutions already in existence which may be viewed as precursors of such a government. Shoghi Effendi eloquently outlined the Bahá'í vision of a world system:

Some form of a world Super-State must needs be evolved, in whose favor all the nations of the world will have willingly ceded every claim to make war, certain rights to impose taxation and all rights to maintain armaments, except for purposes of maintaining internal order within their respective dominions. Such a state will have to include within its orbit an International Executive adequate to enforce supreme and unchallengeable authority on every recalcitrant member of the commonwealth; a World Parliament whose members shall be elected by the people in their respective countries and whose election shall be confirmed by their respective governments; and a Supreme Tribunal whose judgment will have a binding effect even in such cases where the parties concerned did not voluntarily agree to submit their case to its consideration. A world community in which all economic barriers will have been permanently demolished and the interdependence of Capital and Labor definitely recognized; in which the clamor of religious fanaticism and strife will have been finally extinguished; in which a single code of international law—the product of the considered judgment of the world's federated representatives—shall have as its sanction the instant and coercive intervention of the combined forces of the federated units; and finally a world community in which the fury of a capricious and militant nationalism will have been transmuted into an abiding consciousness of world citizenship—such indeed, appears, in its broad outline, the Order anticipated by Bahá'u'lláh, an Order that shall come to be regarded as the fairest fruit of a slowly maturing age.[19]

While the realization of the vision in this passage is still some distance in the future, a few thinking people now recognize that only such a global solution can hope to resolve the intractable problems we are now facing. The superpower military confrontation and arms race, the depletion of the world's natural resources, the desecration of the environment, the economic inequalities and social unrest of the less-industrialized countries—all can only be resolved at the supranational level. However, the number of leaders of thought who have openly come to this realization is small, and their advice is neither popular nor widely accepted. Bahá'u'lláh, more than a hundred years ago, wrote: *"Let your vision be world-embracing, rather than confined to your own self."*[20] While many of His other teachings are now generally accepted and have been gradually incorporated into the social systems of modern countries, His emphasis on global solutions to economic, political and military problems can still be regarded as visionary.

A number of thinkers about world problems and a few groups in the industrialized countries, after analyzing the dangers of nuclear war and military confrontation, have come to the conclusion that the problem can only be avoided through greater human understanding. As Margaret Thatcher, Britain's Prime Minister and a leader not usually known for pacifist statements, said in early 1984: "The important thing is that you simply must make an effort the more to understand one another, and secondly, if, as the President [of the United States] wishes, and as all Europe wishes, you want to get down the tremendous expenditure of armament, then you can only do it if you both agree on it. Now you can only both agree on it if you do more talking to one another."[21] Understanding, dialogue, mutual encouragement, and appreciation have been central Bahá'í principles since the last century. But the ability to communicate with and understand people different than oneself does not come quickly. In this area, too, Bahá'ís have an advantage: they have been developing their communication and consultation skills for many years through the daily functioning of diverse Bahá'í Communities.

It is important to realize, however, that Bahá'u'lláh's prescription for world peace does not rest solely on the attainment of spiritual attributes by world leaders or on a greater dialogue between conflicting states. On the contrary, Bahá'u'lláh clearly envisioned a world government with institutions to resolve disputes. As outlined in the passage quoted above, these world institutions would need both moral and military force to keep order and enforce a measure of justice in relations between nations.

Let us not be naive as we strive for a better world system. The world has an ample supply of greedy, ruthless and powerful people—both in governments and in private commerce—who are accustomed to exploiting their fellow men for their own selfish ends. At least during a transition period, and certainly as long as this generation is alive, any viable peace must include provision for a police power with overwhelming force and authority—one able to act quickly and decisively in cases where the agreed code of international behavior is violated. The United Nations was never given such authority. For this reason it has not fulfilled the original expectations that it would be able to keep peace in the world. Eventually we must take the next, all-important step. Only through a firm international pact, involving the establishment of institutions for conflict resolution and the just administration of international relationships, can we hope to avoid another world conflict—conflict which would threaten the devastation of civilization as we know it.

When we have established world institutions and abolished war, whether as the result of the cataclysmic effects of a nuclear holocaust or a preventive measure, the enormous resources now expended on military preparedness will need to be directed elsewhere. What better or more urgent challenge than the elimination of the extremes of poverty and wealth in the world? However, even the briefest contemplation of this possibility reveals that the available resources would be far greater than what could be wisely and effectively spent. Enormous sums of money poured into development programs would only strengthen the patterns of corruption and exploitation which characterize the existing social system in most countries. As we saw above, experience with aid programs has led many thoughtful observers to conclude that development is a human process which is not always aided by the expenditure of financial resources, particularly if these resources are not wisely administered or not in proportion to other elements of the development program.

Thus a world government may face, not a lack of resources, but a lack of understanding of how to organize a constructive program of external assistance reinforcing and encouraging local initiative and human growth. The work now progressing at the local level in Bahá'í Communities and among many other non-governmental groups, both local and international, to better understand the process of human and social development—to work with developing populations to define objectives and devise practical means of achieving them—may prove an invaluable resource for efforts on a much larger scale when the world is ready to devote more attention to these problems.

In a more equitable world system, imperialism, whether military or economic, would be controlled and the rights of relatively defenseless nations would be safeguarded. The Bahá'í teachings foresee a world system enjoying a single currency, freedom from trade barriers, a world auxiliary language, and a single system of weights and measures, all encouraging free commerce to the benefit of all nations. Some may object that an open system of this nature would only give more latitude for the economically strong to exploit the weak. Undoubtedly the world authorities would have to be alert to such abuses. But the great success in the United States during the postwar period in bringing about greater interregional equality within the country, rather than the polarization into rich and poor regions forecast by some economists, gives empirical evidence that a system of free competition and free flow of capital, coupled with legal safeguards for business contracts and a federal government able to redistribute a certain portion of output from rich to poorer regions, can produce a rapid narrowing of the gap between rich and poor. Such an outcome on a world scale would be one of the most important early challenges of a world government.

Let us not, however, concentrate our attention entirely on the material aspects of development. The people in the rich countries of the world are increasingly plagued with problems of alienation, stress, disintegration of family ties, and the loss of a sense of purpose and self-fulfillment, all stemming from the excessive materialism of these countries. Such problems are not found to the same degree in the less-industrialized countries. One can hope that these countries can pursue a path of material development coupled with spiritual undestanding that will help them avoid the pitfalls of materialism. Their greater spiritual receptivity, as demonstrated in the relative size and strength of their Bahá'í Communities, gives hope for such an outcome.

So, too, do the outstanding human qualities that one often finds in village people around the world: a high sense of generosity and hospitality, of courtesy and human diginity, of the importance of family bonds, of humility, and of the role of religion in life. My own experience living in a less-industrialized country—which I believe is shared by many others—has been one of immeasurable enrichment through observing these qualities and the manner in which people far less well off materially find hope, joy and happiness in their lives. This process is like Bahá'í consultation on an intercultural plane: through observing the approach that different peoples and cultures take toward the problems of life, we come much closer than we could by ourselves to understanding the true human condition.

It is not only Bahá'ís, of course, who see opportunities for constructive international dialogue. Ronald Leger, the Director of the International Non-Governmental Organization Division of CIDA, has written: "Most developing countries' populations have a traditional and active religious respect for life and afterlife and a profound respect for cultural diversity—the foundations of dialogue among nations and a precious antidote to materialism."[22]

Thus, we can visualize a two-way interchange developing in the context of a global society composed of different but equal nations. Through such a cooperative endeavor the world would be much more likely to achieve a balance and synthesis of spiritual and material, of the outer and inner life, so essential to human happiness and progress.

Conclusion. We have seen above that the Bahá'í teachings provide a conceptual framework for understanding social and economic development at both the local and international levels. It is based on a belief in the spiritual purpose of human existence, while at the same time it gives practical guidelines and tools for pursuing development objectives. Within this framework much remains to be done in working out practical programs for human progress in a spirit of global cooperation combined with local initiative and self-reliance. Good intentions are not enough; action is required, and experience must be gained. The problems facing humanity are enormous and will not be easily solved. But effort will bring rewards, both large and small, as those who are already laboring in this field will testify.

One important theme runs through this chapter and deserves emphasis by way of conclusion. It is the importance of knowing our objectives. We cannot reasonably hope to arrive at a desirable destination unless we know where —or what—it is. While we must also have the road map and the plan for our trip, a vision of the destination is most important. As we read in Proverbs: "Where there is no vision, the people perish."[23] It is for lack of clearly defined objectives that many worthy efforts are dissipated and many lives wasted. It is here that the Bahá'í approach to human problems begins: with a clear concept of the purpose of human life and a vision of the future. Others may disagree with this concept or with the Bahá'í aim of a unified world encompassing and encouraging human diversity. Let us, then, openly debate the merits of these objectives. For not until leaders of thought and organizers of action can agree on objectives can we hope to put the world in better order.

Notes

Since an understanding of the process of development in a Bahá'í context is itself part of the continuing development of the Bahá'í World Community, no one can pretend to understand at this early stage in that development what *the* Bahá'í approach to any aspect of life is. Nor can any individual Bahá'í claim any particular authority on these subjects. I have only presented here my own views and thoughts in the hope that others will find them of some value. These views have been heavily shaped by those of fellow Bahá'ís working in the development field, to whom I am deeply indebted for many insights. The responsibility for any errors of fact or interpretation in the pages above, however, is solely my own.

I am particularly indebted to Amatu'l-Bahá Ruḥíyyih Khánum, especially her talk given at the Annual Meeting of the Association for Bahá'í Studies in 1982 (which is available from the Association as a tape recording); to Counsellor Farzam Arbab, particularly his article "Development: A Challenge to Bahá'í Scholars" in *Bahá'í Studies Notebook* (February 1984)); and to Dr. Glen Eyford. It has been my pleasure to work with all three in Haiti.

1. *Gleanings from the Writings of Bahá'u'lláh* (Wilmette, Ill.: Bahá'í Publishing Trust, 1951) pp. 316, 328, 342–43, and 272.

2. Ibid., pp. 214 and 140.

3. *Tablets of Bahá'u'lláh* (Haifa: Bahá'í World Centre, 1978) p. 51.

4. *Gleanings*, p. 215; *Tablets*, pp. 51–52.

5. *Consultation: A Compilation* (Wilmette, Ill.: Bahá'í Publishing Trust, 1980) p. 9.

6. *Synopsis and Codification of the Kitáb-i-Aqdas* (Haifa: Bahá'í World Centre, 1973) p. 47; *The Hidden Words* (Wilmette, Ill.: Bahá'í Publishing Trust, Rev. ed., 1957) Persian, No. 5.

7. Ibid., Arabic, No. 68.

8. Ibid., Persian, No. 53.

9. Poona Wignaraja, in Ann Mattis, ed., *A Society for International Development: Prospectus 1984* (Duke University Press, 1983) p. xii.

10. Ibid., p. 23.

11. *Tablets*, p. 26; *Gleanings*, p. 202.

12. Ibid.; *Hidden Words*, Persian, No. 49.

13. *Gleanings*, p. 260.

14. See *Bahá'í Studies Notebook*, vol. 3, nos. 3 and 4 (February 1984) for the proceedings of the confernce.

15. *World Development Report 1983* (Oxford University Press, 1983).

16. *New York Times*, October 10, 1983, p. 4.

17. A. W. Clausen, President of the World Bank, quoted in *New York Times*, January 26, 1984, p. 45.

18. *Gleanings*, p. 218.

19. *The World Order of Bahá'u'lláh* (Wilmette, Ill.: Bahá'í Publishing Trust, 1955) pp. 40–41; see also, pp. 203–204.

20. *Gleanings*, p. 94.

21. *New York Times*, January 22, 1984, p. 1.

22. In *Prospectus 1984*, p. 176.

23. Proverbs 29:18.

Marxism: A Bahá'í Perspective

by John Huddleston

MARCH 14, 1983 MARKED THE hundredth anniversary of the death of Karl Marx. The occasion was signaled by a number of new books and articles on Marxism, adding to an already formidable literature. A further commentary from a Bahá'í perspective might be useful for at least two reasons.

The first is that a Bahá'í review of any movement or event in history will untimately relate it to the worldwide spiritual and ethical evolution of society. It would thus have a more direct and consistent standard of reference than is found in a normal academic review. It would also differ from reviews written from a political point of view, left or right, because a Bahá'í is obliged to be completely detached from party political interest.

The second point of interest is that both Marxism and the Bahá'í Faith are radical movements, one political and one religious, which arose in the nineteenth century at almost exactly the same time in response to the corruption and injustice of the period.[1] Since then Marxism has gone on to capture the imagination of a large part of mankind. It has become the official creed of states whose citizens total about one-third of the world's population. On the surface, the history of the Bahá'í Faith has been less dramatic. But it should be remembered that religions, which historically have a deeper and longer lasting impact on individuals and

191

on society than political movements, usually take longer to develop to their full potential.[2] What is significant about the Bahá'í Faith is that it has attracted adherents from just about every strata of society in just about every nation, people and tribe in the world. It is recognized by a growing number of outsiders as well as by adherents as having principles and teachings which are in tune with the times in a more comprehensive way than can be said about other movements. And it has the potential for exploding into prominence at any time because of these facts and because modern communications permit ideas to travel through the whole of world society with lightning speed.

Bahá'ís themselves have perhaps an additional interest in such a review because they are called upon by the teachings of their Faith to be friendly with peoples from all backgrounds. In order to give depth to this endeavor, they need to know and appreciate the common ground between themselves and others. For this reason it is clearly important to have some appreciation of a system which is accepted by large numbers of peoples in both the First and Third Worlds, beyond those in the Second World socialist countries.

In making such a review it should be stated quite clearly from the beginning that there are very few references to Marxism or Communism in the Bahá'í Writings.[3] This review is, therefore, mainly a personal commentary, with no official standing, in which Marxist philosophy and practice are considered in the light of general Bahá'í principles.

Background to the Ideas of Karl Marx. An appreciation of any philosophy or movement would be incomplete without reference to the historical context in which it came into being. Karl Marx lived in Western Europe for the greater part of the nineteenth century, a place and time where there was a great consciousness of the themes of liberty, equality and fraternity thrust on the world by the French Revolution of 1789. Society was deeply divided between those, on one hand, who wished the revolution had never taken place and who wanted to turn the clock back to an earlier time, and those, on the other hand, who wished to see these principles put into practice everywhere and wondered why the revolution had apparently failed.

An equally important development of the time was the industrial revolution started in England in the second half of the eighteenth century. By the middle of the nineteenth century it had spread to Western Europe and North America and had brought with it—besides new goods and great wealth—ugly smoke-covered industrial cities that housed, in appalling conditions, thousands of workers brought in from the countryside to man the new factories. Pride in the success of science was mixed, at least for a minority, with a deep concern about the aggravation of existing extremes of wealth and poverty.

As a thinker in these circumstances, Marx was greatly affected by three great themes of the intellectual life of the time: (i) the ideas in current philosophy, particularly those in Germany, his native land, and those associated with the French Revolution; (ii) the socialist movement, especially in France where it was initially the strongest and most developed; and (iii) the early English economists of the free trade school who were associated with the first phase of the industrial revolution. From these three sources he developed his ideas on the nature of man, the purpose of life, the materialistic and dialectical interpretation of history, class struggle, tactics for revolutionary change, and the labor theory of value.

The ideas in current philosophy which attracted the interest of Marx had developed in Europe over a period of two or three centuries. During the Middle Ages, the Roman Catholic Church had dominated intellectual life. Its views were a combination of selected Greek philosophy and Christian theology. One important element was the view of Aristotle that the world has a purpose. That purpose gives everything a place in the world. Physical bodies are naturally at rest and motion is abnormal, only occurring when bodies are disturbed. This view of the universe was also reflected in feudal society with its rigid hierarchy of class and place.

The first cracks in this intellectual system began to appear before the Reformation as educated people took an increasing interest in ideas from the East and the full spectrum of Greek thought. The cracks were widened by the Reformation when large numbers broke away from the Catholic Church because of their indignation at growing corruption and materialism. This time of questioning led to developments in science which raised challenges to orthodox philosophy. The Church was shaken by the idea, originally suggested by Nicolas Copernicus (1473–1543) and then proven by Galileo Galilei (1564–1642), that the earth revolves around the sun and not vice versa. This theory, by removing man from the center of the universe, seemed to undermine the Church's teachings about the intimate relationship between man and God.

Galileo's theory that matter is in constant motion added further to the dismay of church leaders. Ultimately, it contradicted their basic philosophy of a static hierarchical society inside a static universe. Giordano Bruno (b. 1548), another advocate of the Copernicus theory, was executed in 1600; Galileo was put on trial before the Inquisition in 1635 and forbidden to propagate his views. This persecution was in vain: science could no longer be guided and suppressed when it deviated from official philosophy.

There followed an age of great mathematicians and physicists—Johann Kepler (1571–1630), Rene Descartes (1596–1650), Robert Boyle (1627–1691), Christiaan Huygens (1629–1693), and Sir Isaac Newton (1642–1726)—

whose discovery of physical laws gave a mechanistic, materialistic and self-generating picture of the universe. This reinforced a trend toward less emphasis on an intimate relationship between man and God. It clearly did not fit with biblical stories, which if taken literally, portray a God continually directing and intervening in the affairs of man. At best the new discoveries relegated God in the minds of many in the educated classes to the role of the Great Clockmaker who had constructed a beautiful machine, the universe, and then had stood back to let it work by itself according to built-in laws.

The British philosophers George Berkeley (1685–1753) and David Hume (1711–1776) and others of the empirical school concentrated their studies on physical matters which could be tested by the senses and were sceptical of all things spiritual. Others took an even more radical position and argued that the new scientific knowledge explained the universe fully and made it unnecessary to believe in God.

These developments in mathematics and physics attracted widespread attention and prestige. Soon the same methods were being applied in theories about man and society. The English philosopher Thomas Hobbes (1588–1679) theorized that man is essentially concerned only with his own material well being and that there would be a return to the law of the jungle if a strong authoritarian government did not keep order. On the other hand, John Locke (1632–1704) rejected the old Aristotelian theory of natural inequalities and argued that all men are the same when born, and only changed by experiences during the course of their lives. This idea of equality was used to justify the Glorious Revolution of 1688 which limited the power of the English monarchy. It was later to be an important source of inspiration for the American Revolution.

Somewhat similar ideas were embraced by the French philosophers of the Enlightenment, who believed that man is naturally good and that suffering and oppression are caused by ignorance—quite different from the Church's teaching that man had been a sinner since the fall of Adam and could only be saved by the sacrifice of Jesus, the Redeemer. The French philosophers believed that, just as there are laws governing nature, so there are also rational laws for society. If applied, these laws would bring out man's true nature and create universal happiness. It was the duty of educated men to find these laws and then to teach them to the whole population. Such a process, Voltaire (1694–1778) in particular argued, required that man be given complete freedom of thought, unrestricted by the authority of the Bible and the institutions of society. The Enlightenment philosophers claimed that the church and the aristocracy both had a vested interest in keeping the rest of the population ignorant of such laws. One of them, Baron d'Holbach (1723–1789) remarked: "As soon as man dares to think, the priests' empire is destroyed."[4] The ideas of the Enlightenment captured the imagination of a large portion of the French educated classes. This contributed significantly to the outbreak and course of the Revolution of 1789.

The materialistic and mechanistic theories which imbued thinking in France and England in the seventeenth and eighteenth centuries were received with more caution in Germany. Here there was more emphasis on a natural or living model of the universe. For instance, Goltfred Wilhelm Leibnitz (1646–1716), inventor (along with Newton) of calculus, believed that every substance and idea had within itself the seed of its own future development. It was not, therefore, totally molded by external factors. Emmanual Kant (1724–1804), though recognizing the importance of the environment, said that men had the ability to raise themselves up above the limitations which it imposed. Moreover, when they did so they became more truly themselves. He also believed that the existence of God could not be proved or disproved by rationalist methods and that attempts to do so only served to undermine the beliefs of the common man since it is always possible to compose a rational counterargument or antithesis.

George Friedrich Hegel (1770–1831) believed that rationalist and mechanistic theories of society could not explain history because they implied that in similar circumstances similar societies should emerge. He argued that this is not the case and gave as an example Italy, where conditions in the eighteenth century were very much like what they had been in the first century, and yet the societies of the two periods were very different from each other. The laws of society are not like the laws of physics which imply repetitiveness. They are more like those of geology or botany where the impact of past experience is cumulative. History is essentially about developments and changes in prevailing ideas and cultures. It is a nonrepetitive process which develops in a series of cataclysms followed by periods of quiet. The individual is part of the time he lives in, deeply affected by the ideas and culture of his society. Culture affects all aspects of human endeavor and every aspect of society: politics, law, education, history, literature, the arts, science are all intertwined. Every idea and culture breeds within itself an opposite (antithesis) with which it will struggle until suddenly the tension will break with cataclysmic force. At this point a new idea or culture (synthesis) drawn from the others will emerge, which in time will breed an opposite—and so the process continues without end.

Some of the great cataclysms of history, as quoted by Hegel, have been the times when there was acceptance of the ideas of Socrates, Jesus and Newton. It was the job of philosophy to identify these underlying forces so that there could be a real understanding of what was happening in society. Man could only achieve true freedom and fulfillment by aligning himself with the underlying forces in his culture. If he attempted to improve ideas by force before their natural time, as during the French Revolution, then the result would be frustration and failure. Hegel's ideas almost amounted to a denial of an independent morality and an assertion that what is is what ought to be.

The magnificent sweep of Hegel's dialectical historicalism captured the imagination of many of the educated classes in Germany and Russia in the years following the Napoleonic wars. Conservatives saw in them a justification for the post-Napoleonic reaction in Germany. German culture and the Prussian state were, they thought, the latest developments in history and therefore, the most advanced. If what exists is reality, then it was both wrong and futile to oppose it.

Soon, however, the conservatives were increasingly opposed by others, known as the Young Hegelians, who argued strenuously that reality is what is rational, not what actually exists. Existing society, they insisted, was full of contradictions. It was the duty of thinkers to be critical and to point out what was rational. Criticism would create tensions which would eventually lead to a revolution in the ideas which guided society and its actions. Such a revolution need not involve mobs or violence which the Young Hegelians, for the most part, considered irrational and counterproductive.

The Prussian government kept close watch on the universities where these debates were raging. As a result, the Young Hegelians, many of whom were professors, avoided linking their ideas directly with politics for fear of losing their jobs, or worse. Instead, much of the debate was expressed in terms of religion which by this time could be discussed fairly openly in Prussia without fear of sanctions. One of the most famous contributions to the debate was the publication in 1835 of *A Life of Jesus* in which the author, David Friedrich Strauss (1808–1874), methodically analyzed the Gospels and identified many of the stories as myths and only a few as based on historical facts. This book was attacked by others who felt it was too moderate.

More radical was an assault on Hegel's theory by Ludwig Andreas Feuerbach (1804–1872). He asserted that all ideas and culture are determined by the material conditions of society and, therefore, what must be studied are these material conditions. Religion develops as a result of the material needs and fears of society. He dismissed Hegel's *Idea* as just another word for God.

The second group influencing the ideas of Marx was the early French socialist movement. The call for communally-held property and greater economic equality has a long history and can be traced at least as far back as Plato. However, it was not until the nineteenth century and the coming of the French and Industrial Revolutions that the idea graduated from being the occasional dream of fringe eccentrics into a serious political alternative supported by a substantial number of people.

Though the objective of most of those involved in the French Revolution was political and social equality, there were others who also fought for economic equality as well. A small group called the Company of Equals led by Gracchus Babeuf (1760–1797) issued a manifesto saying that all men should enjoy the goods provided by nature, that all men should work, that all had a right to education, and that extremes of wealth and poverty should be abolished in the interest of human happiness. Public ownership of all land and industry could only be achieved by force in a revolution led by a small and ruthless group of professional revolutionaries who would then wield dictatorial power until the dispossessed classes were ready to run affairs for themselves. Babeuf was executed after the government discovered the group's plans for a coup.

The idea of a socialist society achieved by a dedicated

group of revolutionaries was later taken up by Jérome Adolphe Blanqui (1798–1881), who published his views in a journal called *L'Homme Libré*. After leading a failed coup against the Orleanist monarchy in 1839, he spent most of the rest of his life in the prisons of each succeeding regime. It was Blanqui who first coined the phrase "dictatorship of the proletariat," later adopted by Marx.

Other French intellectuals concerned about economic justice, but appalled by the excesses of the French revolution, believed that a socialist society could be achieved by peaceful means. The Comte de Saint-Simon (1760–1825) advocated social ownership of the means of production and the direction of the state by those with the greatest scientific and business knowledge. Wages and rewards should be graded according to merit and degree of contribution to the general good. The state should provide work for all, and all should work to the best of their ability. There would be no room for parasitical nonproducers as in the past. Saint Simon believed that with advances in education and technology men would recognize the rationality of his ideas and would set up a world society organized along these lines.

Somewhat different was the view of Francois Marie Charles Fourier (1772–1837), who was convinced that the competitive spirit encouraged by capitalism, which he believed inevitably lead to lower wages and longer working hours for the poorer classes, was not natural. He included in a list of man's twelve basic passions a desire for love, friendship and cooperation as well as material satisfaction. He proposed that the state be gradually replaced with a network of cooperative settlements, essentially agricultural in nature, to be called "phalanteries," each with about 1,500 persons, which would be federated into increasingly larger units to carry out functions too large for the individual cooperatives. Men and women would be equal, personal property would be permitted, and the emphasis would be on pride in working voluntarily for the common good.

Pierre Joseph Proudhon (1809–1865), a typesetter from a peasant family, took a more radical position. He saw accumulation of capital in private hands as the source of exploitation which he summed up in the expression, "What is property? Property is theft." He believed that only a minimum of possessions are necessary for each individual's independence, and for his moral and social dignity. He too advocated a "mutualist" cooperative system, essentially based on agriculture, which he believed could be more civilized and efficient than the capitalist system. He said that the workers should set up their cooperatives by themselves and not become involved in politics where they would always be manipulated by the more sophisticated bourgeois. Nor should they try violent revolution which only resulted in control by evil men. His ideas were to a large extent adopted by the syndicalist movement which came to prominence in France, Italy, Spain, and South America in the late nineteenth and early twentieth centuries.

Yet another important French socialist of the time was Louis Blanc (1811–1882). He believed that the state should be organized as a parliamentary democracy, that it should give recognition to the right to work for all men, and that it should provide capital for national workshops under public ownership and managed collectively by the workers. He coined the phrase, "From each according to his abilities, to each according to his needs," taken up later by the Marxists.

The third group of thinkers who influenced Marx were the early English economists of the free trade school, most notably Adam Smith (1723–1790) and David Ricardo (1772–1823). Adam Smith maintained that job specialization and concentration on what one can do best is a practice which is both natural and conducive to efficiency and maximum benefit to society. (Here he differed from some of the French enlightenment philosophers who believed that man was in his most natural state when living in a small primitive community where each person had a balanced all-round range of tasks.) This division of labor theory he applied to countries as well as to individuals. Therefore, the existing mercantilist practice of restricting imports to protect home industries and to build up a surplus of gold was contrary to the real interests of a country and mankind in general. Instead, there should be free trade between countries so as to allow each country to maximize its wealth by buying and selling goods at the lowest world price.

Of particular interest to Marx were Smith's theories on price and value. Smith said that there is a natural price for everything at the point where supply and demand are in balance. The main elements on the supply side were profits for the capitalist, wages for the worker, and rent for the landowner on whose land the product had been made. Of these elements, Smith said, labor was the ultimate and real standard by which the value of all commodities can at all times be measured and compared. David Ricardo developed this theme by arguing that rent was not a real factor. He regarded capital as stored up labor and assumed that the proportion of capital to labor was roughly the same for the production of all goods. On this basis he discounted capital also as a cost factor and maintained, accordingly, that the normal price of goods tended to be proportional to the amount of labor required to produce them. Ricardo deduced from these theories that the interests of workers, capitalists and landowners are antagonistic because an increase in the proportion taken by one of the three parties would lead to a reduction in the amount available for the other two.

A Summary of Marxist Philosophy. Perhaps the starting point for Marxist philosophy is the idea that the history of society is the history of man striving to attain mastery over himself and over the external world through creative labor which transforms nature and distinguishes him from animals. In other words, history is about man's struggle to achieve freedom from physical circumstances and to reach his own full potential. In the most primitive societies man is occupied with the most basic struggle to obtain the minimum essentials of food, clothing and shelter. In response to the harsh challenges of this time, man invented improved ways of obtaining what he needed. One of the improved methods was the division of labor whereby each individual specializes in what he does best and exchanges his products for those made by others, rather than struggling to be self-contained and to fulfull all of his own requirements. Specialization meant increased efficiency so that total wealth could exceed the minimum necessary to survive.

But division of labor also meant inequality between men. The more efficient could produce more than others and then take advantage of their position to further increase their wealth by dominating those who were weaker than themselves. The result was the division of mankind into two broad groups: the exploiters and the exploited. As material things necessary to sustain life are the most important factors in being, it follows that a man's position in society, or his class—whether he is an exploiter or one of the exploited—is far more significant than other factors, such as nation, culture and religion, which are all superficial reflections of the fundamental relationship.

Marx then takes these theories a step further. History is about the continuous struggle between the exploiters and the exploited—about the continued efforts of the exploiters to take increasing advantage of their situation, and of the resistance of the exploited. History is a single continuous process and does not proceed in cycles or otherwise repeat itself. It follows certain laws, but these laws are not like the laws of physics which are unchanging. They are rather like those of the natural sciences which take account of a changing environment. History does not proceed along a straight line of progress; the struggle between exploiters and exploited may, in the short run, swing to the advantage of the exploiters. Eventually, however, the exploiters push their advantage to an extreme; and then the exploited, in sheer desperation, find the strength to overthrow their tormentors. There is a cataclysmic change in society and a new group acquires dominance and in turn becomes a new exploiting class. This dialectical process involves a force (thesis), and a counter force (antithesis), and out of the struggle between them a third force (synthesis) emerges. This law was named historical materialism.

Marx identified the first phase in history as the primitive stage where there was little significant division of labor beyond the family. The second phase was that of slave owning societies, as in ancient Greece and Rome. Here the dominant group obtained economic advantage by forcing the subservient group to give up every aspect of freedom and become in effect their property, along with land, buildings, goods, and chattels. This was succeeded by a third "feudal" phase in which the dominant group, the aristocrats, developed a more complex relationship of rights and duties with the subservient group. Here the latter were obliged to work for the former and provide them with a multitude of goods and services in return for a range of protective services. The character of each historical phase is determined by the level of technology of the time and each succeeds the last as technology advances. The first three phases in history were only outlined briefly by Marx as a background to his main interest—the emergence of a fourth new capitalist phase.

In the modern age new machines make it possible to farm the land with fewer laborers. As a result, many of the latter move to the towns in search for work. At the same time, bourgeois entrepreneurs build factories powered with new engines which greatly increase productivity. The factory owners are able to sell their products more cheaply than ordinary artisans. The latter, accordingly, are unable to sell their products. In order to survive, they have to sell off what equipment and property they have, and ultimately to sell themselves, that is, to sell their labor to the factory owner or capitalist. They become a class of property-less employees—the proletariat. A man's labor is an expression of himself, indeed part of himself. When he sells it and its product is no longer his to dispose of as he likes, he is deprived and depersonalized in a very profound sense. He can have no interest in the system and becomes totally alienated. As the capitalist class acquires more and more wealth, it becomes even more powerful than the feudal landowners and demands a change in the political and social structure to reflect that power, as happened for instance in the French Revolution.

Marx argued that labor is the source of and determinant of real value in a good or service. A material thing has no value unless it has been worked on by man, modified in stucture, or transported, etc. Marx defined labor as the average amount required to make a socially needed product. He recognized that the amount would change as the tools used improved. The vast wealth of the capitalist gives him a leverage over his employees whereby he is able to force them to accept wages which are no more than is sufficient to keep them efficient and productive workers. The difference between these wages and the amount he is able to sell their product for, which Marx called the surplus value, he keeps for himself.

As noted earlier, man's inventions, including the division of labor, have meant that the average person can produce more with his labor each day than is necessary just to survive. The capitalist may use some of this surplus value to acquire unnecessary luxuries, but he will use most to acquire more buildings and equipment to increase the efficiency of his employees. In this sense he is playing a useful, necessary, and progressive role in potentially increasing the total wealth of society. The capitalists have to compete fiercely in order to survive. They struggle to acquire more employees and more equipment in order to be able to undercut the prices of the products of their rivals. Those who lose in this struggle, like everyone else in society, gradually sink into the property-less class of the proletariat.

Trade goes through a cycle of alternating depressions which are caused by overproduction, and booms which are caused by shortages. During the depressions marginal capitalists become bankrupt and have to sell their machinery at bargain prices to those who are successful; more workers become part of a reserve army of unemployed which makes it easier for the capitalists to force down wages. At first, during the booms, the successful capitalists prosper as a result of the gains they made in the depression. But soon they need more and more capital to finance the additional equipment they need to increase efficiency in order to compete. As the extra capital can only be acquired by increasing profits from the real source of value which is the labor of their employees, they increasingly force down the wages of the proletariat, adding to their misery. The system builds to a crisis. To defend themselves, the remaining big capitalists form temporary alliances to manipulate the market. So in fact they undermine the principles of laissez faire and economic freedom which are the foundations of the system's efficiency. The ups and downs of the trade cycle become increasingly disastrous and eventually lead to wars between nations. Suffering the most from these crises is the proletariat which has grown to be by far the largest segment of the population and is massed and disciplined in the factories and cities.

Eventually there will be a cataclysm. The hollow political and social system, now supported by only a small minority, will collapse and a new classless era will begin. The collapse of the capitalist class will leave only the proletariat. Because it does not own any property, it will not give birth to a new exploiting class as has happened in the past. After the revolution, all property will be owned in common for the benefit of all,[5] the right of inheritance will be abolished, there will be more taxes, production will be increased, work will be compulsory, and there will be free education for all. This will mark the end of man's prehistory and the beginning of a time when man will be free at last of economic insecurity. Society will be organized according to the principle, "to everyone according to his need, from everyone according to his capacity." Men are naturally good, and when freed from economic oppression will work together to develop their full potential.

These underlying historical laws, Marx claimed, have been obscured by superficial aspects of society. People have been misled into believing that history is the result of the workings of God, or accidents, or ideas and philosophies, or culture, or the actions of great and powerful individuals. Social institutions and practices have been constructed by the ruling class, sometimes unconsciously, for their own benefit. The structure of the state and the law are there to strengthen and confirm their privileges. When a new class of exploiters rises to the top, the state and the law have to be changed accordingly. If this is not done peacefully with the assent of the old dominant class, then it is achieved by violent revolution. Marx admitted, however, that the state is not always the creature of the ruling class, and can sometimes acquire a semi-independent life of its own in the interest of its own bureaucrats.

The culture and morals of a society will reflect the interests of the ruling class by justifying its privileges and the exploitation of the lower classes. One example is the free trade theory which argues that there will be maximum efficiency in the economy, which will benefit all classes, if the capitalists are given complete freedom from state control. Another example is the family, the inferior position of women, and the prominent position of the eldest son—all of which strengthen inequalities in society. Yet another is nationalism which is used to split the working classes. Culture and ethics are also used to disguise the economic realities and divert attention to other matters. One of the most important devices in this respect is religion which promotes obedience and acceptance of inequality and misery in this world by promising a better balance in a future heaven. Like opium it dulls the critical faculties of the people.

In short, all morality is relative and is determined by the class structure. There is no independent ethical system. Marx did not condemn capitalists on grounds of morality. The capitalist is only following the laws of history, as will the proletariat when it establishes the classless society. Like Hegel, he argued that the only morality is to work in step with history. In this sense *is* and *ought* are the same. In this age, morality means to assist the fall of capitalism.

This brings us to the next step in the development of the Marxist system. The materialistic dialectic is clearly a deterministic view of history and implies that even without conscious action by man society will inevitably move from the feudal system, through capitalism, to communism. But as in many other deterministic systems, men have the freedom to speed up or slow down the historical process. Marx argued that men have a duty to promote the cause of the proletariat in order to counter the activities of the capitalists who will do all in their power to slow down history. By speeding it up, the misery and suffering of the proletariat will be reduced.

It is the responsibility of the intellectual and the philosopher to tear aside the superficial veil of culture and morality and expose the exploitation of the proletariat.[6] They then should show the workers how to achieve power by acting in unison. The proletariat are like the fingers of the hand—weak when extended but powerful when curled into a fist to smash the capitalist system. They should also be shown what the new world would offer when capitalism has been finally overthrown. It is not enough to talk. Philosophers and intellectuals must be men of action. This is the core of

Marxist philosophy. His writings for the most part assume the materialistic dialectic and say little about the future communist society. They are mostly concerned with the details of the rise and fall of capitalism and the tactics necessary to promote its fall.

Raising the consciousness of the proletariat requires the organization of a communist party to act as a vanguard for the working class. It should not be another political sect, but ultimately should be representative of the whole proletariat. The party should not be secretive and conspiratorial because such methods are ultimately ineffective. Instead, the party should be open and frank about its objectives and methods. Every means should be used to forward the interest of the working class. Trade unions should be formed and strike action should be taken whenever feasible, not just to raise wages and improve working conditions, but to put maximum pressure on the capitalist system so as to hasten its decline.

The party should seek to have its representatives elected to bourgeois capitalist parliaments where they should eventually have a majority—after all, the proletariat will become the biggest class in the capitalist society. The party may make temporary alliances with bourgeois parties, including nationalist movements, to help overthrow the feudalistic systems where they still exists. This will speed up the inevitable rise of capitalism, and thus shorten the period before the achievement of a communist society. However, there can be no reconciliation between the interests of the capitalists and the proletariat. The party must under no circumstances compromise its basic principles and support reforms within the capitalist system. This will only serve to strengthen it and delay the desired revolution. It should always be remembered that the proletariat is the only truly revolutionary class because it has no property and, therefore, no vested interest in the present system. All other classes, including the petit bourgeoise, skilled artisans, and most of the peasantry will tend to look backward hoping that history will be reversed so that past privileges will be restored. This is not possible.

But action should not be restricted to trade unions and parliamentary politics. If the opportunity presents itself, for instance during an economic crisis or a war, the proletariat should not hesitate to organize a revolution. If these tactics result in the overthrow of capitalism before it has reached its nadir and collapsed of it own accord, there may remain a proportion of the population which is still property owning and which will therefore be resistant to the revolution and the establishment of a communist society. To insure achievement of the ultimate goal of a classless society, it would be necessary in such circumstances to have a transitionary socialist period under a dictatorship of the proletariat.

Marx struggled with the question, raised by his Russian followers, of whether or not it was possible for a socialist revolution to be achieved without going through the full capitalist phase. Clearly, there would be the great difficulty that the real revolutionary class, the proletriat, would be a minority. The most numerous class would be the peasantry who are not concentrated physically for collective action and who are divided between those who have property and those who do not. Experience in the French revolutions of 1789, 1848, and 1870, was that the peasantry would be conservative and sympathetic to the ruling classes unless driven to extreme misery. Nevertheless, Marx concluded that a successful revolution might be possible in Russia, but only if it sparked revolutions in the fully developed capitalist countries; otherwise, such a revolution would fail.

There were certainly many connections between Marx's philosophy and those of others, and there have been critics who have tried to dismiss Marx by showing that he said little that was original. Marx himself was modest on this issue. For instance with regard to the class struggle he said:

> And now as to myself, no credit is due to me for discovering the existence of classes in modern society or the struggle between them. . . . What I did that was new was to prove 1) that the existence of classes is only bound up with particular phases of the development of production, 2) that the class struggle necessarily leads to the dictatorship of the proletariat, and 3) that this dictatorship itself only constitutes the transition to the abolition of all classes and to a classless society.[7]

Such attacks do not detract from the power of the total scheme of Marx's philosophy which has not only inspired revolutions and new political systems, but has deeply affected a whole range of thought in the modern world in such fields as law, philosophy, economics, sociology, and history.

A Bahá'í Perspective on Marxism. Some Bahá'í commentary might be made on four broad aspects of Marxism: religion and the nature and purpose of man, the structure of history, the just society, and how the just society is to be achieved. However, before discussing these, some comment should be made about the general concerns and motivation of Marx. It is apparent that the driving force behind Marx's life was a righteous anger at the contemporary exploitation of the poor, particularly the working classes, by the middle and upper classes. His concern was a burning desire for social justice. This concern should touch the heart of every Bahá'í since justice is the central principle of the Bahá'í Faith.

Marx was from the middle class and could have chosen a comfortable life for himself and his family. Instead, he devoted his life to the cause of those who were less well off than he and suffered much privation. Selflessness in the service of others is also in accordance with Bahá'í principles. Though many Marxists have had very different concerns and motives, there have always been those who had the same ones as Marx himself and justice demands that this be recognized.[8]

Turning now to the aspects of Marxism where some Bahá'í commentary can be made, it is obvious that there are fundamental differences in outlook with regard to religion and the nature and purpose of man. However, it is worth looking into this subject briefly so as to establish more precisely what the differences are and so avoid prejudice and exaggeration on either side.

Marx held to the view of the eighteenth century rationalists that man's nature is deeply affected by his environment. If economic and social injustice are eliminated, he believed that then man would be naturally good and would work for the general welfare. This is a positive and optimistic view often held by those who wish to reform a society. It contrasts sharply with the traditional teachings of the Church which portray man as essentially sinful. Marx saw the main purpose of life as the achievement of freedom from scarcity of essential material things of life. Such scarcity originally resulted from primitive technology, but now, for the most part, results from exploitation by others. Once that freedom is achieved, man can develop all his faculties and reach his full potential. A man's potential is expressed in his creative labor; when he has to work for someone else, and not for himself, and the fruit of his labor is taken from him, he is alienated and frustrated.

The Bahá'í view of the nature of man falls between that of Marx and that of the Christian tradition. It sees both good and evil aspects in the nature of man. The positive aspect, the spiritual, justifies the rationale for reforming society because it recognizes that reform will change man for the better. On the other hand, the recognition that there is an animal, self-centered side of man implies that a just society requires not only changes in the structure of collective action, but also constant effort to develop individual personal qualities. In the Bahá'í view, a just society can only work if its members are themselves just.

This view is not in direct contradiction to that of Marx, only more complex and more realistic. Perhaps one major reason for the failures of the radical left is the assumption that reform can be imposed from above. A classic example is the typical welfare housing scheme where poor people, used to living in deplorable conditions, are suddenly given bright new homes, but with little encouragement to motivate them to take pride in them. The result is that the new homes all too often degenerate into slums little better than the old homes.

Bahá'ís and Marxists agree that the purpose of life is the development of one's own full potential. However, for Bahá'ís, this process is not only necessary for human happiness on earth, but is also an essential preparation for a spiritual life after death. The Marxist emphasis on creative labor is echoed, in slightly different terms, in Bahá'í teachings which require that all should engage in a useful occupation, which state that work is worship, and which hold that work in the service of humanity is the highest form of worship.[9]

Fundamental views about the nature and purpose of man are closely linked to religion. Marx saw religion, like other ideas, as merely a superficial reflection of the fundamental economic conditions of society. It was essentially a device for diverting the attention of the poor from the contrast between their own misery and the privileges of the upper classes with promises of paradise after death. Certainly Marx had good reason to be critical of religion. In his day, as now, Christian churches were divided against each other. They had obscured the original spiritual teachings of

Jesus with a mass of superstition and dogma and, for the most part, they supported the status quo and the privileges of the upper classes.

Bahá'ís also abhor religion when it displays such characteristics. On the question of disunity, for instance, 'Abdu'l-Bahá said:

> Religion should unite all hearts and cause wars and disputes to vanish from the face of the earth, give birth to spirituality, and bring life and light to each heart. If religion becomes a cause of dislike, hatred and division, it were better to be without it, and to withdraw from such a religion would be a truly religious act.[10]

He went on to say that superstition is not reconcilable with true religion:

> Any religious belief which is not conformable with scientific proof and investigation is superstition, for true science is reason and reality, and religion is eventually reality and pure reason; therefore, the two must correspond.[11]

> Religion and science are the two wings upon which man's intelligence can soar into the heights, with which the human soul can progress. It is not possible to fly with one wing alone! Should a man try to fly with the wing of religion alone he would quickly fall into the quagmire of superstition, whilst on the other hand, with the wing of science alone he would also make no progress, but fall into the despairing slough of materialism.[12]

A crucial aspect of the credibility of the churches was their presentation of a God which was too simple for thinking men. 'Abdu'l-Bahá is reported to have said to an agnostic that "the God you do not believe in I do not believe in either." The Bahá'í concept is captured in the following passage:

> So perfect and comprehensive is His creation that no mind nor heart, however keen or pure, can ever grasp the nature of the most insignificant of His creatures; much less fathom the mystery of Him Who is the Day Star of Truth, Who is the invisible and unknowable Essence. The conceptions of the devoutest of mystics, the attainments of the most acomplished amongst men, the highest praise which human tongue or pen can render are all the product of man's finite mind and are conditioned by its limitations.[13]

True religion, though it gives a perspective to life by putting it in a spiritual context, is not concerned with lulling the peoples of the world into acceptance of the way things are. On the contrary, it has as its main thrust their motivation to create a better world. The Bahá'í Faith is committed to the building of a new world based on peace and justice. An important aspect of such a society is the protection of the poor and abolition of poverty.

The second aspect of Marxism on which commentary from a Bahá'í perspective can be made, the structure of history, presents some interesting parallels between the two movements. Both see progress in history, rather than endless cycles of repetition as happens in nature. Both see the progress as coming about in periodic surges at times of cataclysmic events, rather than as a smooth line. Both agree that history has now reached the point of another major cataclysm. When it has taken place, there will be an end to history as known so far and the start of a new phase of man's development. There will be a new world society which will not have the same dynamic of rise and fall as in the past. In both systems there will be a transitional period between the collapse of the old system and the coming of the new.

The details, of course, differ. In Marxist theory the cataclysms come about as a result of the victory of an oppressed class over its oppressors after a long period of struggle. The imminent cataclysm is the one which will result from the struggle of the proletariat to free itself from the exploitation of capitalism.[14] There will be a period of transition when the workers will have made a revolution, but before all other classes have disappeared and there is a true classless society. To protect the interests of the proletariat from outside attack by the remaining capitalist countries and from within by the remaining upper classes, there will have to be a socialist state directed by a dictatorship. Only when these threats have disappeared will it be possible for the state to wither away and for the era of true communism to begin.[15]

Though Bahá'ís recognize the importance of material conditions, they believe that man's cultural and spiritual evolution is ultimately the most significant element of history. The Bahá'í Faith shares with Marxism a special concern for the interest of the poor. Bahá'ís can also recognize that the concept of economic class may be useful in illuminating certain aspects of society and history. Nevertheless, class warfare is quite alien to the teachings of the Bahá'í Faith which are intended to provide for the needs of all mankind, regardless of class or any other division.

As a practical matter, a just society cannot be imposed by one class motivated by hatred of other classes. It must come about with the support of all peoples working according to the highest principles of selflessness instilled by real religion. In addition, an extreme emphasis on class has the danger of creating insensitivity to the individual and basic human rights. This tendency is aggravated by dismissing individualism as bourgeois and seeing the proletariat as having interest only in economic matters and collective action.

For Bahá'ís the cataclysms which have been mentioned above are caused by the periodic appearance of Manifestations of God. These prophets bring new teachings for changing conditions and a revival of spiritual awareness in response to the needs of the old society which is suffering because of the decline of the previous religion. The present cataclysm is centered around the coming of Bahá'u'lláh. As a result of His teachings, for the first time in history, the creation of a democratic and spiritually-based world government and the establishment of the Most Great Peace become possible. As in Marxism there is a period of transition. The Bahá'í period of transition is the Lesser Peace during which the countries of the world gradually adopt collective security on a world scale. They will be forced to do so to avoid total disaster, but they would not yet have reached the stage of world spiritual unity which will underpin the permanent Most Great Peace.

The third aspect of Marxism for our discussion is what one would expect to be its heart, the model of the ideal society which it advocates. In fact, Marx wrote comparatively little about this subject. To a large extent it is necessary to rely on the practice of established Marxist governments—particularly those long established—to obtain a reasonably full picture of the type of society Marxists wish to create. A review of this subject can perhaps be grouped around three broad themes: economy, development of the mind and spirit, and world unity in diversity.

Like the Bahá'í Faith, Marxism stresses that in a future economy, cooperation should be a principle feature and that extremes of wealth and poverty must be abolished. Most Marxist countries have tried to achieve these ends through provision of a comprehensive welfare program and almost total government ownership of all means of production, distribution and banking. Absolute control of the economy by a Marxist central government was first practiced under the War Communism policy of the Russian civil war period, and then later institutionalized by Stalin in the Five Year Plans. However, Marx did not state that such centralization must be an essential feature of the socialist state. Lenin himself abandoned War Communism at the end of the Russian Civil War in favor of the New Economic Policy which gave a greater role to both the independent peasant and to private industrial capital. In Yugoslavia, local communities and individual factories have been given a considerable degree of independence; and some local initiative was encouraged in China during the period of the Great Leap Forward. Marxist theorists of both East and West have for some time pressed for greater decentralization and diversity in the interest of efficiency, even if such a policy might lead to greater inequality.[16]

In the ultimate communist state it was hoped that there would be sufficient wealth to pay each according to his needs. But during the transitional socialist phase, in the interest of productivity, it was recognized that payment would have to be according to effort. For instance, Lenin insisted on piece work rules, and Stalin introduced the Stakhnovite reward system for those whose production exceeded the norm. Generally, and perhaps inevitably in view of the special role of the proletariat in creation of the new society, Marxism seems to have put most emphasis on industry as the engine for the production of wealth, and left agriculture with a purely secondary role. As a result, agricultural policies in many communist countries have not been successful.

What we can see of a future Bahá'í economy indicates some parallels with and some differences from Marxist practice. In terms of organization, it is clear that Bahá'ís advocate a comprehensive welfare program and allow the state some role in the economy, seeing to the fair distribution of natural resources—partly through ownership of key enterprises at international, national and local levels.

However, there would also be considerable decentralization and diversification, with roles for cooperatives, profit sharing companies, and individual entrepreneurs. Complete equality would not be attempted, but the abolition of poverty would be sought through such policies as universal compulsory education, voluntary giving, and progressive taxation, public ownership of minerals in the ground, as well as by the system of organizing enterprises. The welfare of the population depends not only on organizational structure but on what the economy produces. The Bahá'í teachings put emphasis on those goods and services which are essential for the physical and spiritual well being of man and discount luxuries, waste, and above all—those destroyers of the human body, mind and spirit—alcohol, tobacco and drugs. Partly on account of these factors, it is envisaged that agriculture would play a central role in the economy.

With regard to the development of mind and spirit, Maxism has always stressed the importance of education as a means of realizing greater equality and releasing human potential. Lenin wanted to raise the status of the teacher, and he saw education as a means whereby the proletariat could learn to govern itself and so do without a specialized party bureaucracy which might serve its own separate interests. In practice, however, education in Marxist countries has put most emphasis on teaching Marxist theory and on practical skills which would benefit the economy rather than on encouragement of independent thinking about social issues. Marx viewed philosophy as essentially a reflection of the economic relationships in society. It is only a short step from this idea to discouraging any thinking within a socialist society which is not directly supportive—the development of censorship and state guidance of intellectual life. Furthermore, the danger to freedom of thought has been exacerbated by the practice of establishing a highly centralized political, economic and social structure which, by its very nature, tends to be resistant to a diversity of ideas. This trend reached an extreme point in the Soviet Union under Stalin when all independent public expression was silenced, history was systematically rewritten, the arts were limited to social realism, and even the sciences were guided, sometimes with disasterous results, as in the Lysenko case.[17] It is true that there are many Marxists with a more liberal approach to intellectual freedom, but so far they have been a minority and have not held power.

The develoment of mind and spirit is of greatest import in the Bahá'í Faith. The role of the teacher in society is elevated. Education must be balanced between the practical sciences, the arts, and spiritual education. Intellectual integrity is seen as essential in the search for truth, regardless of the subject. There is no official Bahá'í art, though with the passage of time it may be expected that the work of Bahá'í artists will increasingly reflect Bahá'í values.

The theme of world unity is found in Marxist philosophy to a limited extent. Marx did not specifically mention world government, but he was international in his outlook. This is conveyed by his exhortation, "Workers of all lands unite; you have nothing to lose but your chains." This is a call which finds a response in every Bahá'í heart, though no doubt Bahá'ís would prefer the wider term *peoples* rather than *workers*. Marx believed that class interests crossed national boundaries and gave full support to the First International Workingman's Association. International solidarity was shown by the First International, by socialist members of the Prussian Bundestag in connection with the Franco-Prussian War of 1870–71.[18] Also, by the Russian Bolsheviks at the beginning of the First World War when they refused to support the Russian war effort and called for "revolutionary defeatism."

The international view of Marxism did not seem to imply a monolithic culture, beyond the issue of economic organization. Though Marx himself showed little interest in national cultures, the Russian communist party when it first came to power was actually fairly liberal in its attitude toward minority nationalities. All this changed drastically with the coming of Stalin. He adopted a policy of socialism in one country, and used the communist parties of other countries in the interests of the Soviet Union, rather than in the interests of the workers of the world as a whole. Trotsky's efforts to promote international revolutionary solidarity were defeated; he was exiled and eventually assassinated. Respect for minority nationalities within the Soviet Union has declined also, as indicated by the treatment of the Russian Jews since the end of the Second World War and by the increasing predominance of the White Russians.

For the Bahá'í Faith, the goal of one united world is central to its social teachings. Such phrases as, "The earth is but one country and mankind its citizens," and "Ye are the leaves of one branch," are among the most well known statements of the Faith. Already in its own internal administration it has a Universal House of Justice, an embryo world government elected by all the National Assemblies of the world community. Its representatives at the United Nations, and at the earlier League of Nations, have consistantly advised on the basis of a wide-world perspective. The idea of world unity is combined with respect for the rights and cultures of minorities; the greater the diversity the richer will be society as a whole. Conscious elimination of prejudice between peoples of different cultures is a major Bahá'í principle. Special pride is taken in the number of different tribes and nations represented in the Faith.

The fourth and final aspect of Marxism we will discuss is the practical matter of how the desired society is to come about, a subject which occupies a dominant place in Marxist literature. The theory of dialectical materialism implies that the capitalist system will collapse from its own internal inconsistancies. This determinist view of history is tempered with a call for action to the working class, which should use all of its power to speed the coming of cataclysm so as to reduce the suffering of the poor in the last stages of the capitalist system. The communist party would be the vanguard of the workers in this struggle.

At first, there was some ambiguity about the correct form of the party, but under the influence of Lenin it eventually developed into an elitist organization—a dedicated band of ruthless, professional revolutionaries, rather than a mass workers' party embracing all who accepted its principles. Later it became a tightly organized movement with appointments emanating from the top downward. There were separate isolated cells at the base of the system which had little lateral communication. This style was justified as necessary to counter infiltration by spies and agents provacateurs. Decision-making and discussion gradually became more secretive and conspiratorial. In the early days of the party there was much genuine internal debate, but this practice was suppressed by Stalin during the 1920s. In its most authoritarian phases, the Marxist system has produced a great leader—larger than life and free of error— a personality cult, which seems to be the direct opposite of the original intentions of Marx. Such leaders, with an arrogance rivaling the most absolute despots in history, have tried to impose their own revolutionary will on their countries. In so doing, they have made a disaster of worthwhile programs, like agricultural cooperation (collectivization in Russia), and minimization of bureaucracy (the Chinese Cultural Revolution), which might have been successful if supported and initiated by the mass of the people. The disasters also involved the destruction of large numbers of people who had given their all to bring about the revolution in the first place, the unfortunate irony of so many violent revolutions.

Like Marxists, Bahá'ís have a determinist view of history. They believe that, in accordance with the principles of progressive revelation, the present system will collapse of its own and that the Bahá'í Faith will inevitably be accepted by all mankind because its teachings are in accord to the needs of the time and there are no alternatives. There is also the call for action found in Marxism. Bahá'ís cannot sit back and wait for events to take their course, but must bend every effort to bring forward the time of change so as to minimize the growing suffering of the peoples of the world in the last stages of the present system. The Bahá'í Community is, therefore, seen as being in the vanguard of change, but its nature is very different from that which the communist party has developed. The Bahá'í concept is one of community: with universal participation in its affairs, with appointments coming from the base upward, and with encouragement of lateral communication and consultation. All institutions are collective; individuals have no independent source of authority. It is recognized that throughout history individual leaders have been corrupted by ego and fear. This open system has functioned in Iran, and elsewhere, despite persecution and attempts at infiltration by deeply hostile forces.

There are important details with regards to strategy and tactics to bring about change. Marx urged workers' organizations, including trade unions, not to waste time on short-term goals (such as improving wages and working conditions), but to concentrate on the long-term goals of harassing and weakening the capitalists and their governments. This so that when the opportune time arrives, the revolution will be that much easier. He was strongly opposed to any attempts to reform the capitalist system because he believed this would add to its strength. Marxists have been ready to form tactical alliances with other parties, even those of the bourgeoisie and aristocracy. But they have a long tradition of suspicion and hostility toward other socialists, who they see as potential rivals, rather than allies in achieving a new world society. Typical examples of such hostility are Marx's fierce attacks on the so-called utopian socialists, the refusal of the German communist party to ally with the Social Democrats to defeat the National Socialists in the 1930 elections, and the bitter infighting of the communist party against the other Republican parties in the Spanish Civil War.

Marxist parties have dismissed the idea of a morality independent of class welfare as bourgeois sentimentality. They have generally embraced the idea, in day to day tactics, that the end justifies the means, that anything which helps the revolution is legitimate. Lenin, for instance, was not concerned when fellow Bolsheviks robbed banks to fund the party before the First World War. Stalin and his successors used foreign idealists to steal military secrets from their own governments for the benefit of the Soviet Union—idealism was turned into treason. Though Marx and many of his followers hoped the revolution could be achieved with little violence, they recognized that there was a strong possibility that considerable violence might be necessary. Violent revolution was justified on the grounds that the capitalist system was already extremely violent in the way it treated the masses and that one clean sweep was needed to end this evil.

Bahá'ís agree with the Marxist view that time should not be wasted on short-term issues. It is partly on account of this principle that Bahá'ís do not become involved in party politics and do not believe in spending their time trying to patch up the present system. Instead, their main efforts are directed at the long-term goals of spreading knowledge of Bahá'í principles and practices and of building up an alternative system within their own community to which the world can turn in time of need. However, this does not preclude rendering services to the community at large, or giving support to other organizations which are striving to achieve goals which are compatible with those of the Faith (e.g., United Nations associations, peace movements, human rights organizations, women's organizations). Bahá'ís do not see others' efforts to reform the present system as a threat, but rather as a positive step toward establishment of the Lesser Peace. This is a stage on the way to the establishment of the permanent Most Great Peace. Bahá'ís also differ very much from Marxists with regard to the ethics of revolution. For a Bahá'í there can be no compromise with principles in the struggle to achieve the just society. There must be a positive attitude of love and empathy for all, rather than hatred—even for those who are opponents of the Faith. Above all there can be no question of violence. 'Abdu'l-Bahá stated:

> Fighting, and the employment of force, even for the right cause, will not bring about good results. The oppressed who have right on their side must not take that right by force; the evil would continue. Hearts must be changed.[19]

Bahá'ís believe that the just society can not be firmly established by force, but requires a change in values which only religion can achieve. 'Abdu'l-Bahá made the contrast explicit:

> In the Bolshevistic principles equality is effected through force. . . . But in the divine teachings equality is brought about through a ready willingness to share.[20]

To summarize, a Bahá'í can wholeheartedly approve of some aspects of Marxism, particularly its original motivation for social justice and the goal of abolishing extremes of wealth and poverty. Bahá'ís can also have a positive view, qualified to a greater or lesser extent, of other aspects of Marxism, such as its views of the purpose of man, the pattern of history, economic organization, world unity, and the need to concentrate on long-term issues. However, there are other aspects of Marxism which are not in accordance with Bahá'í principles. Most notably these include the absence of a spiritual dimension, the lack of commitment to intellectual integrity and an open society, encouragement of class hatred, hostility to other organizations with similar motivations and goals, the theory that the end justifies the means, and its acceptance of violence as a legitimate means in the struggle to achieve a new society.

Conclusion. One of the most important questions that springs to mind from such a review is: Has Marxism, on balance, added to the general well-being of human society and contributed to the advance of civilization? Such a question raises immense issues. It involves weighing, for instance, such positive factors as improvements in the material condition of the poor in many socialist countries, and such changes as the introduction of the welfare state in other parts of the world—which may have been partly prompted by fear of Marxism or the influence of its ideas—against other less positive factors such as authoritarianism, excessive suppression of freedom, bloody agricultural collectivization, the Great Purges in Russia, the Cultural Revolution in China, and genocide in Cambodia. Perhaps it is too early to try to answer such a question. Certainly it is one which will require much new research and a totally objective and detached approach. Perhaps it will require the political detachment and spiritual perspective of Bahá'í scholars.

A personal view is ventured that Marxism did have the potential for having a positive impact on the general well-being of human society because of its deep concern for social and economic justice. Initially it was not committed to an authoritarian style and need not necessarily have become hostile toward all religious concepts. It might be speculated that if Marxism had been adopted first in Germany, instead of in Russia, it might have become more democratic and more ready to take spiritual values into account. Failure to incorporate spiritual values into the system has been the fatal flaw of Marxism in practice. If this failure had been avoided, there may have been more humility in the leadership and a more humanitarian outlook.

It has been common in many Western countries, particularly in the United States, to treat Marxist ideas as no better than those of that other powerful authoritarian political movement of the twentieth century—fascism. It is suggested that Bahá'ís should take a very sceptical view of this facile and no doubt politically motivated judgment.

This view may seem to be contradicted by the following statement of Shoghi Effendi:

> The chief idols in the desecrated temple of mankind are none other than the triple gods of Nationalism, Racialism and Communism, at whose alters governments and peoples, whether democratic or totalitarian, at peace or at war, of the East or of the West, Christian or Islamic, are, in various forms and in different degrees, now worshipping. Their high priests are the politicians and the worldly-wise, the so-called sages of the age; their sacrifice, the flesh and blood of the slaughtered multitudes; their incantations outworn shibboleths and insidious and irreverent formulas; their incense, the smoke of anguish that ascends from the lacerated hearts of the bereaved, the maimed and the homeless.[21]

However, it is interesting that in this passage, although both fascism and communism are abhorred for their materialism, totalitarianism and violence, fascism is additionally abhorred for two of its fundamental characteristics: nationalism and racialism. There is no condemnation of the fundamental purpose of Marxism which is the abolition of extremes of wealth and poverty. Marxism, for all its faults, has been motivated, as noted earlier, by a profound concern for social justice. In response to that concern, it has advocated not only the abolition of the extremes of wealth and poverty, but also such Bahá'í values as an international point of view, recognition of minority cultural groups, and equality between men and women.

Fascism, on the other hand, is fundamentally dedicated to injustice; it is concerned with obtaining special privileges for certain nations or races at the expense of others. It is by nature authoritarian, intolerant of minorities, and hostile toward internationalism. It embraces the idea that war is necessary to ensure the survival of the fittest and the elimination of those who are weak. In its extreme form, National Socialism, the philosophy was taken to its logical conclusion with policies of genocide against Jews and Gypsies, systematic killing of the mentally and physically handicapped, and medical experiments on or enslavement of many others.

It might be argued that fascism is less atheistic than communism. Superficially, this may have been true in such countries as Spain and Italy where there was some relationship with the Catholic Church. But it should be noted that this relationship was only with that part of the church which was most reactionary in its social commitment, intolerant, and least concerned with the fundamental teachings of Jesus. In Germany, the National Socialists scorned Christianity for its "decadent sentimentality" and cultivated interest in the Nordic myths.[22]

A second important question which must arise in the context of an essay on the Bahá'í perspective on Marxism concerns thoughts (or perhaps speculation) on the future. In the context of the broad history of man, the coming of the Faith is seen by Bahá'ís as a crucial event. In the great cycle of the rise and decline of religions, it brings another time of spiritual renewal and advancement in civilization. This time, however, there is a unique quality to the phenomenon. After a long period of preparation by the prophetic religions, man has now reached maturity. The advance of civilization which is associated with the coming of the Bahá'í Faith is to be extraordinary insofar as it involves the establishment of world peace on a lasting basis.

Within this broad canvas, it is perhaps interesting to look at the Bahá'í Faith in the narrower perspective of modern times using the dialectic approach of Hegel. Thus it can be seen that established religion has become corrupted and hollow. It is challenged by a new atheistic force which in turn fails to satisfy human spiritual needs. As a result, a new religion emerges which confirms the universal spiritual principles of all religions, but which believes that religion and science must go hand in hand, which has ethical teachings adapted to the needs of the modern age, and which is free of corruption and superstitution.

On the social and economic level, an industrial laissez faire capitalist system created unduly harsh conditions for the poor. This led to a new force based on collective principles. But this force, in turn, has severe drawbacks, including excessive restraints on freedom, major inefficiencies, and an inability to envisage and exploit useful innovation. A synthesis of these two forces is provided in the Bahá'í Faith which advocates an economic and social system based on spiritual values, provides for man's desire to cooperate for the common good, and at the same time makes allowance for individual initiative and enterprise.

History has shown that religions often adapt and change according to local conditions and culture. This process has its dangers. Often in the past it has created disunity and allowed man-made corruptions to creep into the original pure teachings of the Founder of the religion. However, such diversity, if combined with unity in essential principles, can add to the richness of civilization. There are strong indications that the Bahá'í Faith may develop in this direction. On the one hand, there is the Bahá'í emphasis on the ultimate authority, with regard to principles and general practices of the Faith, being vested in the Writings of Bahá'u'lláh, the interpretations of 'Abdu'l-Bahá and Shoghi Effendi, and in the guidance of the Universal House of Justice. On the other hand, there is also an emphasis on decentralization, diversity, and appreciation of the positive aspects of all cultures. Though a broad picture of a Bahá'í world economy clearly emerges, the actual weightings which might be given to different factors—community enterprises, cooperatives, profit sharing companies, individual entreprenuers—is not laid down. Inevitably, it seems there will be some variation from region to region. Perhaps it is not unreasonable to speculate that in those countries of the world where there has been a socialist system which has had the approval of the majority, there may in the future develop a Bahá'í economy with more of an emphasis on community enterprises than in other countries where the majority have a preference for a more competitive system. Such variety would add to the total experience of the world community, making it more flexible, and more responsive and adaptive to changing conditions—the sign and essence of a healthy civilization.

Notes

1. Karl Marx was born on May 15, 1818, six months after Bahá'u'lláh. He died some nine years before Him, on March 14, 1883.

2. Christianity, for instance, took some three hundred years to have an important impact on society.

3. So far as the author is aware, there are no direct references to Marxism as such in the Bahá'í Writings. The most important references to communism are quoted in this paper. Other references in the writings of Shoghi Effendi which have relatively minor significance are: *Bahá'í Administration* (Wilmett, Ill.: Bahá'í Publishing Trust, 1928) pp. 105 and 160; *World Order of Bahá'u'lláh* (Wilmette, Ill.: Bahá'í Publishing Trust, 1938) pp. 181–82 and 190; and, *The Promised Day Is Come* (Wilmette, Ill.: Bahá'í Publishing Trust, 1941) p. 57.

4. Quoted in Alex Callinicos, *The Revolutionary Ideas of Karl Marx* (London: Bookmarks Publishing Cooperative, 1983) p. 46.

5. By property is meant the means of production, including land, banking and distribution. It is apparent that Marx did not

mean that individuals should not have their own personal items, such as clothes and various household chattels.

6. The intelligentsia may be drawn either from the working class, or from the auxiliaries of the capitalist class—much as doctors, lawyers, teachers, etc.—who have understood dialectical materialism and have gone over to the side of the workers.

7. Marx to Joseph Weydemeyer, March 1852, quoted in *Revolutionary Ideas.*

8. Reference to the character of Marx surely calls for some comment on Friedrich Engels, his lifelong partner. Engels' complete lack of ego and constant support for Marx, both emotionally and financially, over a period of nearly forty years is a model which is impossible not to respect and admire.

9. The Marxist theme of labor as man's expression of himself is closely linked with the labor theory of value. This theory, though refined to meet obvious problems with the role of capital in the creation of wealth, is not taken seriously by practical economists as the basis for explaining or setting prices, even in communist countries. For a short time, Robert Owen (1775–1858), the British socialist, ran a labor exchange where goods were traded for labor notes which represented the amount of time spent producing the goods, but the system soon failed because the prices did not take into account demand, that is, many goods were priced at a level consumers would not pay. Though Bahá'ís might recognize a crude sort of justice in the theory, there is nothing in the Bahá'í teachings which bear either way on its validity.

10. *The Bahá'í Revelation* (London: Bahá'í Publishing Trust, 1955) pp. 289–90.

11. *Paris Talks* (London: Bahá'í Publishing Trust, 1912), p. 143.

12. Ibid., p. 136–37.

13. *Gleanings from the Writings of Bahá'u'lláh* (Wilmette, Ill.: Bahá'í Publishing Trust, 1939) p. 62.

14. One of the principle criticisms which has been made of this Marxist theory is that the predictions that the capitalist system would be increasingly dominated by a decreasing number of extremely rich capitalists, that the proletariat would grow in numbers and suffer a declining standard of living, and that the system would soon collapse have not proved correct. Keynsian

economics, large increases in production, and the welfare state have gone a long way toward ameliorating conditions, and the standard of living of working people in industrial countries has risen rather than declined. Large corporations are a major element in the capitalist system, but they have been balanced by the emergence of a continuous stream of small new enterprises responding to changes in technology and a myriad of other factors. As a result, not one advanced industrial country has become Marxist of its own accord. Marxism has in fact been most accepted, contrary to Marx's own expectation, in essentially nonindustrial countries where the proletariat was a relatively small part of the population.

15. Marx did not say how long the period of transition might last. So far it has lasted sixty-five years since the first successful Marxist revolution in Russia and in the light of the world's political situtation there does not seem to be much chance that it will come to an end in the forseeable future. If ever the theoretical conditions do arise for the state to be dismantled, it might be speculated that there would be considerable bureaucratic inertia, if not to say resistance.

16. One of the standard criticisms of communism as practiced is the inefficiency of an overcentralized and bureaucratic economy. A recent example of left advocacy of greater decentralization is *The Economics of Feasible Socialism* by Alec Nove.

17. As disturbing as these activities of Stalin was the systematic destruction of a large number of records of the past going back for thousands of years during China's Cultural Revolution.

For decades, Russian biologists were forced to follow the principles of Lysenko who had, on the basis of poor research, put extreme emphasis on environmental factors as opposed to inheritance. This approach was thought to be more in conformity with Marxist principles. But it did not conform to reality.

18. It might be noted, however, that both Marx and Engels were happy to see a Prussian victory since they considered the Second Empire to be more reactionary—a fine point which is not too convincing in historical perspective.

19. *Pattern of Bahá'í Life* (London: Bahá'í Publishing Trust, 1948) p. 42.

20. *Foundations of World Unity* (Wilmette, Ill.: Bahá'í Publishing Trust, 1927) p. 44.

21. *The Promised Day Is Come*, pp. 117–18. It might be noted that this passage was written in 1941, following such events as the collectivization of agriculture, the Great Purges, the Nazi-Soviet Pact, and the outbreak of the Second World War.

22. Though Bahá'ís wholeheartedly abhor fascism, their teachings concerning intellectual integrity and the brotherhood of man give them understanding, and indeed some empathy, for those who were caught up in its false values. Many of these were the most hardworking and solid members of society: the lower middle class and skilled workers, who in the period after the First World War suffered greatly as a result of the economic dislocation which brought mass unemployment and hyperinflation, who were confused by the breakdown of established values, and who were fearful of communism and felt abandoned by the established political parties.

A Dialogue with Marxism

By Nader Saiedi

I T IS COMMON AMONG Bahá'ís to believe that Marxism and the Bahá'í Faith oppose and contradict one another in all their major principles. It is supposed that the two movements can find no common ground in their basic philosophical, social, economic, and political approaches. Underlying this conception, however, are the basic assumptions that there is only one form of Marxist theory and only one correct and orthodox interpretation of the Bahá'í Faith. Different assumptions may well lead to a different conclusion.

It can be argued that the Bahá'í Faith is not a static, closed, and rigidly defined set of teachings, but a vital and dynamic theoretical structure with a deep historical consciousness. The Bahá'í worldview has its basis in humanistic and democratic premises and is open to diverse interpretations and possibilities. Similarly, there exists no single Marxist theory or ideology. Marxism, as primarily a dialectical method, has experienced a variety of developments and interpretations which make it impossible to speak of Marxism in general as though it were one thing.

From this perspective, one may find that the Bahá'í Faith shares much in common with some versions of Marxist theory, particularly those of recent development. Therefore,

235

Marxists and Bahá'ís can, at least potentially, learn from one another and contribute to one another. Such mutual learning is one of the essential preconditions for the creation of a new world order based upon justice, unity and development.

DIALECTICS IS the fundamental philosophical ground of Marxist theory. Although most Marxists emphasize the significance of a dialectical approach, its precise meaning and location in Marxist ideology are matters of serious disagreement and controversy. Hegel's philosophy advocated a dialectical approach in which a concept passes over into and is preserved and fulfilled by its opposite. This approach in turn influenced Marx's theory and method.

One important area of debate among Marxists concerns whether dialectics is to be regarded as a specific theory and system or merely a method of analysis. Advocates of dialectics as method argue that it is a neutral approach which is compatible with a variety of theoretical systems. They maintain that this method can be used by both idealistic and materialist analysts. They argue that Hegel, for instance, believed in both idealism and the dialectical approach, while Marx called for a materialistic dialectic.[1]

Against this position, there are those who consider dialectics to be a theory, rather than only a method. These argue that dialectics is a theory of history that inevitably leads to belief in God, and is virtually an argument for God's existence. They insist that this theory can only be idealist and that there is no possibility of building a materialistic dialectic. These advocates of dialectic as theory ultimately reject the validity of dialectics altogether and find Marxism opposed to any true dialectical approach.[2]

Another area of debate concerns continuity and change in the writings of Marx himself. According to some theorists, the thought of Marx in his later years is entirely different from that of his early years. The young Marx, they argue, was Hegelian and accepted a Hegelian dialectic, whereas the older Marx rejected these ideas and developed a distinct dialectic of his own. Opponents of such an epistemological break in Marx's thought, however, argue that his approach was essentially the same after 1844, and that his notion of dialectic is always Hegelian.

Moreover, there is disagreement even among those who believe in a break in Marx's thought. Some prefer the early and some the late phases of the alleged developments. Structuralist Marxists, for instance, agree with the late Marx and reject the young Marx. Historical, critical, existentialist, and humanist versions of Marxist theory reject the late Marx and emphasize the young Marx. The latter pay particular attention, generally speaking, to the totality of human existence; they emphasize the significance of individual consciousness and cultural frameworks in historical change; and, they define socialism as a democratic and humane strategy to overcome alienation and estrangement in contemporary society.

Theories that are oriented toward the late Marx, on the other hand, reject the significance of the individual, of culture, and of religion in historical development; they deny the notion of progress and development in terms of human fulfillment; and, they equate socialism soley with changes in technology, productivity, and the forces of production.[3]

It is not necessary to discuss other areas of debate over the meaning and significance of dialectic in Marxist theory to demonstrate that there exists no single form of Marxism and no unchallenged dialectical approach. Moreover, it is clear that some versions of Marxism and dialectic are incompatible with Bahá'í philosophy, while others are not. The limited scope of this paper does not permit a full discussion of this question. It will only be possible to briefly discuss here some elements of the dialectical approach and to argue that the Bahá'í Faith is explicitly and unequivocally founded on dialectical method.

ATTEMPTS HAVE BEEN MADE to define dialectics in terms of a set of rigid and dogmatic Marxist formulae, as exemplified in Stalinist philosophy. I do not accept that method. In my own selective definition, I emphasize first and foremost that dialectic is philosophy which defines the structure of being and reality. The most important ontological statement of the philosophy is the assertion of the primacy and reality of *becoming* over *being*. In other words, it is the assertion that reality is not static, but is a process incessantly moving and changing. Being and nothingness are, therefore, mental abstractions of various moments in this concrete becoming.

Hegelian philosophy argues that pure being is devoid of any determination and is, therefore, only nothingness. For Hegel, both being and nothingness are partial aspects of the same underlying reality which he calls becoming.

It is customary to think of dialectics as the law of change and movement through the contradiction between a *thesis* and its opposite, the *antithesis*, to result in a higher level of reality, the *synthesis*. But if reality is understood as becoming, and not static being, then history and totality are the locus of truth. The thesis is only a partial and limited presentation of reality, while the antithesis reflects another aspect of the same totality—also partial and limited, but not touched by the thesis. Synthesis is, therefore, a more comprehensive, though still partial, representation of reality because it comprises more aspects of the whole.

To insist on the primacy of becoming over being is equivalent to approaching reality in terms of relationships, rather than fixed and solid objects. Relations, in this view, are not the secondary products of already existing objects, but the primary reality of the objects themselves. In fact, single objects are only the embodiments or crystalizations of an underlying system of relations and interactions. Unity, similarly, is not something opposed to diversity. It is, in fact, nothing but the full mutual reciprocity of the contradictory and opposing elements of the same totality.

In Hegel's philosophy it is argued that true reality should not be sought in isolated objects of empirical human perception. While at the immediate level of impressions we might think of single objects as autonomous, real and independent entities, at the level of understanding we discover the interdependence and multuality of even contradictory elements. Appearance and essence, for instance, become unthinkable without one another. For Hegel, both essence and appearance are aspects of a higher and more complex totality which comprises true reality. This higher reality, according to Hegel, is the absolute, and ultimately spiritual, ground of being.[4]

Dialectic must also be understood as a normative philosophy. It is an approach which proposes certain human standards. According to dialectical theory, truth and value are ultimately to be sought in the category of becoming. Since everything is in the process of change, truth and the totality of any reality lie, not only in the present, but in future potentialities and possibilities. The present itself, therefore, can only be understood by reference to what can and should be. The movement toward totality is the movement toward the realization of the potentialities and possibilities of present reality.

And so, to accept a dialectical approach is to be discontent with the present order of things, to envision possibilities, to welcome change, and to strive for the realization of the highest potential to be found in the present.

Moreover, the dynamic, changing and historical character of every individual and society implies that values cannot be absolute. The vision of good or bad can have no meaning outside the context of historical development. At each moment in history, values must be defined in terms of the specific possibilities of being at that particular stage of development. What is good for today may not be good for tomorrow.

This does not mean, however, that an historical consciousness must lead to an ethical relativism where right and wrong are determined solely by individual whim. There remains an objective ground for moral preference. The synthesis is a morally superior state of being relative to the thesis.

Such a short article must omit the discussion of other elements of a dialectical approach. Dialectic as a theory of the development of human knowledge, or as a theory of the unity of subject and object, must remain unexplored. Instead, let us turn to a discussion of Bahá'í ideas.

BAHÁ'Í PHILOSOPHY is explicitly and systematically based on a dialectical worldview. This is, by itself, neither surprising nor particularly important. What is significant, however, is the implications of such a dynamic theology on the activities of the Bahá'í Community in its efforts to achieve the goal of a new and egalitarian world order.

The concept of progressive revelation, which is central to the structure of Bahá'í philosophy, indicates that the Bahá'í Faith is fundamentally, structurally, and systematically dynamic and dialectical in its approach. It stands in no need of the imposition of new interpretations or external categories to make it look modern or relevant to our discussion.

It is no accident that Bahá'ís reject the idea that their religion is the last step in the discovery of spiritual truth or the final chapter in a closed system of religious progress. The very notion of progressive revelation is based on two fundamental assumptions. The first is that all reality, including that in the human and social realms, is in a perpetual state of flux and change. This unconditional historical consciousness underlies the Bahá'í conception of human nature, the structure of society, and religious values. The second assumption concerns the relation of religion and spiritual development to various social institutions. Bahá'ís believe that religious truth does and should correspond with conditions of space and time and conform to the requirements and potentialities of social and historical development. Nor should the concept of progressive revelation be thought to apply only to changes between religions. This principle applies, as Bahá'u'lláh Himself explained, even within the dispensation of each Prophet.[5]

Such a progressive theory excludes the possibility of the dogmatic isolation of religion from the logic and dynamic of social and historical change. Religion, in the Bahá'í view, is not regarded as the final and absolute presentation of divine truth imposed on human society. Rather, such a conception is seen as a distortion—a false understanding of religion itself.

ACCORDING TO THE classical philosophy of Aristotle, movement and change apply only to the attributes, and never to the substance, of objects. In this static view, an ideal and unchanging substance is the ultimate reality that underlies all outward manifestations of change. Therefore, the substantive strata of existence which is postulated by Aristotle—stable, permanent and unmoving—is regarded as the primary, while change and relationships are the secondary phenomena of reality.

In Persian philosophy, it was Mullá Sadrá (1572–1641) who first advocated the theory of *substantive movement*. According to Sadrá, change and evolution are permanent features of substance. He maintained that substances are nothing more than the temporary crystalizations of the ever-unfolding potential of a dynamic existence. Such a theory is a hallmark in the development of a dialectical worldview.[6]

Bahá'í philosophy supports the dialectical theory of substantive movement and rejects Aristotle's static approach. 'Abdu'l-Bahá has explained:

Absolute repose does not exist in nature. All things either make progress or lose ground. Everything moves forward or backward, nothing is without motion. . . . Thus it is evident that movement is essential to all existence. All material things progress to a certain point, then begin to decline. This is the law which governs the whole physical creation . . . Movement is essential to existence; nothing that has life is without motion.[7]

ONE OF THE MOST fascinating aspects of Bahá'í philosophy is its stark historical consciousness. This consciousness defines human beings as products of history, accepts human nature as dynamic and transcending of particular forms, and recognizes in human reality the fundamental urge for the realization of potential. From a Bahá'í point of view, everything, including social reality, is ceaselessly changing and evolving. This means that the order of society and the forms of social institutions must also change in order to permit the actualization of individual and social potentials. 'Abdu'l-Bahá has repeatedly stated that everything can be resisted except the requirements of the age.

This historical consciousness of Bahá'í philosophy leads to a strong belief in the relativity of truth. If reality is infinitely complex, and if particular forms of cultural or religious order correspond only to a specific stage in the historical development of society, then it follows that each system of truth can only be partial, limited and relative. Such a stance is an essential principle of the Bahá'í Faith.

Bahá'u'lláh has metaphorically asserted the principle of the relativity of truth, even religious truth. Such a position creates a revolutionary approach to theology which rejects any form of orthodox dogmatism within the Bahá'í system. Shoghi Effendi, the Guardian of the Faith, referring to Bahá'u'lláh's metaphor, has explicitly declared that there can be no absolute in the realm of spiritual truth. He writes of

 . . . the fundamental principle which constitutes the bedrock of Bahá'í belief, the principle that religious truth is not absolute but relative, that Divine Revelation is orderly, continuous and progressive and not spasmodic or final. . . . Bahá'u'lláh testifies to this truth in one of

His Tablets revealed in Adrianople: *"Know verily that the veil hiding Our contenance hath not been completely lifted. We have revealed Our Self to a degree corresponding to the capacity of the people of Our age. Should the Ancient Beauty be unveiled in fullness of His glory mortal eyes would be blinded by the dazzling intensity of His revelation."*[8]

Such an historical consciousness must have far-reaching consequences for the structure of Bahá'í thought and the nature of the Bahá'í Community. One of the progressive implications of this relativistic historical outlook is that it creates an open, tolerant and liberal system of thought which cannot be tied to any fixed and unchanging definition, interpretation or orthodoxy. A dogmatic approach to Bahá'í ideology is impossible.

The Bahá'í Sacred Writings, for example, must be seen as a source of infinite meanings, understandings and possibilities which will only be discovered through a confrontation with future events and the diverse perspectives of the believers. This approach to the Holy Writings is made explicit in Bahá'í theology. Bahá'u'lláh wrote:

It hath been decreed by Us that the Word of God and all the potentialities thereof shall be manifested unto men in strict conformity with such conditions as have been foreordained by Him Who is the All-Knowing, the All-Wise. We have, moreover, ordained that its veil of concealment be none other except its own Self. Such indeed is Our Power to achieve Our Purpose. Should the World be allowed to release suddenly all the energies latent within it, no man could sustain the weight of so mighty a Revelation. Nay, all that is in heaven and on earth would flee in consternation before it.[9]

Bahá'ís believe in the metaphorical and symbolic character of all sacred writings, including their own. Such an explicit admission of symbolism in the Holy Texts leaves no space for the kind of textual fundamentalism which has afflicted other religions.

It is correct to point out that the Bahá'í concept of the Lesser Covenant infuses the scriptural interpretations of 'Abdu'l-Bahá and Shoghi Effendi with special significance and authority. But even these interpretations are themselves symbolic and subject to alternative understandings, representing as they do only one form of the historical realization of unlimited potentialities.

That the interpretations of the Center of the Covenant and the Guardian of the Faith do not exhaust the totality of meaning latent in the Sacred Texts is easily demonstrated. First, they did not interpret all passages. Second, those passages which have been explicitly interpreted may be subject to alternate interpretations which are equally valid—a fact witnessed by the diverse interpretations of the same Biblical statement by 'Abdu'l-Bahá himself. Finally, the explanations of 'Abdu'l-Bahá and Shoghi Effendi must themselves be interpreted by the believers, using their own reason and in changing historical contexts.[10]

The basic principle of the agreement of science and religion, and the central significance of consultation as the cornerstone of Bahá'í practice are paramount. Within the context of an open, tolerant and liberal theology they provide unlimited possibilities for development. Such unique privileges are to be guarded by Bahá'ís against any future invasion of orthodoxy or dogmatism.

A BAHÁ'Í APPROACH finds reality as a set of underlying relations and dynamic interactions, rather than an enumeration of separate and static facts. Moreover, 'Abdu'l-Bahá has defined nature, love, religion, and knowledge in terms of necessary *relations*. The Bahá'í teachings define true unity as unity in diversity; this is the ontological and normative principle of its philosophy of history.

In dialectical fashion, unity in diversity is a synthesis of crude uniformity and antagonistic conflict. In historical terms, Bahá'í teachings confirm the movement in history from primitive communalism toward the antagonisms and conflicts of stratified and hierarchical class societies. There are philosophical and sociological implications as well to the idea of unity in diversity. As a philosophical principle it asserts that unity is nothing more than the structure of mutual and reciprocal interdependence of diverse elements within a system. Unity, therefore, for Bahá'ís transcends both simplicity and diversity. As a sociological principle it implies the dynamic movement of history in the direction of increasing complexity *and* integration.

The challenge of history is the creation of a synthesis. Complexity and integration are usually contradictory forces. The realization of an integrated diversity is the historical task of contemporary society.

It should be noted that the Bahá'í principle of unity in diversity must reject any new formulation of uniformity. The implications of such a radical philosophical and sociological position exclude the establishment of authoritarianism within the Bahá'í Community. The Bahá'í Faith offers a vital, complex and sophisticated worldview which must disallow any attempt to impose a crude uniformity of thought or action among the believers in the name of cooperation or unity. True unity within the community requires, by definition, the full actualization of individual potentials and possibilities. Any attempt to create a single Bahá'í orthodoxy and impose it on the individual Bahá'í degrades the Bahá'í system and threatens to reduce it to a soulless corpse devoid of spiritual reality.

Another implication of Bahá'í dialectical philosophy concerns the theory of value and the relation of truth to value. Of course, the Bahá'í Faith strongly advocates the independent investigation of truth as one of its essential principles. What is less frequently discussed is the nature and meaning of truth within the Bahá'í system.

Bahá'í philosophy regards knowledge and the formation of knowledge as a product of the interaction of a concrete

historical subject and a dynamic reality. It follows, therefore, that the question of truth cannot be separated from
human interests, human values and human development.

Conventional correspondence theories of truth maintain
that the criterion of falsehood or truth is solely the agreement (or correspondence) of thought with external reality.
However, such notions overlook the complexity of reality
and the historicity of human existence. When these are
considered, truth becomes a social, existential and practical
question which is conditioned by historical developments
and possibilities.

'Abdu'l-Bahá transcends simple correspondence theories
of truth in his conceptualization. He defines truth in terms
of social and human values. Those values are, in turn, defined through the logic of concrete potentialities at the present stage of history. When asked on one occasion, "What is
truth?" 'Abdu'l-Bahá replied that truth is the unity of mankind, universal peace, and the other requirements of the
age.

The relative character of the Bahá'í conception of truth
corresponds with the relative and historical nature of the
Bahá'í value system. The idea of progressive revelation rejects any absolute system of values. Rather, values must be
defined in terms of possibilities and their realization within
a particular stage of social and historical evolution. But this
relativity is conditional. Although there cannot be any abstract or absolute moral judgment, with regard to specific
conditions there exists a clear and objective basis for judgment and preference.

This historical approach means that Bahá'ís must see the
present as a bearer of future possibilities. The acquisition
of knowledge, then, is the understanding of these possibilities and the exercise of moral preference or value judgment. The search for knowledge and understanding is,
therefore, a responsible and committed enterprise requiring
action.

Within the Bahá'í Community, such action takes the form of steadfastness in the Faith and active teaching. Both of these follow from a love of beauty as reflected in the system of possibilities. Teaching is emphasized as a means of active participation in the realization of historical potentials inherent in the structure of the present age. These issues are explained by Bahá'u'lláh in the first passages of the Most Holy Book, the *Kitáb-i Aqdas*:

The first duty prescribed by God for His servants is the recognition of Him Who is the Dayspring of His Revelation and the Fountain of His laws, Who representeth the Godhead in both the Kingdom of His Cause and the world of creation. . . . It behoveth every one who reacheth this most sublime station, this summit of transcendent glory, to observe every ordinance of Him Who is the Desire of the world. Thus hath it been decreed by Him Who is the Source of Divine inspiration.

Say: From My laws the sweet smelling savour of My garment can be smelled, and by their aid the standards of Victory will be planted upon the highest peaks. The Tongue of My power hath, from the heaven of My omnipotent glory, addressed to My creation these words: "Observe My commandments, for the love of My beauty." Happy is the lover that hath inhaled the divine fragrance of his Best-Beloved from these words, laden with the perfume of a grace which no tongue can describe. By My life! He who hath drunk the choice wine of fairness from the hands of My bountiful favour, will circle around My commandments that shine above the Dayspring of My creation.

Think not that We have revealed unto you a mere code of laws. Nay, rather, We have unsealed the choice Wine with the fingers of might and power. To this beareth witness that which the Pen of Revelation hath revealed. Meditate upon this, O men of insight![11]

THE PRECEDING DISCUSSION has argued that all of the major premises of a dialectical approach and an historical consciousness are systematically present in the Bahá'í teachings. However, the notion of dialectic has been used as the methodological ground for the theory of historical materialism in Marxist thought. Let us turn to a discussion of the Bahá'í position on this matter.

Historical materialism is a Marxist theory usually assumed to be contradictory to Bahá'í teachings. First, the very word *materialism* seems antagonistic to any spiritual worldview. And second, there is the general idea that any religious philosophy must see religion as an antonomous and determinant force in history which functions independently from other social forces.

In fact, both of these assumptions are incorrect. The theory of historical materialism has nothing to do with materialism in its common sense. Moreover, Bahá'í theology advocates a revolutionary view which demands a dynamic interaction of religion and social structure as the very foundation of its theory of revelation.

It should be admitted that one major area of confusion among Marxists themselves is the distinction between historical materialism and dialectical materialism. This confusion has caused a good deal of misunderstanding in Marxist analysis. In fact, the same word *materialism* has two entirely different meanings when applied to the two theories.

Dialectical materialism is a philosophical theory which maintains that matter, and not consciousness, is the primary element of reality. Materialism in this sense is opposed to any belief in God, soul, or the spiritual character of human beings. This materialism rejects any idealistic theory. It insists that matter exists independent of mind and consciousness and that it is the only real substance of reality. Clearly, this materialism has no place in Bahá'í philosophy.

Indeed, this materialistic approach is a naive philosophical conception which is not essential to Marxist theory. Nor can it be seriously defended. While it is easy to make the claim that matter is the only real stuff of being, the attempt to define the nature and meaning of matter without reference to consciousness is more difficult. Engels, who emphasized a mechanistic form of Marxism, is puzzled by this very question. He maintains that matter is independent from mind and reduces consciousness to an epiphenomenal level. But, when he attempts to define matter he describes it as something capable of being perceived or known.[12]

It will not be necessary to enter into a metaphysical argument at this point. Suffice it to say that Engels' definition of matter, like all others, presumes mind and consciousness as preconditions of material existence.

On the other hand, the word materialism in the context of the theory of *historical* materialism denotes an entirely different idea. Historical materialism is a social theory which is concerned with the interaction of various social institutions and the laws of historical change. A simplistic statement of the theory of historical materialism would be that it is change in the economic institutions of society—not change in ideal institutions, such as art or religion—which determines social development. Adjustment to change in these material institutions is what shapes developments in ideas and ideal institutions. Material institutions are defined as the forces and the relations of production, or more crudely as the economic structure of society. Ideal institutions are said to be such things as art, politics, religion, state, and other cultural and ideological systems.

However, a moment's reflection is all that is needed to recognize that cultural institutions—such as the apparatus of the state, the practice of religion, or works of art for that matter—are as material as is economic structure. And, conversely, the relations of production is as ideal a concept as is state apparatus, etc. The study of history concerns various social institutions, none of which can be seen as purely material or purely ideal.

Anyone familiar with Marxist theory will readily admit that it is materialism in its historical sense that is critical for Marxist politics and sociology. Moreover, it is logically consistent to believe in historical materialism without any belief in dialectical materialism. The word *materialism* is simply used in two different ways and neither presupposes the acceptance of the other. Dialectical materialism is not taken seriously by most philosophers, while historical materialism is a very significant social theory which is increasingly influencing the direction of the social sciences.

IT IS NORMALLY assumed that any religious philosophy must interpret history as a theater for the realization of God's will and, therefore, must explain historical change in terms of God's intervention and volition. Such an approach leaves little space for the importance of social institutions and structural variables. God's will is regarded as absolute, static, unchanging, unrelated to the material world. It is imposed from outside of history and is indifferent to secular change.

The Bahá'í theory of progressive revelation is the first systematic religious critique of this ahistorical paradigm. According to Bahá'í teachings, society is a dynamic system which presents a specific set of potentialities at each stage of its development. Religion, as a social institution at least, must function in accord with this historical dynamic. Religion, in the Bahá'í view, addresses the specific social conditions of its time and attempts to realize the specific potentialities of the age. Society is conceived as a totality, a system, composed of diverse interacting institutions. Real change requires fundamental movement in all the dimensions of social existence.

Consequently, religion, although it is defined as divinely inspired, must respond to the internal dynamics of society. Religion, in other words, is affected by historical change; and, in turn, it affects the direction of social development.

The theory of progressive revelation insists that religion must change in accord with the development of social institutions. Otherwise, it is not a progressive force, but a hindrance to progress. This approach rejects the Great Man theory of history and cannot support a passive resignation in the face of social, economic or political dynamics in history.

The interactionist outlook of Bahá'í teachings should not be confused with either individualism or structuralism. For the former, society is a fictitious entity; only the individual is real; and, social institutions are only the reflections of a static human nature. Individualists maintain, therefore, that the agent of social, historical change is individual consciousness, values and ideas. Social development is accomplished by a strategy of changing individual ethics and ideology.[13]

Structuralist theory, on the contrary, regards individuals as the passive embodiments of social relations and the structure of society. Society is the underlying reality that precedes individuals and individual consciousness. Like the grammar of language which predetermines the speech acts of individuals and is not created by their speech, individual acts are embodiments of the structure of society without the conscious knowledge of the individual actor. The laws of structural change, it is argued, lie within the structure and are not affected by individual consciousness.[14]

The principles of the Bahá'í Faith are incompatible with both extreme individualism and any such reified structuralism. From the interactionist perspective of Bahá'í teachings, both the individual and society are real, and both are effective forces in the determination of social development. The dialectical interaction of the individual and society corresponds to the Bahá'í belief in the dialectical interaction of various social institutions. Bahá'ís, therefore, regard cultural, ideological and political factors, as well as religious factors, as significant for social growth and development.

As opposed to the fatalistic determinism of structuralism, which implies individual resignation, the Bahá'í approach acknowledges the necessity of critical consciousness within a given structure of historical possibilities. It calls for the active participation and interference of human beings in the dynamics of history and for an active critical and theoretical outlook.

The Bahá'í approach, moreover, demands change on both the individual and institutional levels. If society and the individual are both real and important, then the establishment of a new world order requires a strategy of change for both individual consciousness and values and for economic, cultural and political institutions. This is of critical significance.

The reified conception of economistic Marxism overlooks the significance of the individual personality, human values or differences of culture in its endeavor to create a just society. It is assumed that by the elimination of private property, a new socialist man will automatically be created. The present crises in socialist politics testify to the bankruptcy of such a naive and simplistic worldview.

Similarly, the attempt to change the world through preaching the morality of love and unity to individual hearts, without changing the social institutions which must reinforce those values will ever remain in the realm of abstract dreams and empty words. While this approach may be important and meaningful to the individual, it embodies no social dimension. The failure of Christian ideals to create a just society is ample testimony to this.

The Bahá'í ideal of the oneness of mankind represents a simultaneous change in the individual and the social institutions of which he or she is a part. The implication of such a perspective is the necessity for both individual teaching and deepening and active participation in social and political change. Shoghi Effendi explicitly addresses this question:

Let there be no mistake. The principle of the Oneness of Mankind—the pivot round which all the teachings of Bahá'u'lláh revolve—is no mere outburst of ignorant emotionalism or an expression of vague and pious hope. Its appeal is not to be identified with a reawakening of the spirit of brotherhood and good-will among men, nor does it aim solely at the fostering of harmonious cooperation among individual peoples and nations. . . . Its message is applicable not only to the individual, but concerns itself primarily with the nature of those essential relationships that must bind all the states and nations as members of one human family. . . . It calls for no less than the reconstruction and the demilitarization of the whole civilized world—a world organically unified in all the essential aspects of its life, its political machinery, its spiritual aspiration, its trade and finance, its script and language, and yet infinite in the diversity of the national characteristics of its federated units.[15]

Of course, there are alternative interpretations and understandings of historical materialism within the Marxist tradition. Although some of these interpretations are incompatible with Bahá'í teachings, some recent developments in Marxist theory show strong similarities to the tenets of the Bahá'í interactive perspective.

Historical materialism was accepted as a purely economic thesis by early Marxist theorists. In this view, the economy controls and determines the development of all other social institutions. Religion, culture and politics are defined as functions of economic interests and, therefore, are epiphenomenal in historical change. The economy itself is seen in terms of technology and production, and not in terms of social relations. Socialist revolutions are regarded as inevitable results of the iron laws of economic change. Finally, the ideal society is defined in terms of the development of the forces of production and the level of productivity achieved.

Communism, and especially the Stalinist interpretation of it applied in the Soviet Union in earlier decades, is a perfect embodiment of this economistic interpretation of historical materialism. As such, it was vehemently attacked by the Guardian of the Bahá'í Faith as one of the three destructive evils of world civilization.[16]

Recent Marxist theories, however, reject this economistic approach and its hollow vision of the ideal society. For example, Existential Marxism, Marxist Humanism, Critical Theory, Eurocommunism, and even some of the structuralists reject any economistic problematics. In these recent approaches to Marxist ideology the *relations* of production take precedence over the forces of production; all of the various social institutions interact with one another; the cultural and ideological structures of society are relatively autonomous from the economic structure; culture and ideology affect the direction of social change significantly; socialism is seen not only in terms of the forces of production, but also in terms of democratic and humanitarian principles; the results of social change depend upon the nature of critical theory and organizational structure; the agenda of the socialist struggle is not limited to an attack on poverty, but also includes the creation of a counterculture of humanism; the dominant social institution is not always the economy but may vary according to historical circumstances; no socialism is possible without humanist values and the defeat of alienation; and, it is recognized that human beings are too complex to be transformed by only a change in the nature of private property.

Clearly, the recent trends in Marxist thought have, through a dialectical reinterpretation of historical materialism, moved much closer to a Bahá'í perspective. Bahá'ís would do well to appreciate the enormous potential of their own teachings and reject any dogmatism or undialectical theoretical fixation.

THIS ANALYSIS of the Bahá'í teachings in relation to dialectical materialism and historical materialism must remain abstract and sketchy. In conclusion, I would like to call for a mutual dialogue between Marxist theorists and Bahá'ís in our shared struggle toward the establishment of an egalitarian new world order.

Bahá'ís might learn the necessity of dynamic adaptation to changing world conditions and the value of a dialectical participation in social, economic and political struggles to change a corrupt, outmoded and unjust world society. Marxists, on the other hand, might learn to emphasize a more international approach and to accept the need for a new system of values.

Marxism has usually overlooked the significance of the part and overstressed the importance of the whole, undervalued the individual and insisted on the effectivity and autonomy of institutions. Marxists have generally failed to realize the enormous significance of the structure of nationalism in the questions of peace, imperialism, the nuclear threat, and the development of the forces of production. The Bahá'í Faith accepts a dialectic between the part and the whole, focuses on the need to overcome nationalistic loyalties, and refuses to reduce the logic of international relations to the purely internal dynamics of individual nation states.

The establishment of a new world order will require an egalitarian, internationalist consciousness and structure. Marxists and Bahá'ís must learn from one another. Such cooperation may be the last hope for a world afflicted with oppression, antagonism and injustice.

Notes

1. F. Engels, "Ludwig Feuerbach and the End of German Classical Philosophy" in *Selected Works* (Progress Publications, 1977) vol. 3, pp. 337–76.

2. See L. Coletti, *Marxism and Hegel* (London: NLB, 1973).

3. For an example of works by those who favor the young Marx, see J. Habermas, *Knowledge and Human Interests* (London: Heineman, 1978). For an example of those who prefer late Marx and reject the theory of alienation, see L. Althusser, *For Marx* (London: Verso, 1979).

4. G. W. F. Hegel, *Science of Logic* (London: Allen and Unwin, 1929).

5. Cf. *Synopsis and Codification of the Kitáb-i-Aqdas, the Most Holy Book* (Haifa: Bahá'í World Centre, 1973) p. 5.

6. For an excellent description of Sadrá's philosophy, see F. Rahman, *The Philosophy of Mullá Sadrá* (Albany: SUNY, 1975).

7. 'Abdu'l-Bahá, *Paris Talks* (London: Bahá'í Publishing Trust, 1912) pp. 88–89.

8. Shoghi Effendi, *World Order of Bahá'u'lláh* (Wilmette, Ill.: Bahá'í Publishing Trust, 1938) pp. 115–16.

9. Bahá'u'lláh, *Gleanings from the Writings of Bahá'u'lláh* (Wilmette, Ill.: Bahá'í Publishing Trust, 1939) pp. 76–77.

10. On this general theme see, The Universal House of Justice, *Wellspring of Guidance* (Wilmette, Ill.: Bahá'í Publishing Trust, 1969) pp. 38–39.

11. *Synopsis and Codification*, pp. 11–12.

12. F. Engels, *The Anti-Dühring* (Moscow: Foreign Language Publishing House, 1959) p. 65.

13. For an example of an individualistic approach, see J. S. Mill, *A System of Logic* (London: Harper and Brothers, 1856).

14. For an example of reified structuralism, see L. Althusser, and E. Balibar, *Reading Capital* (London: Verso, 1979).

15. *World Order*, pp. 42–43.

16. Shoghi Effendi, *The Promised Day Is Come* (Wilmette, Ill.: Bahá'í Publishing Trust, 1941) pp. 117–18.

Biographical Notes

CARLTON E. BROWN, ED.D., is an Assistant Professor in the Department of Curriculum and Instruction, School of Education, at Old Dominion University.

JUAN R. COLE, PH.D., received his doctorate in Islamic Studies from the University of California, Los Angeles. He is currently teaching history at the University of Michigan, Ann Arbor.

GREGORY C. DAHL is an economist with the International Monetary Fund and has served as its resident representative in Haiti. He is a doctoral candidate in economics at Harvard University.

JOHN HUDDLESTON serves as the Chief of the Budget and Planning Division of the International Monetary Fund. He is the author of *The Earth Is But One Country*, a book on the Bahá'í Faith.

ANTHONY A. LEE acts as Managing Editor of Kalimát Press. He is pursuing a doctorate in history at the University of California, Los Angeles.

ROBERT T. PHILLIPS owns Consultant Services of Santa Cruz, California. He is a medical management consultant for Stanford University and the University of California, San Francisco.

BRADLEY D. POKORNY works as a journalist for *The Boston Globe*. He is now writing a book about peace issues and the Bahá'í Faith.

NADER SAIEDI, PH.D., obtained his doctoral degree in sociology from the University of Wisconsin. He currently teaches at the University of California, Los Angeles.

ANN SCHOONMAKER, PH.D., holds a doctorate in theology from Drew University. She is the author of two books. She is also trained in marital therapy and is the coordinator of Sunrise House in Eliot, Maine.

JUNE MANNING THOMAS, PH.D., is an Associate Professor in both the School of Urban Planning and the Urban Affairs Programs at Michigan State University. Her degree is in Urban and Regional Planning, with specialization in urban economics and quantitative analysis, from the University of Michigan.

RICHARD W. THOMAS, PH.D., received his doctorate in history from the University of Michigan. He is now an Associate Professor in both the History Department and the Urban Affairs Programs at Michigan State University.